CHALKHILLS
AND CHILDREN

Edited by Chris Charlesworth
Cover designed by Four Corners
Book designed by 4i Limited
Picture research by Chris Twomey & David Brolan

ISBN: 0.7119.2758.8
Order No: OP 46556

Exclusive distributors:

Book Sales Limited,
8/9 Frith Street,
London W1V 5TZ, UK.

Music Sales Corporation,
225 Park Avenue South,
New York, NY 10003, USA.

Music Sales Pty Ltd,
120 Rothschild Avenue,
Rosebery, NSW 2018, Australia.

To the Music Trade only:

Music Sales Limited,
8/9 Frith Street,
London W1V 5TZ, UK.

Printed and bound in Great Britain by
Mackays of Chatham PLC, Chatham, Kent

Front cover Photograph: Kevin Westenberg
Back cover: Renaud Monfourny

Every effort has been made to trace the copyright holders of
the photographs in this book but one or two were
unreachable. We would be grateful if the photographers
concerned would contact us.

A catalogue record for this book is available from the
British Library.

XTC

CHALKHILLS
AND CHILDREN

The Definitive Biography

OMNIBUS PRESS
LONDON · NEW YORK · SYDNEY

CHRIS
TWOMEY

ACKNOWLEDGEMENTS

The author would like to thank the following for their invaluable assistance in writing this book: Barry Andrews, Peter Blegvad, Dave Chambers, Gloria Chambers, Terry Chambers, Al Clark, Dennis Detheridge, Simon Draper, Gus Dudgeon, Neville Farmer, Mark Fisher, Tarquin Gotch, Ian Gregory, Margaret and Roy Gregory, Allan Jones, Andrew King, Jeremy Lascelles, John Leckie, Steve Lillywhite, Limelight, The Little Express, Dave Mattacks, Carol Moulding, Vera Moulding, Hugh Padgham, Marianne Partridge, Vera and John Partridge, Pete Phipps, Ptolemaic Terrascope, Todd Rundgren, Steve Warren, Paul Wilde and, especially Johnny 'make us a cup of tea Chris' Waller.

The author would like to make it clear that XTC's former manager Ian Reid was approached with a view to being interviewed for this book but he declined to cooperate in any way.

I

SENSES WORKING OVERTIME

"As a self-preservation thing I had to stop"
- Andy Partridge

As 1981 turned the corner into 1982, serenaded by the nation's number one 'Don't You Want Me', champagne corks were popping in Swindon. Battling for airspace along with The Human League, and other fellow travellers such as The Jam and The Stranglers, was 'Senses Working Overtime' - a rousing pop anthem, distinguished by its curiously medieval sounding verse. Very eccentric. Very English. Very XTC.

XTC's first Top Ten hit didn't make great waves through the music business, nor did it represent a major landmark in the history of rock'n'roll. But it was another minor breakthrough for the first wave of post-punk pop acts (as exemplified by The Police and Dexy's Midnight Runners) and for the band themselves it was a heart-warming reward after a long hard struggle which promised to open up a whole new era for them. XTC were, after all, one of Britain's most consistently underrated groups.

For them it had been a steady but slow progression - a text-book slog. Each of their five albums had sold progressively better than the one before, each tour had witnessed more and more sell-outs. By February 1982 critical acclaim was reaching new heights too. Their new album, 'English Settlement', had been ecstatically received with critics falling over themselves to find superlatives strong enough to describe the songwriting genius of its two main architects, Andy Partridge and Colin Moulding. Its top five placing seemed to confirm the expectation that XTC were finally poised to take their place as the Next Big Thing. Yes, everything was going swimmingly well for XTC. Except in Andy Partridge's head.

Andy had scant regard for the long held convention in the music business that anyone with a new record to promote was obliged to tour. Although initially enthusiastic about the sheer thrill of being on stage and playing live to an audience, five years of routine touring had taken their toll and his distaste for playing concerts was such that a year earlier he had mounted a feeble attempt to knock live work on the head completely. His protests then, as now, were brushed aside by the other three band members, especially down-to-earth drummer Terry Chambers and softly-spoken guitarist Dave Gregory, who weren't involved in the songwriting process and looked forward to touring as their *raison d'être*. The group's manager, Ian Reid, regarded Andy's resistance as a melodramatic artistic whim, and of course their record company, Virgin, were horrified. How could a band like XTC survive without touring? To quit at the very moment you were edging ahead would be seen as pure folly.

Andy's disenchantment with touring had various foundations. For one, he deeply resented the inevitability of the tour-album-tour trap. Secondly, life on the road was often a soulless grind of faceless audiences, gruelling itineraries, featureless hotels, endless waits in airport departure lounges, interviews with journalists who hadn't done their homework properly and a myriad of petty discomforts. It wasn't exactly inspirational and had little to do with being a musician. Churning out the same songs night after night, it seemed to Andy as if he'd been condemned to a life sentence of endlessly repeating himself.

"It was like those times when you arrive somewhere after a familiar journey and you realise you weren't conscious of ever having left," he recalls. "I used to do that on stage. Three songs into the set I'd think 'Blimey! We've played three numbers!' Because you'd done it 25 times before on that tour, you'd put it to some part of the brain that handles mundane chores. I'd see the audience and think 'They're really enjoying this. Why aren't I enjoying it?'

"You'd leave the stage with applause ringing in your ears, and a matter of minutes later you'd be sat in your hotel room in Mooseknob, Wyoming, with a suitcase of reeking, damp washing and a bottle of warm beer thinking 'What am I doing here?'"

Although XTC had partly forged their growing fame on the strength of an impressive live act, Andy felt their reputation was ill-deserved. He believed that they were only really on form during one gig in ten, and as their records grew in complexity he became increasingly less satisfied about the way the group was able to reproduce their newer, more intricate, material in concert. As the group's principal songwriter, he felt trapped, and found himself writing specifically for the limited instrumentation they used when playing live.

2

A far more pressing problem, however, and one which had a demoralising effect on the whole band, was the general lack of money around. For a chart act who could command several thousand pounds per show (the exact sums involved have been very difficult to ascertain, for reasons that will become obvious later) there was a mysterious - some would say suspicious - leak in the financial plumbing. Wherever the money was going, it wasn't into the band's pockets.

"The shows were getting bigger and bigger, but there was nothing to show for it," says Andy. "Or rather there was money, but we weren't seeing it. It was very distressing and we never had time to follow it through because we were always busy writing or recording - or out touring the world somewhere - thinking we were laying down the foundations for our future career. We could see a lot of our contemporaries overtaking us at that time and we were fighting for the recognition we thought we really deserved. All the while our relationship with money was totally negligible."

As the tours got bigger and more prestigious, Andy became progressively more paranoid. The one essential piece of equipment he started taking with him on the road was a screwdriver. As soon as he checked into a hotel he would dismantle the phone in his room and deflect calls from over-zealous fans who had somehow managed to discover where he was staying.

Towards the end of a gruelling ten week American club tour in 1980 he had begun experiencing all kinds of mental warning signs as he teetered on the edge of physical and nervous exhaustion. Out of sight of the others he would suddenly burst into tears for no apparent reason or suffer bouts of acute memory loss.

"I actually forgot who I was once or twice," he explains. "I'd look at the number of my room key in some American hotel, phone the receptionist and say 'Can you tell me who's staying in room 104?' They'd say 'Yes sir, that's Mr Partridge.' 'Oh, thanks . . . by the way, what town is this?' I suppose things like that happen when you bite off more than you can chew."

But the demands of the rock'n'roll circus are non-stop and the show went on regardless of Andy's misgivings. On February 11, 1982, XTC were due to perform live on BBC2's late-night TV rock show, *The Old Grey Whistle Test*, playing two songs from 'English Settlement' - 'Yacht Dance' and 'No Thugs In Our House'. Besides promoting the album, this would also serve as a warm-up for yet another world tour, the European leg of which was due to begin in Brussels on March 7.

As on previous occasions, Andy had again protested about having to tour and again nobody had paid any serious attention. The tour had been arranged and inevitably he was swept up in the machinery of it like everyone else. But despite all Andy's other misgivings, the *Whistle Test* appearance brought him into contact with something he had neither bargained for, nor experienced before: stage fright.

"I was phenomenally nervous and I didn't know why," he says. "I think I was trying to tell myself that I didn't want to do this. The little man inside me was saying 'You said you weren't going to tour, and here you are off on another one. There's an audience out there. They're expecting you to be fantastic'."

The Continent, where their quirky Englishness had previously met with a generally cool response, had always been something of a commercial wasteland for XTC. But now audiences were getting to grips with the British New Wave and 'English Settlement' was at the heart of that. In Europe, as elsewhere, the door was open.

Andy had mixed feelings about XTC's new popularity. The big drawback was that it put even greater pressure on him to excel on stage. As the European tour kicked off, these self-induced anxieties began to manifest themselves physically.

"I'd been dry retching before the gigs and feeling unbelievably nauseous. The physical pain was so intense that it seemed obvious that there had to be a physical cause to it. But it was just a reaction to my own internal arguing. I resented being carried along with this Frankenstein's monster we'd created."

Eventually Andy needed medical attention for stomach pains that everyone assumed were just the result of food poisoning. That diagnosis was unlikely, though, since at the time he was a strict vegetarian and was virtually living off fruit and handfuls of peanuts. But the pain was real enough and XTC had been on the road for little more than a week.

Something had to give and matters came to a head on March 18, a day that passed by in a surreal blur for Andy. The band was booked to play at Le Palais, an elegant, old-fashioned tiered theatre in the less than elegant Montmartre district of Paris. The show was a sell-out and was being broadcast live on French radio and TV. The potential audience was massive.

Andy had agreed to do an interview with *Antenne 2*, the TV channel, that afternoon. For reasons best known to themselves the TV company had chosen to conduct the interview in the caretaker's house,

4

next to the venue. "I was sat in this little caretaker's house feeling weird, feeling very tired and scared stiff at the thought of doing the show that evening," recalls Andy. "I felt like I was on some other planet. I could hear myself answer all these questions and it was like someone else talking. Sitting in the corner of the room was this very sweet elderly French couple - the caretaker and his wife - who didn't speak a word of English, and it felt like we were all stuck inside this old black and white French film. It wasn't real at all."

As show time loomed Andy grew increasingly anxious and by the time he was due on stage, he was in the early throes of a massive panic attack. Thoughts of going AWOL had crossed his mind, but he knew he had to play. He'd be letting too many people down if he didn't. He ran on stage with the others and launched into the opening bars of 'Respectable Street'.

Thirty seconds was all that the audience at Le Palais got of XTC that night. Although from the outside he looked calm enough, Andy's mind was taking him on a terrifying voyage, like a bad acid trip. It was a classic Hollywood horror scenario: the room began to spin as everyone and everything seemed to be drifting further and further away from him. He felt more and more nauseous. Finally he thought, quite literally, he was going to die.

Those thirty seconds felt like three hours. In a daze Andy unplugged his guitar and ran off-stage. The others carried on a few more bars without him, then looked at each other in bemusement. They were just as puzzled by Andy's behaviour as the audience were.

Backstage the band found Andy crouched in a corner of the dressing room, doubled up in pain and sobbing hysterically. He was gripping his stomach and retching so alarmingly that once again everyone assumed he had food poisoning. Andy knew better but a doctor was hurriedly called nonetheless. So alarmed were the local emergency services that the doctor was given a fire brigade escort to the theatre to speed through the heavy Paris traffic. When Andy recovered a few minutes later, he was confronted by the concerned-looking doctor accompanied by a dozen firemen in full regalia. "One part of me was laughing my socks off, while another found the whole situation just too surreal to handle. It was a strange mixture of emotions."

Andy begged the tour manager, Frankie Enfield, to put him on a plane back to England immediately. His greatest urge now was to "curl up and disappear" for as long as it took to recover but the band's

5

manager Ian Reid, present for the first time on this tour, had other ideas. Despite Andy's obvious distress, he tried to coax him back on stage. The audience was understandably angry and needed to be placated. Eventually a compromise was achieved when Andy agreed, under pressure, to a rescheduled show the following night, though privately he never had any intention of going through with it.

When morning came Andy had made up his mind - he wanted to go home. The band's record company, Virgin France, wouldn't hear of it. Their tone became progressively hostile as they tried to impress upon the group that numerous TV and magazine interviews had already been arranged. If they pulled out now XTC's reputation would be ruined throughout the French music industry. But Andy was resolute. By mid-afternoon he was on a plane back to Heathrow.

Back in Swindon, Andy's first priority was to find out what was wrong with him. Although deep down he knew, it didn't seem plausible that so much physical discomfort could stem from an emotional problem. He underwent a battery of tests and had to submit to having an exploratory tube threaded down his throat but even this endoscopy failed to reveal any physical cause for all the horrendous stomach pains. He next sought psychiatric help and was recommended a course of hypnotherapy. A group of sessions with a hypnotist was booked. "The hypnotist would take me back through the build up to gigs. I'd end up in the same condition as I did in Paris. That awful feeling came flooding back."

Hoping that Andy would make some progress through these sessions, Ian Reid postponed the British leg of the 'English Settlement' world tour - eight shows culminating with two nights at London's Hammersmith Odeon - until the summer. But a whole series of American dates could not be dumped so easily. Andy resigned himself to having to do them, though much coercion was eventually needed to get him to pack his bags.

XTC arrived in Los Angeles on March 30, allowing them three days to recover from jet lag before the first show in San Diego on April 3. The weather was unusually wet for the time of the year, and Andy took refuge in his hotel room. Despite its opulent name and location, The Beverley Sunset Hotel on Sunset Boulevard was no palace and as Andy lay on his bed killing time he could hear hookers fighting with clients in adjacent rooms, the nightly chorus of police raids and ferocious rain storms. One night he woke up screaming, imagining that the hotel was burning down; the rain made a crackling noise like fire as it pitched against the palm trees outside his window.

At San Diego's California Theatre, everything was set. The house lights were dimmed, the Philip Glass intro music was playing and the band was standing backstage waiting to make their entrance. Suddenly Andy turned on his heel and began to walk away from the stage but the rest of the band, acting in self-preservation, made sure he went on. Against his will Andy endured the entire performance, virtually on auto-pilot. If the crowd noticed it didn't affect their enthusiasm as a wild stage invasion took place at the end of the set. Andy left the stage feeling badly shaken.

The following day they returned to Los Angeles for a sold-out show at the Hollywood Palladium. After a soundcheck in the afternoon there was a small crowd of fans waiting outside the venue to greet the band but Andy had made up his mind that he couldn't go through with that night's gig, or any other. "We were getting questions like 'Hey Andy! What are you gonna be playing tonight?' - all the usual fan things - and me privately thinking 'There won't be any show. You won't be seeing me later on. Goodbye'."

The four band members had arranged to meet about an hour before the gig at a little diner just up the road from the hotel. Colin, Dave and Terry all arrived on time and ordered something to eat. Back at the hotel, Andy dragged himself off his bed and forced himself to leave the safe haven of his room. It took every last reserve of emotional energy. As he walked along the street he felt as though he were moving in slow motion. By the time he arrived at the diner, there was only ten minutes until show time.

"It took me ages to walk to this diner," he recalls. "I thought 'If anyone sees me they're going to think I'm an old acid case, or a wino who's forgotten how to walk.' When I got there the guys had very glum expressions on their faces. They said 'Where have you been, we've been waiting ages? Come on we're going to be late for the gig.' I just said 'I'm sorry. I can't do it'.

"Colin and Dave knew I really meant it this time, and took me seriously. But Terry's attitude was 'What's the fuckin' matter with you, yer pansy?' That was his style. I felt I was letting them down pretty badly, but as a self-preservation thing I had to stop."

Not again, Ian Reid thought as he convened a meeting back at the hotel. He told the band in no uncertain terms that if they didn't play the show they were likely to have their legs broken by the promoter.

XTC: CHALKHILLS AND CHILDREN

"It's no good me telling him you don't fancy doing the show, Andy," Reid said. "You've got to be ill. We're going to have to get you to a hospital and get you a certificate saying you've got something serious."

So Andy was taken to the casualty department of a nearby hospital and made to wait his turn for an outpatient examination. "I was lying there in the emergency area and on one side of me was a black guy who'd been shot. There was this Oriental individual groaning on the other side. I'm in the middle thinking 'What am I doing here? I don't want to be doing this!' Eventually this young no-nonsense doctor appeared and began to examine me in a very off-hand manner. He just shoved his rubber-gloved fingers up my arse, turned me over and felt my stomach and decided I must have some gastric problem. Then he wrote this indecipherable mess on a form which was what we wanted to stave off the promoter."

The following day the tour was cancelled: Andy and Colin were packed and ready to leave on an afternoon flight back to London; Dave decided to stay in L.A. for a few days to soak up some sun and a disgusted Terry flew straight to Australia to be with his girlfriend.

As they checked out of The Beverley Sunset, Andy was accosted by a man sketching by the desk who was, he claimed, a red Indian chief. He told him that he was the inventor of an invisible ray that could shield cities against nuclear attacks but the US government was trying to hush him up because he'd stumbled across a top secret formula. In Andy's unstable emotional state this bizarre encounter seemed like final confirmation that he was going out of his mind. He was just grateful to be going home.

For XTC though, matters are never that simple. After leaving LA the plane was delayed in Boston for 24 hours due to snow storms. Andy wondered if he would ever see England again. Eventually they touched down in the UK 48 hours later, XTC's live career now at an end. Although very tired, a kind of calm contentment had washed over Andy.

"The relief when I got home was incredible. Although I hadn't, I felt like I'd taken my unsatisfactory career and pushed it off a cliff. And that was it - it had gone away."

2

A NEW TOWN ANIMAL

A mighty storm was blowing in Malta the day Andrew John Partridge was born and Vera, his mother, took that to be a good omen. She was already convinced she was going to have a girl and had named the unborn child Gail. The fact that it was blowing one as she went into labour seemed to be a sign from above.

The delivery of a healthy baby boy, at the Mtarfa Royal Naval Hospital, on November 11, 1953, was a mild inconvenience - if only because the baby suit that Vera's mother had sent her was pink.

John Partridge heard the news of his son's birth on his ship HMS Wakeful, which at the time was engaged in manoeuvres in the Suez Canal. He had been posted to Malta by the Royal Navy six weeks earlier, and he spent much of his time away at sea. As agreed, because the baby was a boy, he had to choose the name. He picked Andrew as it was the slang term for the Navy, as in 'being in the Andrew'.

John and Vera Partridge occupied married quarters in a block of flats in Senglea, just across the majestic Grand Harbour from Malta's capital, Valetta. Although it was a dusty, barren place, still suffering from the most appalling war damage, Vera liked Malta. She liked the people and for her it was also a great adventure. She'd never lived anywhere but Swindon before, let alone abroad, and she confessed to friends that when she first arrived she was surprised that the moon looked pretty similar to the one they had in England.

Andy liked Malta too, as far as anyone could tell. His bleached blonde Aryan looks made him the centre of attention among the locals and his forward, chatty nature earned him the nickname Grampy. When the Partridges were eventually posted back to the UK on Christmas Eve 1956, three-year-old Andy could speak Maltese and English in equal proportions, a legacy of the countless hours spent with Vanna, his Maltese nanny.

Sadly, the glamour of life in the warm Med was soon a distant memory, and after six months in a small flat in Portsmouth the family moved back to Swindon. They were placed on a brand new council estate - the massive Penhill estate which was built with Harold Macmillan's misconceived 'You've never had it so good' ethic in mind. Fifties town planners being fifties town planners, somehow just about all life's essential amenities were missing from Penhill. The Valley, where the Partridge's first house was located, may have overlooked open fields but it had no shops, no pubs, no churches, no community centres, nor was it on any bus routes. Indeed, when the Partridges moved in it was virtually a sea of mud interspersed with identical houses. Many such estates sprang up in post-war Swindon, but Penhill was among the biggest - and the ugliest.

The Valley quickly became the least desirable part of the estate to live on and as a result it developed into a dumping ground for society's underclass: poor Irish families, 'problem' families, alcoholics, drug abusers, pyromaniacs, overspill Londoners and other social misfits. From the beginning the neighbourhood seemed to be dotted with larger-than-life grotesque characters.

John and Vera Partridge, in contrast, were a modest working class couple - abstemious, moral and respectable in their working-class conservatism. They'd both been brought up on a strict set of ethical values and they stuck rigidly to their ways. They loathed alcohol and were suspicious of the sudden proliferation of foreign foods available in the shops. They would say grace at the table without really knowing why.

Many of their habits had a charming old-fashioned ring to them. For instance, although their new house had a modern bathroom, they liked to wash downstairs in the kitchen sink. Likewise, for no particular reason, the front door was never used except on special occasions. Everyone came and left their house by the back door next to the coal bunker. Andy can remember being 'put on guard' outside the kitchen because Vera didn't want anyone bursting in and seeing her 'disabells' - meaning her breasts. (Andy wondered about the origins of this word for many years, and eventually discovered it came from the French *deshabille*, to be in a state of undress.) None of these things was considered unusual. Indeed, some families on the estate actually kept coal in their bath tubs when the coal bunker was full.

Thriftiness was another virtue that the Partridges held dear. The post-war generation had become accustomed to goods being in short supply in the fifties, but Vera had her own way of minimising waste. She would often buy the smallest quantity that she could get away with - half a packet of cigarettes, or half a packet of butter - and so she soon became known to local shop-keepers as Mrs Half!

Andy spent much of his early childhood alone with his mother because his father was away at sea for weeks, and sometimes months, at a stretch. "He'd be this strange man in my mum's bed once every six months," Andy recalls. "I'd like seeing him because he would always have some sort of present for me. A set of Rubba bricks, or a big plastic helicopter."

Vera struggled to be both a mother and a father to Andy, but inevitably it was a struggle. Andy was a sensitive, temperamental child with awesome mood swings. "I was a brat," he admits now, "a terrible tantrum thrower. I had to have my own way and be in control. If I didn't I would throw the contents of the cutlery drawer at my mother or kitchen stools - or something equally violent. When I was angry about something I could be quite psychotic". On one occasion Andy locked Vera in his toy cupboard. She was only saved from possible suffocation by the milkman who heard her knocking when he came to the door to be paid!

For a while Andy had a kind of surrogate father in the family's lodger Gerald - a handsome young man with jet black hair, who looked not unlike Victor Mature, the Hollywood heart throb known as 'The Hunk'. Because Gerald was so dark he would shave two or three times a day - a process which fascinated the boy.

Andy was a solitary child who hated sports and other outdoor pursuits, but he enjoyed drawing and demonstrated a precocious talent for art. While other boys in the neighbourhood would be outside playing football, he would borrow ten shilling notes from his mother and spend hours scrupulously duplicating them with coloured biros. Then, if one of his forgeries was particularly impressive, he would attempt to spend it! On other occasions, Andy would pester Gerald to draw pictures of Spitfires - fat, contented creations that looked a bit like camouflaged cows.

Andy's own artwork - whether plagiarised or otherwise - became a kind of black market currency with kids swapping all manner of things for one of his pictures (which he'd inevitably demand back at a later date). Andy had an advanced understanding of the bartering system and soon progressed to taking cakes and biscuits to school to 'pay' other kids to do the things he couldn't do for himself, like tying his shoelaces. He soon learned that anyone could be bought at a price.

John Partridge was eventually demobbed from the Navy in 1958; from the age of six Andy had his father around him for the first time. After 13 years in the Navy, John found the transition from service life to civvy street tougher than he expected. He shuffled uneasily through a handful of 'fetching and carrying' jobs before eventually finding some stability as chauffeur to the directors of Metal Box Ltd - a big local company. Part of his wages he spent on buying and "fixing up" a succession of three-wheelers and bubble cars.

Vera helped to make ends meet by working part-time in a chemist's shop. She was eventually sacked from this job because her fastidious compulsion to clear up all the time - often when the pharmacist was half way through fixing someone's prescription - drove everyone mad.

After the family's unforgettable Maltese adventure, Vera found life back in the UK dull and routine by comparison. She longed to go back there, and even contacted the Maltese Consulate in London to see if it was possible to work there legally. One day she read in a newspaper that the famous footballer Stanley Matthews had retired to Gozo, Malta's smaller sister island. She wrote to Matthews offering her services as a housemaid, and John's as a chauffeur, saying that she knew the islands like the back of her hand. A few weeks later Matthews wrote back thanking them for their kind offer. Although Vera and John were just the sort of couple he was looking for, he'd been told by the Maltese authorities that he could employ only local people. Eventually, after exhausting every possible channel, Vera gave up her dream of returning to Malta.

After two years in The Valley the family moved to another house on the Penhill estate at 10, Southwick Avenue. Although considered a 'better' area than The Valley, their neighbours were an equally odd assortment who fuelled Andy's interest in the cartoon-like qualities of people. No family suited this description more than the Warrens, who lived across the road from the Partridges.

Sonia Warren was a very large, big-boned woman with rosy red cheeks. By contrast her husband Jack was skinny and frail-looking. He worked nights for British Rail, but on his days off he liked nothing better than to conduct along to brass band records on his stereo-gram.

Sonia and Jack didn't get on. Jack had tried to kill himself a couple of times, and whenever he was hospitalised after such misdemeanours, Sonia would throw massive parties to celebrate. These parties became legendary in the neighbourhood.

The Warrens had three children, a daughter and two sons. The elder son Steve, who grew to be a towering deep-voiced behemoth, became Andy's closest mentor and long-time friend. Whenever the

Partridges went on holiday to either Weymouth or Cornwall, or whenever they had a family outing in one of John's 'embarrassing cars', Steve Warren would inevitably come along too.

Whenever they were together, Andy and Steve almost always ended up in trouble; indulging in adolescent sex-perimentations with willing older girls, or cruelly baiting a neighbourhood mental patient they called Noddy (because of his constant nervous head movements). They once provoked him so far he chased them down the road with a meat cleaver. The boys gave him the slip by running into the local Co-op store and hiding under the check-out counter after begging the cashier not to give them away. As time went on they developed another common interest: music.

During his Navy days John Partridge had been the ship's unofficial entertainer. He was fairly adept musically, an enthusiastic singer who also played guitar or clarinet with the ship's skiffle group. When he left the Navy he joined another skiffle group in Swindon, playing the drums. At home, there was always an acoustic guitar standing in the corner of the living room, gathering dust. John attempted to teach his son a chord or two, but the rusty old strings made Andy's little fingertips crack and bleed, and he went off the idea very quickly. There was also a piano in the living room, but Andy was impressed less by its musical potential than by its squeaking lid, and the fact that you could hide things in its stool.

Young Swindonians, like just about everyone else in the mid-sixties, were gripped by a new sensation, Beatlemania. One day Andy and Steve went to see The Beatles' film *A Hard Day's Night*. The 10-year-old Andy, dressed in his duffle coat and shorts, was shocked by the way all the girls were screaming in the cinema and wondered whether he should be screaming as well. Although The Beatles impressed him, Andy didn't associate the group with anything that had any real relevance to his life. The Beatles were like a celluloid dream - mythical and untouchable - and seemed to have been ordained by divine providence. Years later The Monkees, however - American and, ironically, far more of a Hollywood creation than The Beatles - were another matter. The girls at Andy's school loved the televised madcap antics of Mickey Dolenz and Co, and that made all the difference.

"Although I knew they were crass and there were these rumours that they didn't play their own instruments, and didn't write their own songs, The Monkees connected with me in a big way because I

13

knew that most of the girls at school liked them," says Andy. "Also I knew that I didn't look too dissimilar at that point to Peter Tork. I did everything I could to look more like him. I grew my hair into a pudding basin style and I got my mother to order Monkees-style clothing from her catalogues. Also I'd borrow my dad's Hush Puppies and stuff newspaper in them so they'd fit me - anything to look even more like Peter Tork. I was distraught when he grew a beard!"

Gradually the guitar behind the settee took on a fresh lustre. Pop music was now a nationwide youth obsession and - even though he never bought records, simply because the Partridge family didn't own a record-player - Andy was similarly hooked. In school essays, writing about the future, Andy developed this dreamy idea that he was going to be a pop star, never really believing he'd ever achieve it. Eventually he started carrying his dad's guitar with him everywhere.

"I'd actually take it to school," he remembers, "and walk around the playground not being able to play anything, but it acted like a magnet for girls, especially in Secondary School. You'd carry it along the corridor and they'd flock around you. Of course you were in deep shit when they asked you to play a song because I couldn't. I could just about get through the opening of 'Day Tripper' or 'Last Train To Clarksville'. But it was great as a girl magnet. A musical fishing rod."

In the evenings and during the school holidays Andy would get Steve Warren to bring his portable gramophone over and they'd spend hours in Andy's bedroom listening to singles like 'Itchycoo Park' by The Small Faces, 'Fire Brigade' by The Move, and records by other classic groups of the time, The Stones, The Pretty Things and The Kinks. Whenever Andy could keep the record player to himself for a couple of days, he'd play these records over and over and over at all speeds, absorbing every little thing about them and about how they sounded.

Fantasizing about being DJs, Steve and Andy set up their own pop radio station, Radio Anglo, which periodically 'broadcast' to the Penhill estate out of Andy's bedroom window. An occasional ruse was to crank up the opening hellish sermon of 'Fire' by The Crazy World Of Arthur Brown, timed to coincide with the weekly Salvation Army brass band concerts on the green at the end of Andy's Road. Mostly, though, they just compiled programmes for their own entertainment.

Stereo was just coming to the fore as an exciting new innovation, but owning a stereo record player was way beyond the reach of schoolboys. Between them they devised a way of creating a mock stereo effect on a mono Dansette by plugging and unplugging the speakers in a certain combination. They would take it in turns to lie on a table, head positioned between two mono speakers enjoying the fake stereo results. While this was going on a splurge of overlaid colour slides would be projected onto the ceiling from a Chad Valley 'Give A Show' projector, giving the experience a visual dimension. The whole show would be interspersed with emulated hippy-speak such as 'Are you getting anything?'

As Andy became further wrapped up in the romance of Sixties pop culture his parents, particularly Vera, began to voice their concern. Vera's disapproval of his ever-lengthening shaggy hairstyle - which was getting so long he now had to part it in the middle - grew to obsessive levels. What had begun as an occasional sarcastic parental rebuke had developed into a relentless nagging tirade.

"She would start on about my hair from the very second that I got up in the morning," he says. "I'd be at the breakfast table and she'd be insulting me. She'd say 'You filthy heap. Don't let anyone know that I'm your mother'. She would talk about my hair all the time that I was at home. You couldn't watch anything on TV without her saying 'Now look at his hair, it's really nice. Yours would look nice like that'. It got to the point where I actually had fantasies about murdering her - I even planned how I was going to do it!"

His mother's increasing depression was undoubtedly caused by the virtual collapse of her marriage, brought on by a brief affair John had with another woman in Swindon. The shock pushed the ever-loyal Vera into a state of hysteria. Throughout 1966, the couple's rows became furious and violent, sometimes lasting throughout the night. Indeed, Andy remembers Vera actually lunging for John with a kitchen knife on a couple of occasions. When she eventually had a nervous breakdown she was admitted for treatment at Roundway, the notorious mental hospital in nearby Devizes, and Andy can recall painful scenes there. "I'd visit my mother in this place and she'd be sat next to somebody with an umbrella up, or some woman stroking a stone like it was a baby. I'd think 'Surely my mother's not like these people?'"

Vera's illness, and the generally bad atmosphere at home, rubbed off on Andy who became exceptionally nervous and excitable - at one stage he began going to the toilet every five or ten minutes. Vera remembers the headmaster calling her into the school to discuss Andy's erratic behaviour. Subsequent medical tests and psychiatric assessment failed to come up with an answer to Andy's odd compulsion, and the 12-year-old was put on Valium tablets to calm him down. This "temporary treatment" was to last for the next 13 years.

As he approached his teens, Andy's school reports at Penhill Secondary began to reflect his declining interest in academic work, exacerbated his parents' marriage difficulties and probably the effects of the Valium. In Junior school he had always been one of the brightest in his class, coming near the top in most subjects, but now it seemed he had given up on everything except art, at which he continued to excel, winning almost every art prize the school could muster. Art alone, though, wouldn't help him very much in securing a career. For a while he'd considered joining the police force, but now it was assumed he'd follow his father into the Royal Navy.

Andy never allowed these problems to cloud his dream of pop stardom. Self-portraits featuring him with a pudding basin haircut, and playing the guitar, began to replace the forged ten shilling notes of old. He spent hours in school designing elaborate space-age guitars on the back of exercise books. Eventually he charmed Steve Warren into buying a guitar - a shop-soiled Egmond semi-acoustic model - that they could share. But Andy soon began to monopolise the instrument, and now that he had his very own guitar he wasted no time in looking around for other aspiring guitarists with whom to play.

During his final months at school, Andy met Paul Porter, "a tall, randy looking, half-caste kid" whose trouble making activities were surpassed only by his skill at seducing girls. Much to everyone's intense envy, he once got the two best-looking girls in the class to autograph his penis. That had elevated him to God-like proportions in the eyes of his peers. Porter had also discovered the girl-magnetising benefits of being seen with a guitar and was regularly to be found in the cloakroom of the school youth club, practising on the school's only electric guitar.

To Andy, Paul Porter was someone to admire and respect and he soon forged a firm friendship with him. "He'd sit there probably not playing very well," Andy recalls, "but at the time I thought it was fantastic. He seemed so sassy and because he was bigger than everyone else he monopolised this electric guitar. I'd only get it when he was bored shitless, or when a string had broken."

There was nothing special about the school guitar - it had a neck so thick it was very difficult for small hands to play - but it was a marked improvement on the shop-soiled semi-acoustic model he shared with Steve Warren. In fact, it was the only electric guitar and amplifier Andy could get anywhere near and he resented Paul Porter's monopoly of it.

So one evening after school, Andy hung around the youth club until everyone else had gone home and took the guitar and its tiny amp back home with him. As far as Andy was concerned it was now his. Predictably enough, the school authorities began to investigate the missing guitar and Andy had to restore the offending instrument to its rightful home. As swiftly and mysteriously as it had vanished, the missing guitar re-appeared.

With two all-consuming interests in common - girls and music - Paul Porter and Andy agreed to form their own group with Paul's two brothers. "There'd be one brother on drums, another on bass, Paul singing, and me on this rotten red school guitar that was umbilically connected to the shoe box amp. We'd rehearse in a classroom, and then in a disused house - which was given to the school as a renovation project - which we'd covered inside with all these psychedelic murals."

During practice sessions the group would sit around on mouldy mattresses, Paul Porter usually knocking back a bottle of cheap cider, and discuss The Plan. They eventually came up with an idea that was ingenious, but corny: they would become a kind of 'living jukebox'. The idea was to rehearse a set of songs, mostly contemporary hits like 'Baby Come Back' by The Equals and 'Hi-Ho Silver Lining', and the audience would have to choose what they played from a 'menu'. Andy had an idea for the stage-set, a large mock-up of an old fashioned juke box, which could also be used to hide the group's amps and speakers.

But before they could play live they had to do something about their equipment - after all, they didn't even have microphones to sing through! In a display of bravado, Paul offered to remedy the situation and disappeared in mid-rehearsal. An hour later he returned with half a dozen telephone receivers on his arm, thrust them at the group and said 'There you are, we can sing through these.'

"We were astounded," says Andy. "What Paul had done was wander around the Penhill estate with a pair of scissors, gone into all the phone boxes and snipped off the handsets. He took out the mouthpieces, wired them up and sang through them!"

The unnamed group practised long and hard for the big day, but the big day never came. Not least among their problems was that with only telephone mouthpieces through which to sing, each song was vocally indistinguishable from the next. Without the goal of actually playing live one day, the group simply disintegrated. Paul Porter and his brothers emerged some time after the split with a new group called, appropriately enough, The Bruvvers, but Andy saw little of them again.

In July 1969 Andy left Penhill Secondary School aged 15 and a half with no qualifications. Though he was the only pupil in his class not to go on to further education, the day couldn't have come soon enough for him. He loathed academic subjects, and most of the teachers who taught them, and refused to take any exams. His career options were extremely limited so he applied for a place on the arts course at Swindon College. Their minimum entrance age was normally 16, but the college were so impressed with Andy's precocious talent that they allowed him in immediately.

'Young Sod', as he was affectionately known to his fellow students, enjoyed college life initially. It gave him far more freedom than he was used to, and he now mixed with a class full of people in their late teens and early twenties. While he'd always been popular at school, he now found himself the centre of attention and was encouraged to make everyone laugh - which he could do with ease.

There were other advantages to being at college, most especially a girl who was every sexually inexperienced young man's dream - a virtual nymphomaniac. Though recently married, she took a perverse delight in sharing her sexuality with her male classmates on the arts course. Andy's age and naïvety made him particularly vulnerable and she lavished special attention on him. He was frequently at the receiving end of her lewd sexual advances.

"She'd hide in the dark room during photography lessons. You'd think you were in there alone and suddenly you'd feel this hand going down the front of your trousers. She'd make me tell her these dirty stories and I got the feeling she had a hand down her trousers as well. Of course, when you're a 16 year old virgin this is shocking stuff."

Quite unknown to her husband, she and Andy enjoyed a bizarre quasi-sexual relationship for several months. Although Andy (just) held on to his virginity throughout, it was a highly enlightening experience for a young boy who'd previously been unable even to talk to any girl he fancied without breaking into a sweat.

The demise of Paul Porter's 'slaves to the juke box' left a temporary vacuum in Andy's musical development. He had yet to become proficient as a guitarist, but he was progressing steadily by playing along to records in the student common room. He earned himself the new nickname 'Rocky' after mastering the essential components of 'Rocky Raccoon' by The Beatles, and was often persuaded to stand up in front of the class and play it. On several occasions he was physically lifted on to a desk top by older boys and ordered to perform.

One day in the common room he was heard by a fellow student called Martin Vincent. Vincent was older than Andy by two or three years and bore a passing resemblance to a ginger-haired, goatee-bearded rocker called Ian Anderson and, not-too-coincidentally, was a big fan of his exciting new band Jethro Tull. Fancying himself as a singer and harmonica player, Vincent decided to put his own group together and invited Andy to audition.

Andy turned up to the audition in some lock-up garages in Swindon's Old Town with a borrowed electric guitar and watched in dismay as a guy in his mid-twenties, also auditioning, raced through songs with the flair and abandon of Jimi Hendrix. "When I saw him I thought 'That's it, I haven't got the job. I can't play like this.' I could play a couple of chords and a few lines, which was pathetic compared to what this guy was doing."

But Andy's rival was eventually judged *too* good (and too old) because no-one in Vincent's band could play very well, and the last thing they wanted was a flash guitarist whose playing would emphasise their own limited ability. Despite his shortcomings, Andy was ideal: he was young, he looked more the part and he certainly wasn't in danger of showing anyone up with his dazzling guitar trickery. For these reasons he was in. Stray Blues (named after The Rolling Stones song 'Stray Cat Blues') had - like many of Andy's early groups - bags of enthusiasm but very little ability. They were an unlikely rabble with little in common. Martin Vincent, despite his rock star aspirations, was a fastidious character who kept his harmonica collection in the loops of a modified gun belt. Tony Hancock, on guitar or bass, was a kindly country yokel who was oblivious to the fact that Andy was poaching his girlfriend whenever he got the chance. And Mick, the drummer, was a naval cadet who frequently sat in rehearsals in his uniform.

Only Andy, with his Peter Tork pudding-basin haircut and roll-neck sweaters, had any whiff of charisma. It made up for the fact that he was still a pretty poor guitarist and had somehow managed to learn the 'wrong' three chord sequence - E, A and D as opposed to E, A and B.

Stray Blues (or The Gods as they contemplated calling themselves) naturally had delusions of grandeur. They saw themselves as a capable blues/rock outfit, but the rest of the world thought differently. Most of their set relied heavily on improvisation and when they attempted the occasional Fleetwood Mac or Jimi Hendrix cover it was rendered virtually unrecognisable - or jarred horribly - thanks to Andy's use of the wrong three chords. Despite weeks of rehearsal they only played three gigs. The third, and most eventful of these, took place in the spring of 1970.

McIlroy's, a large department store in the centre of Swindon, used to house a ballroom where professional groups would play when they came to Swindon. The Beatles played there in July 1962, and received a lukewarm reception 'because they were from up north'. Monday was disco night at McIlroy's - a 'Hop' as these events were known - during which a 45 minute show-case slot was given over to local bands who earned themselves £8. These slots were much sought after because they guaranteed a captive audience of several hundred and a good performance could lead to further bookings around town. A bad set was like a rodeo ride: the challenge was to stay on for as long as possible.

Stray Blues didn't have much gear and Andy had to hire a huge Marshall stack but even with the extra amplification they came to grief. After finishing their first number they had just begun a second improvised riffing piece when the DJ noticed how badly they were going down. He put a record on straight away and ordered the band off stage.

"Poor old Martin Vincent," Andy remembers. "He was so distressed. He was literally on his knees in tears begging the DJ to let us go back on and do another song. Even the audience were calling out for more. I think it was a case of 'They're so awful, we want to laugh some more'."

The DJ relented and allowed them to play one more song. Almost immediately a bunch of skinheads in the audience started throwing pennies at the group. These hurt like hell when they found their targets and Andy, not wishing to take any more humiliation - and fearing for his safety - sheltered behind the Marshall stack and played the guitar on his lap with a plastic bottle-neck.

"There was quite a lot of applause afterwards, but the records went on straight away, so we got to play two and a half songs in total. Martin left early and went home, leaving us to pack away the stuff. He was very upset that his glorious show-case gig had been pulled. I think he thought that this was going to be the start of the big time," says Andy.

Instead it was the end of Stray Blues. Everyone was demoralised by the night's events and the band simply disintegrated. Andy never saw Martin Vincent again. Although short lived, Stray Blues had given Andy a taste for being in a rock'n'roll band, and he never doubted that this was what he really wanted to do.

3

REAL BY REEL

With Stray Blues in disarray, Andy began looking around for other like-minded teenagers with whom he could indulge his two unfulfilled obsessions: music and sex. He won £10 in a 'draw your favourite Monkee' competition (he drew Mickey Dolenz), bought a second-hand reel to reel tape recorder and began experimenting in his bedroom without much success. Equally, on the girl front, his progress was rather limited - he'd managed a clumsy grope inside his latest girlfriend's blouse, but this left him feeling even more frustrated. Then he met Spud.

Michael "Spud" Taylor was one of life's ordained beatniks with a casual outlook on everything, which impressed Andy immensely. Shortish with long greasy fair hair that flopped over one eye, he wasn't what you'd call handsome but he had a self-assurance that girls found attractive. Spud had girls taking their clothes off and climbing into the bath with him! If this weren't impressive enough, he also played the bass guitar.

Spud Taylor gradually became a kind of guru to Andy. He seemed so sophisticated in many ways, and his musical taste was miles ahead of Andy. His record collection was full of highly obscure imports by avant garde artists such as Hans Bennink and Eric Dolphy. The nearest he had to anything 'conventional' was a copy of Captain Beefheart's 'Trout Mask Replica'. Initially Andy was resistant to such experimental sounds, but he grew to genuinely appreciate many of them when Spud insisted that he borrow them. Not that Andy had much choice: many of his own records had been taken away by Spud on the pretext of a loan and never returned.

"Because of Spud I had this weird split musical upbringing where one side of me wanted to learn the chords to 'Lazy Sunday' and the other side of me wanted to sit in with Sun Ra and his Solar Arkestra. He was tremendously influential."

Like Andy, Spud lived on the Penhill estate. The two of them regularly got together to jam, attempting to peel back rock's dis-

22

sonant horizons in their own inimitable way. In the main this involved hours of experimenting on Andy's reel to reel tape recorder. Spud's record collection was the main source of reference for their challenging avant garde 'pieces'. Typically these were 20 minute recordings of feedback noises over which they would improvise strange spacey blues riffs with Andy on his trusty Egmond guitar and Spud on bass.

"We thought this stuff was fantastic!" Andy admits. "It was right 'out there' and only people on the very fringes of 'out there-ness' would ever get into it, but we thought we were really cool making this music.

"It had a lot to do with these bands Spud was introducing me to. I got the feeling that some of them were making these avant garde noises to cover up for the fact that they couldn't play very well. It was great because I could play just like them. I was the ape with the guitar. I could make these squeaking skwonking noises too!"

In the early summer of 1970 Spud and Andy finally emerged from the bedroom, teaming up with drummer Tony Climpson to form their own group. Previously a member of a rival Swindon group called Orange, Climpson was an ex-public schoolboy-turned-hippy. Always over-compensating for his impeccable middle class background, Climpson worked as a conductor for Swindon Corporation buses but his main contribution to the hippy revolution was letting people off their bus fares! He also took every chemical substance he could lay his hands on.

Although surrounded by several soft drug users, Andy's notion of an 'altered consciousness' meant getting drunk and doing way out things like lying in a field with his guitar, and improvising to the star patterns. He never once touched drugs, except the legally prescribed variety, fearing the consequences if he did. His mind was quite capable of working overtime on its own without chemical assistance.

"I wouldn't tell people about these Valium tablets I was taking," he admits. "I felt very illicit about them and I was a bit worried that they wouldn't mix with anything else. It was a mixture of fear and concern that if I did take anything it would make me like the idiots I'd encountered at parties".

The unlikely trio of Spud, Andy and Tony Climpson named themselves Stiff Beach and, modelled rather hopefully on Cream, attempted to master a heavy blues sound. This meant they didn't have to worry about writing songs, since their own "original" material was simply a succession of lumbering, thundering chord progressions.

Stiff Beach played only two gigs and both were disasters! The first at a W.H.Smith staff dance, and the second at the British Legion club at Stratton, a tiny village near Swindon, where they got the thumbs down from the open-mouthed audiences who failed to appreciate the very loud, improvised, triangular riffs that Stiff Beach peddled. Even the non-original material they played - bad Cream and Taste covers - went way above the heads of people whose idea of pop music was easy listening fare like 'All Kinds Of Everything' by Eurovision winner Dana.

Soon after these embarrassments, Spud pronounced Stiff Beach dead. In July 1971, Tony Climpson quit, leaving the musical nucleus of Spud and Andy who renamed themselves Tongue in celebration of "the most exploratory part of the body". The idea was that they too would aim to become more exploratory - but Tongue was essentially the same old rambling blues-rock outfit.

Sure, there were changes - Spud had moved from bass to alto-sax and Tony Climpson had been replaced by Tony Hill, who was at least 15 years their senior and, by their standards, amazingly straight. Andy and Spud were still firmly resolved to making way-out music, though Tony Hill's family background - the Hills were well known local cement magnates - and social status made him an unlikely ally for Spud and Andy. "He was horrendously square in all attributes," says Andy. "Except he did have this passion for jazz music. I remember us rehearsing a song called 'Pterodactyl'. It was typical of what we'd do. We'd pick an obscure word, put it into an obscure riff, and play it obscurely! It was great fun if you were doing it, but you really had to be of an altered consciousness or very pretentious to get into it."

Tongue spent a few weeks jamming and rehearsing together, occasionally at Tony Hill's house, but the group never got to play any gigs. Whenever they phoned local pubs to arrange their début gig, they would be asked what kind of music they played. The reply "free-form, experimental jazz" would be closely followed by the sound of the phone being put down. Gradually the rehearsals became fewer and fewer and by the end of the summer of 1971 they had ceased altogether.

Mostly Spud lacked the patience and sense of routine to organise rehearsals and gigs. He was an impetuous character who changed his opinions and views at the rate most people changed their socks. Andy felt he was too preoccupied with his latest craze to care about the band and became exasperated by his utter unpredictability. "I couldn't keep up with Spud. He had these phases and he'd go wholeheartedly into them, buy all the paraphernalia, then a little while later he'd move onto something else. He'd be into Zen Buddhism one week then he'd want to be a Hell's Angel the next - that kind of thing. Being his friend was a real rollercoaster ride on your emotions, but it was inspirational at the same time."

Andy valued Spud's friendship, and still liked him tremendously, but he was fast realising they didn't share the same goals and ambitions. As Tongue fell apart Andy began thinking about forming a new group. Through his old mate Steve Warren he had met Dave Cartner, another Penhill resident, and they decided to form a group together. Dave owned two electric guitars and a 100 watt Carlsboro stack - ample reason for Andy to want to know anyone in those days - and, in contrast to Spud, he was down-to-earth and practical.

When they first met, Dave couldn't play guitar very well which would exclude him from Andy's various bands. But times were changing: Andy was fast improving as a guitarist and so was Dave. They had similar tastes in music and they both looked quite good. Cartner was a little on the large side but he had long hair and Charles I-style ringlets, which gave him something of a Cavalier appearance.

Soon Andy was spending most of his spare time at the top-floor council flat where Dave lived with his widowed mother. The days together seemed to revolve around three things - beer, sex and music. They rehearsed at deafening volume in Dave's bedroom and upset the neighbourhood night-shift workers with Partridge originals such as 'Sperm Whale Rock' - a title chosen because it sounded heavy! And when they weren't rehearsing they'd be waylaid in the local pub, getting drunk. This would result in Andy having to spend the night at Dave's because his mother - ever fearful of the demon alcohol - wouldn't let him in the house.

Andy and Dave recruited several other local musicians into their group and christened it Clark Kent, reflecting Andy's obsession with American comics. Like most of Andy's early groups Clark Kent existed mainly for rehearsals, and weren't very good. They often rehearsed in the Penhill library common room and finally managed to arrange a gig at an end-of-term bash at Headlands School in Swindon, with a line-up featuring Andy and Dave on guitars, plus a rhythm section, with Andy also handling vocals.

It was an inauspicious occasion: 'Sperm Whale Rock' - along with other comic-influenced Partridge compositions like 'My Baby Was A

Reptile' - was not hailed an instant classic by the youthful audience and gradually they made it clear what they thought of Clark Kent. Eventually the whole crowd disappeared - except for one drunken dancing figure.

"We'd emptied the hall the noise was so horrible," recalls Andy, "and the lights were on full blaze when the doors swung open and this character staggered in drunk with hair down to his waist and a bottle of cider in his hand. That was my first sighting of Colin Moulding."

Colin Ivor Moulding was born in the front room of his parents' home at 2, Hinton Street, Gorse Hill, Swindon, on August 17, 1955. His mother Vera (evidently a popular name in Swindon before the war!) elected to have her second child at home as was the fashion in those days and Charlie, her husband, was happy to agree. As was usual then, he wasn't present at the birth.

Both born and bred Swindonians, the Mouldings were typical of young working class couples in the Fifties. In many ways they were the quintessential Mr and Mrs Normal - no grand ideas, no outstanding aspirations. They didn't have much but they weren't left wanting for much either. Vera seemed content with her lot, and as long as Charlie had enough spare cash to go to the pub each evening he was happy too.

Charlie was constantly in and out of work. British Rail was the principal employer in Swindon in those days and he alternated between long spells as a coalman on the Great Western Railway and periods as a caretaker at various schools around town. Vera did her bit in between raising their two children by working part-time as a laundry woman. They lived with Charlie's recently widowed mother in her modest two up and two down terraced house in Gorse Hill, an area sandwiched between the town centre and the Penhill estate.

Colin was just five weeks old when the family were at last allocated their own council house, but they were less than happy when they discovered it was on the edge of The Valley, the notorious corner of Penhill. Vera hated their new home at 13, Minety Road, a house on a steep hill with no nearby shops, and with no family car she found the constant journeys up and down the hill exhausting. After only eight months the couple applied for another council house and moved back to Charlie's mother's place in Hinton Street.

Two years later they were back at Penhill and resigned to making a go of it this time. Their two bedroom house at 9, Tilshead Walk was a bit small - especially as Charlie's still-grieving mother kept coming to stay - but at least it was in a better area, far enough away from the undesirables in The Valley.

Colin grew up a happy, unassuming and contented child. Although he was by no means a loner, he was painfully shy and always afraid of stepping out of line. He got on okay with his brother Graham most of the time but Graham was five years older than Colin and, although normally kind-hearted and generous, he had an explosive temper. Whenever the brothers argued, Colin would lock himself in the bathroom to escape Graham's wrath. The Mouldings' bathroom door was forever being patched up where Graham had then tried to kick it down.

Outside the home Colin was content with his small group of friends and had become especially close to a boy called Alan Watts. "He was pretty big in my life," Colin explains. "He was one of these people who was into everything. I tended to follow those sort of people."

Spurred on by Alan Watt's infectious enthusiasm, and the total lack of recreational facilities on the estate, young Moulding's interests were impressively diverse - cycling, fishing and astronomy took up most of his time. He also became keenly interested in local history and topography and frequently went off by himself on field trips. Apart from these occasions, the only other time he got away from Swindon was during the family's annual summer holiday to Weymouth. Colin's dad especially liked Weymouth. He constantly suffered from chest complaints, aggravated by his heavy smoking, and claimed the Weymouth sea air did wonders for his lungs.

By 1960, steam locomotives, and therefore railway coalmen, were rapidly becoming anachronisms and Charlie was made redundant by the GWR. He soon got a job as a delivery man for an upmarket grocery firm called Masons and Gillets. Colin loved going with him on his rounds, dropping off supplies for well-to-do local households. As he grew older it was obvious Colin took after his father much more than his mother. He shared his father's temperament and many of his interests.

If there is such a thing as the male menopause then Charlie Moulding experienced it. As he reached his forties he resisted middle age as if it were some contemptible virus and he began to dress in the flared trousers and brightly coloured shirts that were *de rigueur* for the younger generation. His friends noticed that he was deliberately turning his back on many of his old haunts and then, almost inevit-

27

ably, he had an affair with a school cleaner which lasted several years. The very proper Vera, who adhered rigidly to her Victorian values, watched all this from the sidelines unable to do much about it, but stood by him.

Charlie had been a singer with several bands in his time and regularly performed in the pubs and clubs around Gorse Hill. Even when he wasn't officially appearing with a band, if he was in a pub and had downed a pint or two he could be persuaded to get up and do a turn. And his interest in music didn't end with the crooners he imitated - unusually for someone of his generation he liked a lot of the so-called 'beat' groups of the Sixties.

"My dad was into The Kinks before I was," says Colin. "One of his favourite songs was 'Autumn Almanac'. He was well into the Sixties thing. Bob Dylan was another of his favourites - he knew all the words to the songs on 'Freewheeling'. It seemed as though he was always singing. He'd usually break into song when we had people round, much to my mum's embarrassment. After a few drinks he'd be in his own little world singing these songs with my mum telling him to shut up, and me and me brother cringing in the corner. It became quite a family joke."

The Sixties music scene mostly passed Colin by. He was too young to appreciate anything other than the occasional chart hit, which he would hear at the weekly Penhill church hall hop. He went regularly to the hop as it was a good place to look at girls (he was too shy to chat them up) and watch amateur local bands on stage.

On one occasion he stumbled into the church hall when a well-known local group called Oozy was rehearsing and he ventured in to take a closer look. "They were recording themselves," Colin remembers. "They had one of those old reel to reel tape recorders at the back of the hall with a microphone dangling over the push bar of the fire exit. That was my first brush with recording, and I thought it was so revolutionary. Until then I'd never equated recording with making records."

After eight years at Penhill school Colin transferred to Headlands school in September 1969 - the same time, coincidentally, that Charlie was installed as the school caretaker, having lost his job with Masons and Gillet a year earlier. A bungalow in the school grounds went with the job, and the Mouldings willingly moved the mile or so from Penhill.

In June 1970, Colin heard a record that changed how he thought about music. Free's first hit, 'Alright Now', was a full-throated blues anthem which reached number two in the pop charts. Colin rushed out and bought the band's album 'Fire And Water' and from that point he was hooked. In the ensuing years Free was the band by which all others were judged.

Colin began pestering his father to let him have a bass guitar, and Charlie relented on condition that he took bass lessons to prove that he was serious about learning to play. They visited Kempsters, the local music store, and picked out a second hand Shaftesbury Rickenbacker-copy - which turned out to be Spud Taylor's old bass - plus a WEM speaker cabinet and amplifier. These were bought for £65 on a hire purchase agreement with the Victoria finance company in Swindon and because Charlie didn't own his own home, one of Colin's relatively well-off aunts reluctantly agreed to stand guarantor.

"I became a total gear freak, as I think a lot of people did around that time," Colin recalls. "If you knew someone who had a Marshall stack it really impressed you. I lost interest in school work. In my early teens I had pretty high hopes of doing something academic, but once I'd discovered music it all went out the window. I started growing my hair and got totally engrossed in the scene."

His parents were surprisingly easy-going about Colin's long hair, but were less tolerant of his declining interest in school work. He'd always been a consistent, diligent worker and Headlands prided itself on being an ex-grammar school, turning out pupils that were a notch above most other schools in the area.

But Colin was more interested in Free and Led Zeppelin than French and Maths. He managed a slightly disappointing three 'O' Level passes but he was sufficiently encouraged to return to the sixth form, and it was widely assumed that he would eventually get a sensible steady job with one of Swindon's insurance firms. All that was now falling by the wayside, and all he could talk and think about was rock music. He was a regular at local rock gigs and at the school end-of-term dance he witnessed the only performance by Clark Kent, the group fronted by Andy Partridge.

During the summer school holidays Colin's hair (which grew exceptionally quickly) had become very long. It had grown past the psychologically important shoulder-length stage and Colin was rightfully proud of the way he looked. His mind had become fixed on more glamorous prospects than a 20 year career with Hambro Life, and he was reluctant about going back for sixth form in September. But, typically, he was wary of upsetting his parents.

On the first day back the headmaster caught sight of Colin's cascading mane and ordered him into his office. He was reminded that the school rules forbade long hair and told that if he wished to stay on and complete his education he would have to get it cut to a 'respectable' length immediately. "There was a big thing because my old chap wanted me to stay on at school - wanted me to get my hair cut and take my 'A' Levels, as any normal father would I suppose. It was extra difficult because I was the caretaker's son and the headmaster didn't want to expel me, but at the same time he couldn't favour me."

This confrontation proved to be an ideal opportunity for Colin. He refused to get his hair cut and so he was expelled - which, of course, was what he wanted. Charlie was disappointed but didn't make a big issue of it - it was his boy's life after all, even if he was going to be on the dole.

After four months of signing on, Colin finally got his first job. In January 1972, he started work as a milkman - or rather a milkman's assistant, as he was still too young to drive the milk float legally. Despite the anti-social hours, Colin quite enjoyed the work. He was fast coming out of his shell and soon discovered several other "long-haired freaks" working "on the milk". He befriended several of his colleagues, notably Paul Henry, and by working extra shifts they could accumulate days off and then treat themselves to a long weekend off, hitch-hiking around the countryside and sleeping rough overnight.

Very occasionally, Colin would also meet up with his old mate Alan Watts but they had grown apart almost from the moment Colin had discovered music. Watts was still heavily into cycling and was a member of the Swindon Wheelers Cycling Club. Tragically, it was this interest that was directly responsible for his untimely death. At the age of 17 he was knocked off his bike one day by a passing car and killed.

By the early seventies Swindon's principal rock venue, McIlroy's Ballroom, was regularly playing host to the new breed of heavy rockers - groups like Atomic Rooster and Uriah Heep. Everything about these groups - their image, their hair and the sheer ferocity of their music - left Colin gobsmacked. There was something menacing in their awesome power and the row of tall stacked speaker columns that experienced fans like Colin knew was called the 'back-line'.

A good way of getting in free to some of these shows - and to meet the bands - was to hang around outside McIlroy's in the afternoon and help to unload their equipment from the trucks into the venue. Mott The Hoople had recently had a hit with the David Bowie-penned 'All The Young Dudes' and when they came to town, Colin was there, eagerly waiting with the small group of unofficial roadies. Soon he and another local guy were carrying singer Ian Hunter's piano up a flight of stairs into the hall. Suddenly it slipped from their grasp and it went crashing to the bottom of the stairs. "We didn't hang about, we just ran," says Colin. "We couldn't bear the embarrassment of having to face Ian Hunter and tell him what we'd done. I didn't get to go to the gig because I was so frightened that he might spot me in the audience!"

1972 was a magical year for Colin: for the first time in his life he had money of his own and could get around to a succession of rock festivals - Weeley, Buxton, Reading - watching groups like T Rex and Coliseum while knocking back huge quantities of cider. He and his fellow "freaks on the milk" had discovered alcohol in a big way, and whenever the opportunity arose they would drink themselves into near oblivion. More significantly, Colin was able to afford a brand new bass guitar - a mustard coloured Fender Jazz - and get into the serious business of trying to emulate his heavy rock heroes.

Around the same time that he acquired the bass he met an aspiring drummer called Terry in his local pub.

Terry Chambers was born on July 16, 1955, at a nursing home on Westlecott Road, Swindon. The youngest of three children, his parents were already in their forties when he was born. His dad Pete Chambers managed a dry cleaning shop for a while, but spent most of his life working as a taxi driver. His mother, Eileen, spent most of hers raising the children as there was a twelve year age gap between Gloria, the eldest, and Terry.

The Chambers were reasonably well off by Fifties working class standards. They owned their own house and were able to afford many of life's creature comforts. When Terry was three they moved into a three bedroom detached house on Swindon's Whitworth Road (his parents still live there today) where he shared one of the bedrooms with his brother Dave who was two years older. Apart from the occasional brotherly scrap, they were quite close, sharing some of the same interests and some of the same friends. Gloria, being so much older than Terry, was a remote figure by the time he was old enough to notice. It seemed she was always either at work at the hairdresser's or getting ready to go out - wafts of her perfume or jazz records tumbling down the stairs most evenings.

As a child Terry was very quiet and was quite happy to be left to his own devices. "Having two brothers I suppose I was able to notice how quiet Terry was," says Gloria. "David was the outgoing one - always bored and not knowing what to do. But Terry was quite content to sit and read a book."

His first real passion in life was football which grew to monopolise his waking thoughts. When he wasn't playing football he was fantasizing about it - dreaming of one day playing for his favourite club, Chelsea, or transporting himself to the Lilliputian world of Subbuteo table soccer. He went through his school days convinced that he was destined to become a professional footballer, much to the detriment of his academic studies.

In July 1971 he left Heriod Burner secondary high school, aged 16, with no academic qualifications. He'd been suspended from school, along with several others, for drinking a couple of bottles of potent cider and relieving themselves in a garage near the school. Spotted by the proprietor and forced to stand in an identity parade, the culprits were collared and immediately suspended just before they were due to sit their 'O' Level exams.

During a three month spell on the dole, Terry took his single-minded ambitions to the gates of Swindon Town FC who were sufficiently impressed with his skills to offer him a trial but he was turned down because of his slight build. Terry had a stubborn streak which often manifested itself in perverse ways and, disillusioned by Swindon's rejection, he chose not to approach other professional clubs. Instead he gave up hopes of a soccer career and, indeed, lost much of his interest in the game generally.

Terry's next employment was at a firm of builders' merchants called Bamburgers. After a year there he took an apprenticeship as a printer for Thorns, the electrical company, sticking with that job for the next five years. (His printing skills were very useful to XTC in the run-up to getting their record deal. Terry would often stay on after hours and print up posters, leaflets and stickers).

By 1972, like Colin, he had discovered the heavy rock scene and frequently went to see bands at either McIlroy's Ballroom or the Corn Hall in Devizes. Led Zeppelin's drummer John Bonham became one of his big heroes, and the thunderous sound that Bonham got out of his drumkit was the initial inspiration for Terry to start learning the drums himself. With money he'd saved up he bought a second-hand Pearl kit and started practising. He would set the kit up either in the family living room (dampening down the sound with tea towels!), or in his dad's garage. The noise upset the neighbours from time to time, but Terry's commitment was unshakeable.

Drumming rapidly replaced soccer as the main passion in his life. He taught himself to play by banging along to records by some of his favourite bands like Free, Jethro Tull, The Pink Fairies (who had two drummers!) and, most especially, Led Zeppelin. "If Terry took anything up he stuck at it," says his brother Dave. "Like with his football - he had nets made up and he spent hours just kicking the ball around and practising. It was the same with the drums; he'd stay in night after night and practise."

The once shy, reticent Terry opened up noticeably. Like his father and older brother before him, he immersed himself in the Swindon pub scene. Drinking and socialising became an attractive respite from the mundanity of day to day life. He started going out with girls - eventually finding himself a steady girlfriend in Lynn Fowler, who co-incidentally was a cousin of Colin's wife-to-be Carol.

Through the pubs he met other aspiring musicians like Steve Phillips, who had just started to learn to play guitar through a tiny 40 watt WEM amp. Phillips wasn't brave enough to throw himself into a band with musicians who could play well but was looking for like-minded beginners.

Over several evenings at The Stage Bar Tavern - one of the trendier watering holes in Swindon's old town - Terry got talking to Colin Moulding who seemed to like the same kind of music. Although they had only been learning how to play their instruments for a few months, the bassist and drummer were both dedicated and conscientious in their approach. Terry suggested that Colin, Steve Phillips and he should all hook up together and start a band. Colin agreed. He liked Terry even if their relationship was based on superficial self-interest.

"He was a pretty simplistic chap," Colin explains. "Very down-to-earth, very 'Swindon'. But he could be cold and brash. You couldn't approach Terry about emotional subjects - relationships and things. That was all just cissy talk to him. Our conversations would always revolve around women or drink or music."

With Charlie Moulding's permission, the un-named trio began to rehearse primitive covers of Rolling Stones and Pink Fairies songs in one of the classrooms at Headlands school, or at the Bolingbrook Arms at Hook - a pub owned by Steve Phillips' parents. For a couple of rehearsals this trio was augmented by another drinking buddy of Colin's called Steve Percival who modelled himself on Mick Jagger, but no one much cared for his singing. Not surprisingly, they never progressed beyond the occasional rehearsal and both Terry and Colin sensed this embryonic unit was never going to achieve success. However, they made a pact that if one of them was ever invited to join a band, he would make sure the other got in too.

4

DAY IN, DAY OUT

It didn't take long for Andy to tire of college life. The initial attractions of a more liberal study régime and the chance to indulge his creative muse all day soon wore off as he realised he wasn't being stretched and was, in fact, a better artist than the course made allowances for. Neither did he enjoy being permanently broke and having to rely on hand-outs from his parents for everything.

He began to spend more and more of his study time indulging in pranks - infantile practical jokes such as stealing lino from the college stores to make model boats, and then floating them in the town garden's pond. Another favourite pastime was raiding the college cookery department during lunch breaks and glueing the tables and chairs to the ceiling! Boredom always found its own distractions and when Andy wasn't in college, he could be found in the gardens with a bottle or two of cider practising the guitar for hours on end.

It was no surprise that Andy's dissatisfaction with academic life led him to leave Swindon College in February 1971 after only 18 months and, maintaining an academic consistency of sorts, he left without sitting any exams. He'd lost all ambition to become a graphic artist or designer. Indeed, he found it hard to be motivated by anything other than music.

In the wake of his brief college education, Andy settled into a succession of manual jobs and non-jobs. His father now worked as a delivery driver for the *Swindon Evening Advertiser*. One day he noticed there was a vacancy in the reporters' room for a teaboy/messenger and put in a good word for Andy who got the job without even an interview.

Andy proved to be a fast efficient worker, though not through any particular desire to impress his superiors. He regarded work as an irritating inconvenience and swiftly learned ways of minimising his workload. One of his duties involved cycling a mile to and from the central bus station several times a day to pick up packages sent from outlying villages. Andy soon identified the relevant bus numbers and, much to the annoyance of their drivers, intercepted them outside the *Evening Advertiser* by leaping out in front of them, thus saving innumerable back breaking journeys up and down Victoria Hill.

Most of the work defied the original job description. In line with tradition, some of the journalists had drink problems and came to rely on Andy to fetch hangover cures, or pick up car keys from wherever they'd been left for safe keeping. He became as much an emotional crutch as the office dogsbody and one journalist in particular, flamboyant film critic Peter Holmes, took a shine to him.

Holmes regularly received complimentary tickets to the movies and when he was short of a companion he would ask Andy along. He was openly gay before it was acceptable to be so, and his already startling appearance was heightened by recent brain surgery which left his shaven head scarred like Frankenstein's monster. Recovery from the operation coincided with his 'coming out', and he'd gone from being quietly camp to openly gay in the space of a few weeks. He announced his arrival at work each morning with a very theatrical 'I'm here, dahlings', and his wardrobe had begun to resemble a fluorescent light show.

On their trips to the cinema, Holmes would buy Andy as much popcorn as he could possibly want to eat, and in exchange for this and the free ticket, Andy would let Holmes rest his hand on his leg, just as long as it went no further. Although Andy found this rather disturbing, he thought it a small price to pay for getting in to so many new films for free.

When Andy turned 18 on November 11, 1971, the management of the *Swindon Evening Advertiser*, in their wisdom, decided that he was not worth paying an adult wage. Andy was politely but firmly shown the door. He never cared much when a job came to an end. It gave him a chance to relax and enjoy a few carefree weeks on the dole. He spent this extra time practising the guitar, or exploring the quiet Wiltshire lanes on the back of his cumbersome Eastern-bloc moped, which he'd saved up and bought with his wages from the *Evening Advertiser* to eradicate those arduous journeys up and down Victoria Hill. (This was the only motorised vehicle Andy ever owned. To this day he has never learned to drive.)

For a while he had an additional distraction in unpaid work with the *Swindon Free Press* - an amateur pastiche of hip anti-establishment, underground magazines of the day like International Times and Oz. It was the brain-child of a middle aged teacher/crusader called Greg

Wilkinson, and Andy undertook most of the magazine's design and illustration, and had a hand in writing its naïve idealistic articles.

By the spring of 1972 he was back in full time employment, working in the record department of a large store called Bon Marche. This was much more his style - not only could he play music all day long but he could dress however he wanted. The joy of doing something he really liked even made him endure ridicule and victimisation from other members of the staff for his long hair and brightly coloured clothes. It was the music that mattered.

Band-wise, Andy's career had stuttered to a halt. The end-of-term show by Clark Kent had been so abysmal that the whole band realised there was no point in continuing. But Andy and Dave Cartner had vowed to consider new possibilities; in fact, they'd made a pact that from now on they would always include each other in future projects. But since no-one else on the local scene was likely to offer either of them a post as lead guitarist, they decided to take direct action and form a new group themselves.

Star Park featured Dave and Andy both doubling up on guitar and vocals plus a couple of recent acquaintances, Paul Wilson on drums and a character simply known as Nervous Steve on bass. This aggregate did their best to sound like Wiltshire's answer to Free or The Grateful Dead, but fell laughably short of the mark. They were essentially a second-hand pretentious cod-hippy combo with stars in their eyes and holes in their pockets. Although indistinguishable from countless other struggling blues/rock groups of that era, they nevertheless managed to become quite well known around Swindon, a reputation based on the handful of gigs they did play.

The most notable of these was in summer 1972 at Swindon Town Hall, supporting blues favourites Chicken Shack. While Nervous Steve - dressed in a floor length purple cardigan - characteristically kept his back turned to the audience all the way through the gig (hence the nickname), Andy attempted to turn Star Park's set into a mini-Woodstock, a surreal psychedelic happening. He handed out dozens of small plastic containers of soapy 'bubble' liquid, or spare drums and tambourines, urging the audience to become more involved. And over the top of the band's leaden blues-rock riffs, Andy would coax swirling spacey noises from his guitar by feeding it through on a home made 'tone generator'.

Soon Andy was back on the dole. He left Bon Marche under a cloud of suspicion after being falsely accused by an over-officious store detective of stealing and deliberately down-marking records. The job had lasted just six months. Long, empty days stretched before him and on his frequent trips to Kempster's - Swindon's best known music shop - Andy would often meet other musicians and exchange ideas and occasionally accept invitations to jam with them. The volatile nature of these early bands meant that it was always best to consider the possibility of a better offer coming your way. One day towards the end of 1972, while in Kempster's, Andy bumped into Colin Moulding again.

Once they got talking Andy discovered they had in fact crossed paths at various points in the past. Colin's family had also lived on the Penhill estate and, although he was a couple of years younger than Andy, he knew him by reputation. Colin remembered him as the star of the playground at Penhill Secondary school (one of his party pieces was drawing caricatures of the teachers that would have everyone in stitches).

In December 1972 Nervous Steve was unceremoniously dropped from Star Park, and their unsuitably jazzy drummer Paul Wilson left Swindon altogether to join a Scientology commune, so Andy resorted to the usual channels to recruit new musicians. At first Colin Moulding wasn't an obvious choice because he'd never played in a 'proper' band, but when they jammed together something clicked. As always, it also helped that he looked good.

"I don't know how I got to finding out that Colin owned a bass," says Andy. "It was probably through bumping into him in Kempster's music shop. In those days you felt no compunction about just taking an instrument off the wall and playing, much to the chagrin of the owner Jeff Kempster who asked me to leave the premises many times!

"I'd go in there on a Saturday and take a guitar off the wall and plug it in on the pretext of trying out a certain amp. Colin would come in and do the same with a bass guitar. He'd suddenly be underpinning what I was playing. You'd think 'Hey! We've got a little scene going here!'"

But the two didn't instantly strike up an easy rapport, partly because Colin was still rather shy. "He was painfully quiet, he never uttered more than one syllable at a time!" recalls Andy. "It was ages before I actually heard him talk. He'd just nod or mumble one or two words under his breath."

"I'd known about Andy for a long time," says Colin. "He was the type of person who drew attention to himself wherever he went. If you were a musician in Swindon you were bound to come across him sooner or later."

As the jams became more frequent and the talk turned to making their get-togethers more permanent, Colin told Andy that like him and Dave Cartner he had made a pact with another local musician. Andy was pleasantly surprised by Terry Chamber's drumming. Although basic, he had a style much better suited to his kind of music than anyone he'd come across to date.

Star Park (Mark II) began rehearsing in earnest around March 1973 in preparation for live shows. Although they carried the same name as the band that had featured Nervous Steve and Paul Wilson, this was a substantially different animal. Each member brought his own influence to the group, but it was Andy's character and experience that came through the loudest.

"You brought in things that were in your record collection at that time," Andy explains. "Colin would be nutty on Black Sabbath and Uriah Heep that week. Cartner would be into Thin Lizzy or Atomic Rooster. Chambers, The Pink Fairies of course, and I'd just have discovered The New York Dolls and The Stooges . . . it was that sort of thing."

Andy was steadily getting more carried away by the emerging crop of glam bands from Britain and (especially) America. The visual - not to mention musical - rebelliousness of people like Alice Cooper, The New York Dolls and The Stooges was being hurled at young British audiences via the pages of imported American pop mags like Tiger Beat, as well as through the increasingly international coverage offered by Melody Maker, New Musical Express and Sounds. Their appeal hinged largely on the fact that they were sticking two fingers up at everything that had come before them.

For Andy this was an exciting and convenient new vehicle to latch onto. He couldn't be Cream or The Grateful Dead very convincingly, but he could pump out fast, brash three-chord sequences like MC5 or The New York Dolls. In response to this fresh call he encouraged the others to raid their mothers' wardrobes for suitable items of clothing so as to look authentically 'glam'.

There was some dissension in the ranks, however. Colin was willing to go along with it, although Andy had to supply much of the gear, but Dave Cartner's glammy attempts usually made him look more like one of The Bay City Rollers. The ever laconic Terry

Chambers was particularly nonplussed by Andy's efforts to make him look "like a pansy" and his only concessions to the image were a pair of jeans with a lace up crotch and some stack heeled boots.

At least Andy had the courage of his convictions. He lived the part 24 hours a day, wearing a selection of bright androgynous clothing, a touch of eye-shadow and a hint of lipstick and was quietly confident that he wouldn't look totally out of place on the cover of Roxy Music's startling début LP. Most of Andy's strange wardrobe was an accumulation of tacky, sparkly-looking items he'd bought from jumble sales and some of Vera's cast-offs. Vera didn't really mind Andy dressing in her clothes. To her it was just a bit of fun and a passing phase.

At least, she consoled herself, Andy had at last got himself a steady girlfriend. Linda Godwin was an attractive, petite, dark haired girl who worked as a laboratory technician in Swindon's Princess Margaret hospital. They had met socially and she was immediately smitten by Andy's humour and outrageous dress sense. Andy in turn was impressed by Linda's fun-loving laid-back attitude to life.

Linda didn't get on with her parents and meeting Andy gave her the confidence to leave home and find a flat of her own. Over the next couple of years her flats - she had a tendency to move every few months - were also occasionally occupied by Andy. He hadn't fully extricated himself from his parents' clutches yet.

Out of the blue, Spud Taylor phoned Andy one day and told him he'd built his own synthesizer which he felt could be incorporated into Star Park's line-up. Evidently he had ambitions of becoming the Brian Eno of the group. But when he brought it to their next rehearsal the band were not impressed - Spud's synthesizer was a massive steel case, about three feet long, with no keyboard, just a solitary protruding switch. Depending on which way this switch was turned it could make two types of noise, a gurgle or a buzz. Andy inspected Spud's creation with dismay and wondered what had happened to his friend's sense of style and innovation. "I was really disappointed," he says. "I thought 'There's no place in this band for someone with a model of the tomb of Lenin that gurgles'."

Following this rejection, Spud dropped out of Andy's life and the confirmed four-piece line-up prepared for their first gig. At Dave Cartner's suggestion each group member adopted a stage name. Colin was already known as 'Curtains' because his hair came down so far over his face that you could see only his nose poking out. Terry was called 'Blackhand' because for a while he wore a black leather driving glove, on doctors orders, to cover a septic hand. Dave was called 'Dino Salvador' for the dual reasons that he was into Dino from The Flintstones, and because he was impressed by the artist Salvadore Dali's surreal outrageousness. Andy was still lumbered with 'Rocky' which he hated.

In December 1972, when the first incarnation of Star Park was falling apart and Andy was susceptible to all comers and all offers, he was introduced to Dave Bennett. Looking rather collegiate with spectacles and curly thinning hair, Bennett worked in Swindon's Civic Offices and took care of many of the council's arts functions. He was very keen to manage a rock group and promised Andy that he could secure Star Park prestigious support slots. Andy was impressed by this and accepted Bennett's offer on an informal basis.

But there was an ulterior motive for Bennett's offer which became evident as the weeks passed. His wife Valerie, a rather theatrical redhead, wrote poetry and Dave wanted Star Park to back her poetry recitals with a cocktail of spacey, atmospheric sounds, and thereby launch her stage career. Needless to say, the band weren't very keen on this absurdly pretentious idea but they realised Bennett could be a useful ally, so they went along with it for their own mercenary gains.

Determined to learn from past mistakes, Andy wanted Star Park to be much more professional in outlook. In one of the many local pubs he and Dave Cartner used, he had met Martin Church, a music enthusiast who offered to help in any way he could. Although Church had no specialist music knowledge nor talent, he was willing to turn his hand to whatever the band needed and his job at Garrards, the hi-fi manufacturers, gave him access to electrical equipment.

His first task for Star Park was to take a series of promotional photographs of the group. Unfortunately Church had suffered polio as a child and one leg was shorter than the other - thus when the photographs were developed, they were all at an angle! "That was how Martin perceived the world," says Andy. "Unfortunately we had to throw the lot away!"

In order that they could start to play gigs away from Swindon, Martin Church offered to buy a van on their behalf and the band agreed to pay him back in weekly instalments. In the meantime the van would be kept at Martin's house at Church Walk North. After a few months they had paid Church back the full £110 and went round to collect the van that was now rightfully theirs.

"Terry and I went round and told him we'd come for the van to pop it round to Terry's house to get his brother to have a look over it," Andy recalls. "Martin must've misread what we were saying because he flew into this terrible rage on the doorstep. He was accusing us of all kinds of things - trying to do him out of money, out of the van, trying to sack him. Terry and I were totally baffled! Basically, what he was doing was extricating himself from the group and trying to make it look as though we were throwing him out and stealing the van - which he never handed over to us!"

Their other ally, Dave Bennett, was as good as his word and Star Park played their first gig in May 1973 supporting Thin Lizzy in a council-promoted show at Swindon College. Lizzy was fronted by the mercurial black Irish bass guitarist Phil Lynott and they had recently scored their first big hit with 'Whiskey In The Jar', a rock arrangement of an old Irish folk song. Lizzy was certain to draw a large crowd and the gig therefore offered an ideal opportunity for Star Park to reach a wider audience. Andy was determined to make a big impression.

He wore his favourite stage outfit of skin-tight gold fur trousers with a three foot long tiger's tail hanging down the back. These ended about a foot above his ankles which were planted into black stack-heel boots. On his left leg was the image of a penis fashioned from heart-shaped studs and the trousers were cut so they came right up under his armpits, with little kiddies' braces holding them up. Under that was a cut off shirt covered in star shaped studs, a little black corduroy jacket, and the ensemble was topped off with a silver bowler hat covered in mirrors and a pair of glasses made from silver card with lightning flashes which stuck out a foot or so each side of his head like huge antennae. But the band's dream of making a grand entrance was thwarted by Thin Lizzy's own ego trip. "They were real bastards!" recalls Colin. "They wouldn't let us into the dressing room. We had to change outside in the corridor."

A month later Dave Bennett arranged another support slot with Welsh heavy metal band Budgie at Swindon Town Hall which, for the purpose of rock gigs, had changed its name to The Funhouse. Up until now, Star Park was happy with what he'd achieved for them. Besides, there were other advantages. "Dave used to drive us to his house on the Walcott estate and leave us there with his missus," says Andy. "He'd make some excuse about having to go off somewhere. His missus was either a bit of an exhibitionist or just didn't give a damn because she'd wear these mini dresses with no knickers and sit there with her legs up on a coffee table reading her poetry out of a 'J. Arnold of Leeds' exercise book. We would be sitting on the settee opposite, supposedly concentrating on the nuances of her free form poetry, when all we could see was the view up her skirt!

"The idea was she would do this Yoko Ono-style poetry and we were going to feedback contentedly in the background. This never came to fruition because her poetry was fourth form rubbish. But we did quite enjoy going round to Dave's house!"

In July 1973 the group decided to change its name. They felt their music was now far removed from Star Park's turgid blues sound of old and they were now much more inclined towards The New York Dolls' glam-rock approach and needed a title that would reflect this new influence. For a short time they tried Zip Code and The Helium Kidz, but this implied that Andy was 'Zip Code' and that The Helium Kidz were his backing band - which no one liked. So the name was shortened and Star Park became The Helium Kidz. This suited Andy's continuing fascination with American comics and for some gigs he wore a homemade Captain America shield, though this was usually discarded after a couple of numbers because it made guitar playing virtually impossible!

Although he wouldn't admit it to anyone, Andy was obsessed with The New York Dolls, even to the point of writing them a letter offering his services as a replacement for Johnny Thunders, should he die. (Knowledge of his excessive rock'n'roll lifestyle always made this a distinct possibility.) Whilst he never had the gall to send the letter off, he had still scrupulously planned every detail of how he could be incorporated into the band, even designing a 'look' based around a brolly and bowler hatted commuter and rechristening himself Lord Andrew English in anticipation.

If The Helium Kidz image left anyone guessing, their music didn't. Almost every song Andy wrote brazenly displayed his fascination with 'glammy' themes, science fiction and comics, with titles like 'Saturn Boy' and 'Teenage Planet'. In most cases he shamelessly took other people's songs apart and re-constructed them as his own.

"We were too snotty to cover anyone else's material," he says, "so I'd write surrogate songs that were uncannily similar to other songs. I'd just change the lyrics and the title and re-structure the chord sequence. So instead of 'Jet Boy' by The New York Dolls we had one called 'Jet Shoes' which was in praise of platform boots! Silly things like that . . ."

43

Despite his misconceived efforts to side-track the group as his wife's backing band, Dave Bennett continued to work with them and now set up their first show as The Helium Kidz, headlining at The Arts Centre.

Andy was becoming a well-known face on the local music scene, and this had its drawbacks as well as advantages. A large crowd gathered at the Arts Centre and the groans of disappointment were clearly audible as the crowd, filled with the excited anticipation of seeing a new Swindon group, realised it was just "Partridge's mob" again.

From other local musicians there was a begrudging respect. At least The Helium Kidz were more than just another pub rock band: they had ambitions and they had the gall to go against the grain. What they were doing was different; ill-defined maybe, but different.

In an attempt to spread the band's reputation further afield, Dave Bennett set about arranging a London gig for the band and eventually secured a booking at the Fulham Greyhound on a quiet mid-week night in August 1973. This was to be The Helium Kidz' big break: it was the first time any of them had played a gig away from the Swindon area, let alone in the capital, and they had their heads in the clouds.

"We thought, 'Wow, the capital city!'," recalls Andy. "We thought there would be loads of people there from record companies, just sitting having a drink and it would be like a musical where they'd say, 'Hey, where have these guys been all this time?'. And, of course, it wasn't like that at all . . ."

As The Helium Kidz ambled out in front of the small but cynical audience in their lurid stage regalia with only the buzz of their amps and the clumping of their platform boots to break the silence, someone mockingly shouted 'Blimey! It's The Swindon Dolls'. The audience laughed and behind his silver lightning glasses with the two foot wing span, Andy blushed. Instantly he knew they'd been rumbled. Back home in Swindon - barely 75 miles from London, yet in some respects about a decade behind the Capital - most pub audiences wouldn't know who they were plagiarising. But the more sophisticated London crowd couldn't be fooled so easily. The journey home to Swindon seemed like an ignominious retreat.

In October 1973 The Helium Kidz played their last gig under Dave Bennett's management when they supported Island Records hopefuls Bronco at the Town Hall. The night ended with an ugly scene involving Dave Cartner - who was noticeably the worse for drink

- and Bennett, who was accused of having made a financial killing on the evening and keeping it to himself. Blows were exchanged on the steps of the Town Hall during a furious row after which Bennett refused to have anything further to do with them.

Once again, the band were cast adrift and lacked a sense of direction. Things weren't happening nearly as fast as they had hoped. Then, one day late in 1973, Linda Godwin was staying with friends in Tulse Hill, London, when she heard their window cleaner singing to himself outside their flat. She was impressed by his voice and got talking to him and he told her that he was in fact a semi-professional singer called Steve Hutchins. He claimed he had several connections in the music business and said that once he had found himself a proper backing band he was almost sure of signing a recording contract. Naturally enough, Linda told Steve that her boyfriend was in a band and suggested they should get together.

When Linda told Andy about her conversation with Steve Hutchins a couple of days later the proverbial fruit machine in his head registered jackpot. If what this guy said was true, maybe he was the key to The Helium Kidz getting a record deal.

Urged on by Linda, Andy telephoned Steve Hutchins. His initial suggestion was that The Helium Kidz should go to London with a view to becoming part of a backing band he was auditioning. This didn't sit well with Andy and the others, particularly as it would involve dropping at least one member. Instead Hutchins agreed to travel to Swindon and, if all went well at a trial rehearsal, become The Helium Kidz new lead singer.

No-one doubted that Hutchins could sing but his voice had an annoying tremolo 'wobble' that Andy kept asking him to drop, and although his cheeky Cockney barrow-boy charm recalled David Essex, he sang with an irritating nasal American accent. There was also a real problem on the image front. Hutchins was in his late twenties, short and musclebound, and looked not unlike Robin Asquith with a slight hair-lip. A genial happy-go-lucky Jack-the-lad type, he had little potential as a glam-metal heart-throb.

There was no question about it: Steve Hutchins was hopelessly unsuitable for The Helium Kidz. The band's motive in offering Hutchins the job was therefore blatantly mercenary, something they happily admit, and they would welcome him into the fold with open arms - if and until his music industry connections got them a record contract.

45

To give him his due, Steve Hutchins at least had some idea of how to go about getting a recording deal - which the others hadn't. As soon as he joined The Helium Kidz he suggested they make a demo tape which could then be presented to record companies as an indication of their talent. The band had never considered making a tape before, and certainly hadn't the financial resources to do so.

Steve Hutchins was managed by Tony Gordon of Wedge International Ltd (many years later Gordon resurfaced as manager of Culture Club) and he agreed to take on The Helium Kidz now that Hutchins was aboard. When the Swindon contingent went to sign the legal papers formalising Tony Gordon's involvement, they were quietly impressed by the lavishness of his offices off London's Wigmore Street. How could they fail to make it now they had an organization as sophisticated as Wedge International behind them, they thought.

There was nothing sophisticated about their first foray into the recording world, a home demo made in Steve Hutchins' rented house in Morden, south London, in February 1974. Once their gear was set up in Hutchins' front room there was barely enough space for the band to squeeze in alongside. Steve had borrowed a friend's archaic two-track reel-to-reel tape machine on which they recorded six of their own songs - 'In Love With The Hurt', 'Shark In The Pool', 'Café', 'Private Eye', 'Saturn Boy' and 'Adrenalin' - putting all the instruments on to one track and the vocals on the other.

"Steve really must've done something to placate the neighbours," says Andy, "because we were thundering out in there. I'm sure you could've heard the drums and bass up the road. We all slept there overnight next to the amps and cabs. It was terribly cramped."

Despite its complete lack of polish, the band were proud of their first set of recordings. It seemed as though it could be the turning point in their career - they had a new singer, new management and now a demo that they felt captured their raw enthusiasm. However, for two members of the band at least, it was a time of divided loyalties.

That same February Colin married Carol Evans, his first serious girlfriend. They had met in March 1973 at a gig by Mick Abrahams, the ex-Jethro Tull guitarist, at Swindon College and had become virtually inseparable ever since. They had planned to marry on September 7, Carol's father's birthday, but these plans were brought forward when Carol became pregnant. Their son Lee was born in June, 1974, and this inevitably posed problems for Colin, though he still felt committed to The Helium Kidz. "It was often difficult being married and trying to keep the band thing going," he recalls. "The others used to laugh at me when I took sandwiches along to gigs!"

Dave Cartner, meanwhile, was also struggling to balance the demands of both band and marriage. His wife and mother-in-law, a formidable pair, were firmly against his messing around with a rock'n'roll group and instead wanted him to concentrate on being a postman.

With family commitments now vying with band activities for their time and attention, doubts and resentments began to creep into the group's previously ebullient esprit de corps. But response to The Helium Kidz' home-cooked demo tape was surprisingly favourable and with just a little hard sell, Tony Gordon managed to get the Decca label interested in auditioning the group. Hutchins and Gordon also thought the name The Helium Kidz was too gimmicky for a record company to take seriously and the band temporarily re-named themselves Skyscraper.

The audition took place at the Decca studios in West Hampstead in August 1974 - the same studio, as Andy proudly reminded everyone, where The Rolling Stones recorded 'Come On', their first single. They had just one day to record updated versions of the songs they'd taped earlier in the year at Steve Hutchins' flat. "I remember the engineers looking down their noses at us," says Andy. "I felt really uncomfortable. As far as they were concerned we were just country bumpkins in funny clothes. They made it very difficult for us."

In October, while they were still waiting for Decca's judgement on their tape, the band received another invitation to record demos in London, this time for the Pye label who had just lost The Kinks, one of Andy's favourite childhood groups. Everyone was excited about another trip to a London recording studio, but then Dave Cartner broke the news: his wife and mother-in-law actually forbade him to take time off work for the recording session. Reduced temporarily to a four-piece, they set off for the capital.

Discarding the Skyscraper alias and reverting to The Helium Kidz, they recorded four tracks, including two new songs: 'It's About Time We Had Some Rock'n'Roll' and 'Teenage Planet'. Andy had to play all Dave's guitar parts as well as his and, if anything, the engineers at the Pye studios in Bryanston Place were even more condescending towards the group, openly laughing at the sounds they got out of their cheap guitars and transistor amps. Andy now owned a black Guild S50, with one pick up, but the engineers guffawed, saying he made it sound like a Woolworth's guitar.

Dave Cartner's absence from this session hadn't caused any real hardship, but the band knew the situation would only get worse. One evening that autumn, Colin, Terry and Andy piled round to his house in Deburgh Street, Rodbourne and, sitting around his kitchen table, told Dave he was no longer in the group. Cartner did not take the news well and begged the group to let him stay. It was an embarrassing situation for Andy, who felt he was betraying his old friend and breaking their 'one for all' agreement. "It was a case of 'Your gear's in the van. Shall we give you a hand to bring it in?'" Andy remembers. "Actually the van looked pretty empty once his stuff had gone because most of the gear was his. Sadly that was the end of our friendship. I think Dave felt badly let down. I met him again years later when he was delivering a parcel to me. We were having some success at the time, and the atmosphere was very strained. I don't think he ever really forgave me."

For a while, the band considered drafting in a replacement for Dave Cartner. Among those considered was a young guitarist called Dave Gregory who'd played with local bands such as Pink Warmth and Alehouse. Dave was one of those musicians that Andy would often bump into in music shops, and Andy had admired him ever since seeing Pink Warmth play at a Penhill Church Hall 'hop'. Auditions were held in their rehearsal room at Jennings Street school in Rodbourne, Swindon, but none of the contenders really fitted in. Finally it was agreed that Andy should now handle all guitar duties.

Both Decca and Pye rejected The Helium Kidz, but the band didn't let that deter them. In February 1975 they financed their own demo session at T.W. Studio on the Fulham Palace Road in London. They chose three brand new songs - 'Walking Across The Ceiling', 'Yabber Yabber Yabber' and 'Neon Shuffle' - plus re-arrangements of 'Shark In The Pool' and 'Star Park'. The tape was certainly a vast improvement on anything they'd recorded before, less derivative of Andy's musical influences and surprisingly commercial.

For a while Andy toyed with the idea of transferring these recordings to vinyl. He had heard through a friend that special 'record-a-disc' booths could be found at certain major train stations. Although they were designed only for recording speech - and even then the sound quality was poor - the idea was that he would play The Helium Kidz demo into the microphone for as many times as he wanted to make copies of the 'single', then design labels and picture sleeves for each one individually. One of these, he thought, would impress record companies far more than just another demo cassette. Andy wrote to British Rail asking them where these booths could be found, but they wrote back to tell him that the last one in existence had just been taken out of service.

The Helium Kidz waited for Wedge International to use their latest tape to secure them a record deal. Tony Gordon was supposedly taking care of their business affairs, but in reality he was doing very little. Most of the band's gigs were secured through their own efforts - sending tapes around the country and spending hours on the phone running up huge bills, which would result in occasional bookings outside Swindon.

In their recently acquired but still old and battered white Commer van, now kitted out with ex-aircraft seats to make long journeys more comfortable, they travelled all over the country. All external trace of the van's previous owners - a firm of building contractors - had been erased except for two words 'any distance', which they decided would be their motto. Distance was no object, and they'd often return to Swindon in the early hours of the morning, snatch a couple of hours sleep, then get up for their day jobs.

Colin had been fired from his milkman's job in January 1973, when, extremely drunk, he and his friend Paul Henry were caught red handed stealing milk tokens from a rival milkman's round. Colin worked briefly as a building labourer and was now a school grounds-man for Swindon Council. Andy worked for A.E. Tunley & Sons, an odd combination of art suppliers, hardware store and replica gun dealers, while Terry still worked in the printing department at Thorn's factory.

Steve Hutchins, who worked in London as a window cleaner and part time garage mechanic, was becoming increasingly unconcerned in regard to the band. Often he simply couldn't be bothered to come down to Swindon for gigs and rehearsals, and would ask for dates to be re-arranged so that it was more convenient for him to attend. Although the others were fully committed, they also needed their jobs - mainly to earn money to finance the group's ever spiralling expenses - so gigs and other band fixtures had to be scheduled carefully. It was a particularly testing time for Colin who had responsibilities as a family man but was determined not to suffer the same fate as Dave Cartner.

In the spring of 1975 The Helium Kidz received nationwide

exposure for the first time - albeit in a specialist field - via the pages of *New Musical Express*. At that time *NME* ran a column called 'Roadrunner' which gave unknown working bands a chance to promote themselves. The Helium Kidz had submitted their biographical details months before the feature eventually appeared, and the accompanying photo - featuring Dave Cartner in the line up - was well out of date. But the public weren't to know that, and the group were grateful for any publicity they could get. Having mentioned that they were prepared to "work (their) bums off", they sat back awaiting a flood of work. The solitary offer they received, however, was totally unexpected.

A week or so after the Roadrunner feature Andy received a letter from Roger Lavern, keyboard player with The Tornados, the pre-Beatles era quintet who'd distinguished themselves in 1962 by recording Joe Meek's stunning instrumental hit, 'Telstar', the first ever US number one hit single by a British group. Lavern had maintained his contacts with the rock'n'roll journeymen from this distant era and was presently setting up a tour for ex-Shadows bass guitarist Jet Harris, a noted casualty who'd topped the charts in a duo with drummer Tony Meehan, suffered from depression after a much publicised car crash and, at his lowest point, worked as a bus conductor. Now Lavern wanted to know whether The Helium Kidz would consider being Harris's backing group. He mentioned that he was particularly amused by the prospect of the entourage being billed as Jet Harris and The Helium Kidz. He liked their name, writing in his letter "Helium. Gassy element found in the sun. Nice One!" Since he hadn't heard any of their music, this seems to have been the only reason for contacting them.

The band were desperate for a break but wanted to succeed on their own terms. It was common for visiting American artists such as Chuck Berry and Little Richard to use local backing bands when visiting Britain, but they were rock'n'roll legends while Jet Harris, in Andy's view, was "a mediocre guitarist from a long dead era of British pop". All agreed that accepting the engagement might bring in some much needed money in the short term, but could only harm them in the long run. Andy wrote back to Roger Laverne politely declining his offer. "I didn't put it in so many words", he says, "but I sensed that if we'd gone along with it we would've been used. It was too bizarre an offer to take seriously."

Andy had begun to steer the group into fresh musical areas. Glam rock had run its course and The Helium Kidz now switched to a unique brand of pub rock with sci-fi overtones. Newer songs such as 'Spinning Top' and 'Science Friction' were shorter and more compact. Musically they had lost much of their boozy R'n'B influences and gained a futuristic quirkiness. Technically the instrumental nucleus of Partridge, Chambers and Moulding had become tight and confident.

The band's look went through several changes: denims and T shirts, boaters and blazers, and then a 'wear anything white' phase. At one stage Andy kitted the group out in black boiler suits which were offset with white accessories (belts, shoes etc) giving an impression of futuristic factory workers. This space-age garage mechanic look was unwittingly duplicated by the American group Devo over two years later - an acknowledgment to Andy's innovative outlook.

Again defying the fashion of times, Andy had his hair cut short and encouraged the others to do the same. They all complied eventually, but Colin - for whom the sacrifice was greatest - was 'phased in' over several hair cuts to lessen the shock!

With so many changes in the air, the name The Helium Kidz no longer seemed appropriate and in July 1975 the question of a change came up once again. Everyone had their own idea. Tony Gordon at Wedge International suggested Fat Fruit. Steve Hutchins liked the idea of being recognised as the focal point of the group and went for Steve Z and The Zodiacs. These were both dismissed immediately by the Swindon contingent and eventually the choice was narrowed down to two options and the first, The Dukes Of The Stratosphear, was dismissed as being too flowery and psychedelic.

The name finally chosen had little significance except that it suited the band perfectly. It was inspired by a piece of film of Jimmy Durante looking for the lost chord which Andy saw. When Durante found it, he exclaimed in his strong New York accent: "Dat's it, I'm in XTC!" At first Andy didn't understand what he was saying but when he wrote it down phonetically, he thought it looked and sounded great. It was almost like a pictogram of their music; witty and incisive, unbridled by either fad or fashion.

From now, they would be known as XTC.

5

'THIS IS POP?'

With the new name came a new member of the group, a young keyboard player called Jon Perkins, poached from rival local group The Teenage Polecats. Although still in his mid-teens, Perkins owned some impressive gear, including a Fender Rhodes electric piano and Davoli synthesizer, both virtually unattainable luxuries for most musicians of his age. The Perkins were considered one of Swindon's posh families. They lived in a three storey house in the 'right' sort of area - Goddard Avenue in Swindon's Old Town - and enjoyed a typically middle class lifestyle.

Jon - Jonathan to his family - had an older brother, Peter, a medical student who had jammed with Andy on several occasions. At one point they had considered inviting Peter, who also played keyboards, to join the group, but young Jonathan was undoubtedly a better musician and in any case Peter was becoming increasingly serious about being a doctor. Jon Perkins' Davoli synthesizer changed the group's sound significantly, giving their songs a techno-pop quality that enhanced the futuristic themes. It seemed as though they had at last found the missing element in their sound spectrum.

The new five piece XTC - five piece, that is, when Steve Hutchins could be bothered to join them - finally started to get their message across. Andy's songwriting had improved by leaps and bounds, and when they played one of their regular Swindon gigs (usually the Town Hall or The Brunel Rooms) they could sense a steady change in reaction. This and the growing disillusionment with their day jobs made them all the more determined to make the band succeed.

Having lost touch with him for a few years, Andy had become reacquainted with Steve Warren, who was now working as a DJ. Steve had always taken a keen interest in Andy's various musical projects and regularly plugged tracks from his old friend's latest demo tape during his residency nights at The Brunel Rooms. Increasingly these met with audience approval, with more and more people asking Steve what he had just played.

Steve suggested they team up again, and Andy was grateful for the opportunity to supplement his meagre income by roadying for Steve's matt black Mobile Disco. He was now employed as a poster painter and window display designer at McIlroy's department store where one of his tasks was to build Santa's Grotto every Christmas! But it was another dead end job he didn't much enjoy, and he spent most of his time mucking around and chatting up the female staff.

Andy and Linda Godwin had now been together for almost three years, but Linda had become bored with the relationship and was casting her eyes elsewhere by the spring of 1977. Although Andy remained smitten by Linda's bubbly, flirtatious personality, it became increasingly obvious to him that Linda had fallen for the swarthy good looks of Barry Jeffrato who was part of their social circle and had coincidentally been Andy's manager at the Bon Marche record department. The situation came to a head when Linda returned from a holiday in Morocco bearing numerous gifts for Barry and nothing for Andy even though they were still officially 'an item'.

To complicate matters Barry Jeffrato was gay - or at least bisexual - and he made no secret of fancying Andy! For a while Andy, Barry and Linda were trapped in a truly bizarre love triangle. "We did make the interesting, if idiotic, move of all climbing into bed one evening," says Andy. But the impossibly complicated relationship inevitably fell apart, leaving everyone out in the cold.

At McIlroy's there was one girl in particular who had caught Andy's eye, a pretty, petite girl called Marianne Wyborn with whom Andy had fallen instantly in love. The fact that he had never even spoken to her was but a minor hitch. "She walked past me one day looking like a Russian princess in this fur coat and hat. I remember thinking 'I wish I could have a girlfriend like that'," recalls Andy.

Such hankerings were severely frustrated when he discovered she was already involved with someone - a teacher called Ken - and all but shattered when, with a certain amount of family encouragement, she became engaged to him. Nevertheless, Andy's secret longing continued . . .

Towards the end of 1975, XTC entered a local talent contest run by the Bass Charrington brewery group. Competing against an odd mix of amateur showbands, comedians and magicians, XTC were awarded only runners-up spot in the finals in February 1976 at The Globe at Newton St Loe, near Bath. In retrospect it was a minor event, and probably just as well in the long run they didn't win, but it

53

was one of the last gigs Steve Hutchins performed with the band. With another failure to add to the list there didn't seem to be any point in Steve being in the band any more. He'd only been drafted in so that the band could use his alleged record company contacts to get them a deal - a promise that hadn't materialised.

"Steve grew to be a bit of an embarrassment," says Andy. "He never really took the image side of things seriously. I remember one occasion when we were in our glam stage. He came down to Swindon with a girlfriend - of which he had quite a few while we knew him - and they were both dressed in their embarrassing interpretations of the glam look. It wasn't right at all. It looked more like they'd just stepped out of a B-movie version of *Clockwork Orange*. When we went out on the town this attracted all sorts of unwanted attention!

"A while later, in the middle of our boiler suit phase, we were supporting Alehouse at the Town Hall. We were all wearing these black and white uniforms and Steve turned up wearing these shiny red satin mechanics' overalls. He'd unzipped them right down so that the top of his pubes were showing because he thought this turned the women on! I remember we tossed a coin with Alehouse to see who would go on first, and it was decided they would. The hall was packed for Alehouse - they were quite a popular local group. But by the time we came to go on there were only a dozen people left. Half way through one of the songs Steve came over to me and yelled 'This ain't no good, I'm going to get me jeans on'. He ran off stage and came back a couple of minutes later in a T-shirt and jeans. He'd decided it wasn't worth sweating it out in his overalls for only a dozen people!"

By June 1976 - the month when Colin and Carol Moulding finally moved from their council house on the Penhill Estate into their own house at No 565 Ferndale Road - it was decided to fire Steve Hutchins. Because Andy had done most of the dirty work in sacking Dave Cartner, Colin was given the honours. Colin phoned Steve in London and told him of the band's decision. There was no tearful separation this time, only a moment of disbelief as Hutchins phoned Andy to double check whether what Colin had just told him was true.

Two months later, in August, having briefly gone through the motions of auditioning other potential lead singers, XTC financed another set of demoes at Sun Studios in Reading. The songs - 'Science Friction', 'Quicksilver', 'Spinning Top', 'Hang On To The Night', 'She's So Square' and 'Refrigeration Blues' - were the first to feature Andy as their newly elected singer. Although his voice wasn't as professional as that of Steve Hutchins, it suited the frenetic pace of the songs. What he lacked in technical ability he made up for in urgency, although his insecurity led to a delivery that included a measure of Hutchins-style Americanisms.

"I sounded like a junior Steve Hutchins at that point," says Andy. "After a while I found a mannered style that I thought was unique - a bit like Steve Harley on speed. It was all done on purpose, to try and make a stylistic statement so people would remember and say 'Hey, that's the bloke with the hiccupy, shattered, self-dubbed voice.' It was years before I felt comfortable with a completely unpretentious voice - just sounding like me."

A home-spun advertising campaign was devised and copies of the new demo were sent out with individually crafted Partridge illustrations and 'XTC R NRG' stickers.

That same month, Andy finally encountered Marianne Wyborn in a social situation, a mutual friend's eighteenth birthday party at Froxfield just outside Swindon. Steve Warren's mobile disco was providing the music that night and as usual Andy was roadying for him. "I was looking very drippy that night . . . wearing a Laura Ashley dress and some Scholl sandals," Marianne remembers. "I didn't have much to wear because I'd moved all my things down to my fiancé's flat in Brighton. I was meant to be moving in with him the next day, but I didn't really want to because we hadn't been getting on very well."

Neither Andy nor Marianne went home that night. They sat up talking in a broken down Daimler in the middle of a field near the barn where the party was being held and eventually admitted their feelings for each other. By the time Marianne went home dawn was breaking and her mother was in no doubt what happened to young girls who stayed out all night. She immediately ordered her daughter to get into a bath of disinfectant and beat her about for her sins! After explaining her innocent night with young Partridge, Marianne phoned her fiancé to tell him the engagement was off.

A couple of weeks later Andy and Marianne left their respective homes and moved into their own flat at No 7 Gladstone Street which backed on to the railway. It was a pokey little place; two dark, damp rooms which shook every time a train passed by. Andy fell foul of the landlord after spray painting palm trees and Stuka dive bombers on the walls to try and liven the place up! Marianne's father - a commercial artist who owned a prosperous local company called Wyborn

Signs - was disgusted with his daughter's decision to live with a "tuppenny, halfpenny ticket writer" and scruffy rock'n'roller to boot, and refused even to talk to Andy.

Although still working at McIlroy's, Andy's scruffy rock'n'roll career was at last beginning to show signs of life. On September 16 XTC played a gig at a new club in Swindon called The Affair which was owned by Ian Reid, an Army officer drop-out who had found his niche in life managing clubs and cabaret restaurants for Watneys brewery. Although only 31, he was a shrewdly ambitious entrepreneur, valued by his employers because he had a successful track record. When The Birds Nest - a Watney owned club in Swindon - fell into financial trouble, Reid wasted no time in offering to buy it for his own purposes. He sold his house in Birmingham, where he'd been managing the New Cresta at Solihull, and put all his money into the club which he then rechristened The Affair.

For XTC it would've been just another gig except that in the course of packing up they overloaded the club's service lift with their gear and caused it to break down. In a tit-for-tat arrangement Reid offered to waive the subsequent £40 repair bill if the band played another show at The Affair a few days later free of charge.

Reid had an ulterior motive - other than simply getting free entertainment for his club - in having XTC play another show. He liked what he had seen and heard of XTC the first time but because he had no knowledge or experience of the music business he wanted to get an expert opinion. He asked his right hand man cum PR officer, Dennis Detheridge, to check them out.

Detheridge was as qualified to judge as anyone could be. He had been *Melody Maker*'s Midlands correspondent for many years and judged many local heats for their annual National Rock-Folk contests, the winners of which almost always plunged into obscurity immediately after receiving their prize. In the Sixties he had started his own Birmingham based music paper called *Midland Beat* (a poor cousin to the much better known *Mersey Beat*). He had also managed a band called Denny Laine and The Diplomats, from which Laine went on to greater prominence, first as the vocalist on The Moody Blues' first hit 'Go Now' and later with Paul and Linda McCartney as one third of the Wings line-up that recorded 'Band On The Run'.

After scrutinising XTC's performance, Detheridge told Ian Reid that he thought they had potential and could get somewhere. Reid immediately offered them a management deal and the band eagerly signed - without any deep discussion or consideration of the terms. It was the start of a relationship that would take them several times around the world, through tremendous highs and lows and end - ultimately - in a long, bitter and expensive dispute.

Reid and Detheridge soon got down to the business of promoting XTC. A company called Allydor Limited was bought 'off the shelf' for the purposes of managing the group, who were led to believe they would be directors of their 'own' company. Although Detheridge was not given a directorship of Allydor, he had a written agreement entitling him to a share of the company's future profits and was paid a small retainer by Reid for his services.

Ian Reid made The Affair's cellar available to the band for rehearsals and, using their Sun Studio demo, a package was put together for approaching record companies. An accompanying leaflet written by Dennis - in which Andy (at his own request) was described as a nuclear powered Syd Barrett - said: "XTC have established themselves as Wiltshire's best known rock band. Now encouraged by the emergence of punk rock, they are set to gain recognition."

XTC certainly weren't a punk rock band but they saw no reason to entirely disassociate themselves from the movement, especially if it might accelerate a record deal. In November 1976 punk's first single, 'New Rose' by The Damned, was released and the record industry cottoned on pretty fast. The furore that followed The Sex Pistols' infamous early evening appearance on Thames TV's *Today* programme with Bill Grundy threw the industry into a frenzy. Labels were signing virtually anything that moved if it looked 'punk'.

"I remember seeing The Sex Pistols performing 'Anarchy In The UK' on TV in a record store and only being mildly impressed," says Andy. "I liked their attitude, but it wasn't so radically different from what The Dolls and The Stooges had been doing years earlier. I couldn't really see what all the fuss was about."

For a while the group made regular trips to London, often with their girlfriends and wives in tow, during which they would literally walk around as many record companies as they could cover in a day, naïvely expecting to be granted audiences with A&R staff. Rarely succeeding, they would leave a copy of their demo at the reception desk after being assured that it would be passed on to the relevant department. This exhausting and demoralising practice ceased after they made return visits to the same offices weeks later and saw that their demo remained in the pile of other tapes on the same front desks where it had been left.

The first label to respond to XTC's package was Jonathan King's UK records. King and his brother Andrew thought the demo was "quite fun" but, curiously, were hoping they could steer them away from the punk band-wagon. During a meeting at their London office on November 26, King spent much of the time trying to persuade the band they should have Marianne fronting them. It was a bizarre suggestion: Marianne had never sung with anyone before in her life.

The next label to show interest was CBS. The head of A&R there was a guy called Nicky Graham who, as he proudly boasted, was also Andy Williams' producer. Graham wanted to see the band play live but since they didn't have any London dates arranged he agreed to come down to Swindon for a special showcase gig at The Affair. But then, just as a date had been fixed, disaster struck.

It had come to the attention of the others that Perkins was moonlighting with a band called The Stadium Dogs. When Andy and Colin confronted him threateningly and asked him to choose between them and XTC, he asked for a couple of days to think it over and then came out in favour of The Dogs. Perkins formally left XTC on November 30, just two weeks before their showcase gig on December 15.

The band went into mild panic since Nicky Graham at CBS expected to see a four piece XTC and had expressly said he liked the keyboards on their demo. Ian Reid said he knew of a local keyboard player who might be prepared to stand in temporarily . . . enter Bob Hall, a middle aged boogie-woogie piano player who was well known in certain muzo circles and could count Rolling Stone Charlie Watts among his acquaintances. Everyone knew he was totally unsuitable for the group, but they were desperate.

"We went round to see Bob Hall," remembers Andy. "He had this upright piano in one corner of his little council flat and he said 'What sort of songs do you do?' I thought 'How am I going to get this bloke to agree to do the gig?' So I said 'Well, one of them's called 'Boogie Woogie City'. His face lit up and he said 'Great! How does it go?' I remember trying to give him some indication of this song, and basically lying! It wasn't a boogie woogie number at all. It was a really heavy pomp thing that sounded like a cross between Todd Rundgren's Utopia and The Glitter Band!"

Bob Hall agreed to play the showcase gig with them and, with

58

only a couple of days notice, a warm-up gig at the Brunel Rooms on December 8 as well. "He was very badly out of place with us," says Andy. "We turned all our guitar amps up so loud that you couldn't hear his boogie-woogie piano playing - which rather defeated the point of having him!"

But when the big day, December 15, came around Hall couldn't make it. He'd been to Belgium on business and was fog bound at Brussels airport and at such short notice the band were forced to play the gig as a power pop trio and to lie to Nicky Graham that their departed pianist was actually on holiday. Fortunately Graham was impressed by what he heard and invited XTC to do a test recording for CBS the following January 5. It gave them just enough time to audition other - more suitable - keyboard players.

A couple of days later Andy was browsing in a local music shop, the John Holmes Organ Centre, when he spotted on the noticeboard a little card that simply said 'Keyboard player seeks band'. "I asked the assistant in the shop if he knew anything about this bloke," Andy remembers, "and he said 'Oh, he lives out Park North. His name's Barry I think.' We went round there and this funny looking balding character with a London accent came to the door.

"We never auditioned him, we just went out drinking. We plied him with huge amounts of drink in the hope of talking him into doing the next session with us, and ended the evening as drunken mates. I liked his caustic sense of humour. When I got back home, I was as sick as a dog in the sink. Marianne had to put me to bed. He kept his drink down better than I could, so he was in the band."

In the cold, sober light of day there were some misgivings about Andy's impetuous decision. Barry Andrews hardly had what you'd call a rock pedigree. The only bands he'd been in before were cabaret style outfits and cover bands that played in Working Men's Clubs. Furthermore, he was only twenty and losing his hair, a definite dilemma for a band who placed image high on their list of priorities.

Unlike the others, Andrews was not a born and bred Swindonian. His family was among the many who migrated to Swindon from London in the Sixties in search of a better life. They arrived at Park North - one of the innumerable overspill housing estates that surround Swindon - when Barry was seven and he never really lost his London accent. As a youngster he was taught the basics of how to play the piano by his grandfather and soon entertained lofty ambitions of being the next Mozart.

At the Richard Jeffries School in Swindon Barry was a high achiever, coming top of the class in most subjects and attaining 10 'O' Levels. He also took 'A' Levels but as he grew older he treated these academic attributes as an embarrassment and was prone to masquerading as an intellectual yob. After leaving school he worked for Radio Rentals for a while, then packed his bags and moved to Exeter where he spent the long hot summer of 1976 getting nowhere with three different bands. Musically there was more than a touch of the maverick in him, even though it didn't show up immediately.

"The first time we rehearsed with Barry properly I thought 'bloody hell, we've made a terrible mistake'," says Andy. He had an upright piano with pick ups in it which he put through a little amp, and he had this cheap organ that he played through a wah-wah pedal. I sensed he was trying to please us with this Jon Lord Deep Purple style, but it was really clichéd stuff.

"I remember taking him aside afterwards and telling him he ought to play how he wanted. It wouldn't matter, we'd probably enjoy it more. The next time we rehearsed he just seemed to go off the rails. He was playing all these wild runs in any key, strange chord shapes and making gratuitous noises by leaning on the keys whenever he felt like it. I thought 'Hey, this is really interesting!' Some of it was rubbish, but equally a lot was very creative. He was literally the most original, most inspired keyboard player I'd ever come across and he was accidentally in our band!"

With Barry in position, XTC recorded a session for CBS at their studio on Whitfield Street, London, on January 5, 1977. The tracks were 'Star Park' (the only ballad in their set which, although old, had become one of Ian Reid's favourites), 'Statue Of Liberty', 'Monkey Woman' and - most interestingly - a version of The Kink's song 'Tired Of Waiting' arranged in a lazy reggae style. This was followed by a second session on March 8 when they demoed 'Traffic Light Rock', 'Saturn Boy', 'She's So Square' and 'Neon Shuffle'. In what seemed to be a half hearted gesture, CBS subsequently offered the band a bottom of the range 'C' type contract - one which left most of the options open in the label's favour. But by now XTC were an indelible part of the new wave buzz in London and Ian Reid felt they could afford to hold out for a much better deal.

The trickle of live work had now become a flood. Ian Reid and Dennis Detheridge's strong point was their ability to get the band gigs and XTC were either on the road or rehearsing six nights a week.

Dave Gregory at 9 months with Mum and Dad,
June 1953. *(Dave Gregory Collection)*

Colin with Mum and Nan Moulding on holiday in
Weymouth, 1956. *(Colin Moulding Collection)*

Andy Partridge with Mum and Dad, (Vera and John), 1954.
(Andy Partridge Collection)

Andy Partridge playing guitar with Stray Blues, 1970.
(Andy Partridge Collection)

Dave Gregory, 16 years old, 22nd January 1969.
(Chris Hawkes/Dave Gregory Collection)

Alehouse, March 1974. Left to right: Tony McCondach, Tony Green, Dave Gregory, Mole, Rod Goodway.
(Pete Gross/Dave Gregory Collection)

Studio 70 photo session for The Helium Kidz, 1975. Left to Right: Andy Partridge, Dave Cartner, Colin Moulding, Terry Chambers (seated). *(Studio 70/Andy Partridge Collection)*

Brunel Rooms, 1975. Steve Hutchins and Andy Partridge. *(Andy Partridge Collection)*

XTC during the recording of 'White Music' at The Manor, October 1977. Left to Right: Terry Chambers,
Barry Andrews, Colin Moulding and Andy Partridge. *(Wiltshire Newspapers)*

Right: Ian Reid, 1978.
(Andy Partridge Collection)

Far Right: Tarquin Gotch, 1990.

XTC with Talking Heads, early 1978. *(Jill Furmanovsky)*

Andy Partridge, Barry Andrews and Colin Moulding playing live, 1978. *(Pennie Smith)*

The Punk Pose: XTC in 1978. Left to right: Andy Partridge, Barry Andrews, Colin Moulding, Terry Chambers. *(Barry Plummer)*

Steve Warren, Australia, 1979.
(Terry Chambers/Steve Warren Collection)

Andy and Marianne on their wedding day,
28th August, 1979. *(Andy Partridge Collection)*

XTC on *The Saturday Banana*, Southern TV Studios, Southampton. 10th November 1979. *(Dave Gregory Collection)*

Reid had struck up a deal with the Albion agency who managed a few big new acts like The Stranglers and 999 and had a foot in the door at most of the principal new wave venues in London and around the home counties. In exchange for putting their bands on at The Affair, XTC were regularly booked into the 'right' sort of places like the Nashville Rooms, the Red Cow in Hammersmith and the Hope and Anchor in Islington - all of which fuelled the implication that they were a punk band.

To help cope with the sudden deluge of activity, Steve Warren was added to Allydor's payroll and was officially made XTC's full time roadie/handyman. During the first half of 1977 Steve kept a diary with a view to ultimately compiling a roadie's guide to the UK. Certain extracts offer an interesting insight into the day to day activities of a band on the precipice of signing their first record deal:

Monday, January 24, 1977: Bogarts, Birmingham. Band comes on and from the word go Colin is visually amazing. During one number he kicks over his mike stand. I leap forward and catch it, put it back on stage. He kicks me so I punch him back. Then he kicks Andy. Barry is really fitting in with the total sound. The audience (where are they all?) seem to appreciate the band. To me the best gig so far. Colin and Terry plaster their heads with a pot of Brylcreem. I hate the stuff but by God don't they look FAST. I liked the way Andy fell flat on his arse when he came onto the dark stage. Still, he got away with it in true showbiz style.

Saturday February 19: Nashville Rooms, London. We are support to Nasty Pop, but when we arrive there is a band called HGV who also have a contract to back Nasty Pop. After much arguing it is decided to let all three bands play. Place fills up pretty quickly and when XTC go on there's quite a good crowd. Band are great as usual and the crowd gives them a really good reception. Nicky Graham is in the audience and he likes the set. He offers Ian a class 'C' recording contract. HGV are about five years out of date. They come on stage with Wurzels type gear on. Nasty Pop come on and people start to leave. EMI music say they wish they had seen XTC before signing HGV. Don't blame them, they were awful.

(Author's note: The following day, on Sunday February 20, Colin and Carol Moulding's second child Joanne was born.)

Thursday March 3: The Golden Lion, Fulham. Back in London. EMI music here again to see band. The bloke is very free with his expense account. The pub landlord, an Irish bloke, is a sod. He hates the band before they even set the gear up. When they start to play he moans like hell to Ian Reid to turn the volume down. Andy takes no notice and the crowd agrees. The whole gig is great. I am starting to like 'Watchtower' and Andy looks really menacing. I'm sure he looks a bit like Johnny Rotten. Never mind. When I go into the dressing room after the gig I meet Pat Travers (and Andy King). He was very impressed with the set and talks to Andy about trying to get the band to back him at The Rainbow. Also, some guy gives Ian a card and offers the band a month in Mauritius. Rumours that Mitch Mitchell was in the audience were flying about . . .

(Author's note: Pat Travers had actually asked Andy to move to America and join his band.)

Saturday April 2: Naval Rooms, Tonypandy, Rhondda Valley. A gig to remember. The band don't get much of a reception for the first few numbers, but then some of the locals get up and start to dance and the clapping starts. During the break between sets the bingo is called out. Typical British Legion sort of thing. Everyone seems to be smoking dope. More and more people get up and dance and the place starts to go mad. People banging glasses in time to the music. XTC build up to the last number and then say goodnight, but the crowd won't have it. They shout until the band come on again - they are going berserk! Barry's piano falls over but he still keeps on playing it. Terry's cymbal keeps coming off and once nearly slices Andy's head off. I'm on stage as much as the band. During the last encore I'm holding up the PA stack because it's wobbling so much. What a night! Wales didn't know what hit them.

Monday April 4: The Affair, Swindon. In the audience are Jonathan and Andy King of UK records. Andy King is really a great fan of XTC and I swap his Magpie badge for an XTC one. I don't think Jonathan King is so impressed, but then he thinks he's a real star. Had a blazing row with Ian, but never mind. I didn't really mean that I would quit the band.

Tuesday April 19: Upstairs at Ronnie Scott's, London. Not all the people Ian and Dennis promised turn up. Andy King is there plus James Rubenstein from EG music. The band is interviewed by some bloke from *Sounds*. Both the sets are really good - especially 'Crosswires', 'This Is Pop' and 'Radios In Motion' which is repeated at the start of the second set. I have a talk with John Peel who turns up to see the second set. I think he was quite impressed. (Actually he rings up the next day and says that he liked 'Crosswires'.) Barry was seen sniffing some strange substance between sets. He must not drink so much. We have a row at the end of the evening. London watch out - XTC will be back soon.

(Author's note: As a result of this gig the band were offered a session on the John Peel show which they recorded on June 20. The tracks - 'Crosswires', 'She's So Square', 'Radios In Motion' and 'Science Friction' - were subsequently broadcast on June 24.)

Tuesday April 26: Brunel Rooms, Swindon. Swindon Viewpoint come down and film the gig. By the time the band come on the place is packed solid. The extra lights that the Viewpoint team have brought in make it very hot. During one of the numbers Andy's guitar packs up but much to our relief it is only temporary. The band go off to great applause and then come back and do 'Traffic Light Rock' as an encore. Terry really sweated his head off tonight. I bet when the Viewpoint film is shown it will be the usual load of rubbish.

(Author's note: Swindon Viewpoint was an experimental cable television network set up in 1974. Reception was limited to the Swindon area and programmes offered plenty of community access. Despite its very modest audience many local bands pounced on the opportunity of appearing on Viewpoint, including The Helium Kidz on several occasions. One of these performances is still held in a national film/video museum.)

Saturday April 30: The Roxy, London. We are top bill tonight, supported by The Drones. Place gets heavier by the minute with lots of leather, chains and various other strange clothes. Heaviest guy is one with glasses, short hair, no teeth, an arm band, studded gloves, leather trousers and jack-boots. XTC come on and open with 'Radios In Motion'. The crowd like 'Saturn Boy' very much. I cringe with fear when they play 'Watchtower', but it goes down quite well. Dave James and Colin get hit by a glass. Band leaves stage after 29 minutes, thank God. Reid's brother starts smashing some tables up and The Drones' roadie beats up two writers from a paper. Various beer cans and glasses are thrown around. I do like girl in black suspender belt and stockings with the white shirt. Lots of trouble when the place closes. No one wants to leave. Heavy scene at the end of road and later we find out Reid had his car smashed in.

(Author's note: Dave James [real name Albert Bartlett] is a Swindon based singer songwriter who was once a runner up on New Faces. The band had a long association with him - Andy especially - regularly backing him at gigs and playing on his demos. Dave

accompanied the band on several early gigs and was the man responsible for their first Affair booking.)

Saturday May 14: Barbarella's, Birmingham. One of the keys on
Barry's piano was broken so I got some superglue to fix it. No problem
after that. Ian and Dennis arrive at about 10.15pm. Ian has a tussle
with a punk who tries to put a pint of beer on the PA amps. Reid
comes off best. The band are on at midnight. Starting with 'Radios In
Motion' then straight through 'X Wires', 'Science Friction',
'Refrigerator Blues', 'Fireball XL5', 'Star Park', 'She's So Square',
'Watchtower', 'Do What You Do', 'Let's Have Fun', 'Spinning Top'
and 'Neon Shuffle'. Barry was his usual energetic self and he looked as
mean as ever. Colin stamps his leg up and down. Terry just beats hell
out of his kit. Andy moves well across the stage. Panic sets in when
half way through 'Neon Shuffle' Andy's mike packs up. This brings
the show to an abrupt end and Andy walks off in disgust.

Friday May 20: The Rock Garden, London. We are supporting a
band called Woman. Quite a few people have come to watch XTC
including Andy King, Brian Eno and publisher James Rubenstein
from EG music. When Woman come to the end of their set Andy,
Barry and Terry get up on stage and have a jam with the band for a few
numbers. Barry looks great pogoing and Andy seems to be taking
over on vocals. He won't let the band leave the stage, but a good time
was had by all. Manager very pleased and he buys us all a drink. Says
XTC are the best band he's had on since Chicken Shack and Talking
Heads, and he wants them back for more money.

Thursday June 2: Nashville Rooms, London. Back at The Nashville supporting a group called Squeeze. XTC are the better of the two
bands by miles. Lots of record companies turn up to see us. Our friend
Pat Travers turns up again and he enjoys the gig. Squeeze were a band
without conviction or real direction. Bass player had a glass of beer
thrown at him which hit him on the head. After gear packed away we
went back to Ian's brother's house where I had a row with his wife.

Monday June 6: The Nags Head, High Wycombe. Fred Cantrell
from Beserkley Records comes to see the gig and is very impressed.
With Fred is John Foxx of Ultravox fame. I have a chat with him
before the band go on stage. Great applause at the end of the gig. They
come back to do an encore and as they leap into a very fast version of
'Route 66' the pub manager turns the power off. Foxy came into the
dressing room afterwards to say how impressed he was. I think he was
quite genuine.

Tuesday June 14: The Rochester Castle, Stoke Newington. Audition time once again. Nearly all the interested record companies - Island, Virgin, EG Music, UK Records etc - are here. In fact there are probably as many record company people as there are ordinary punters. Luckily Barry's equipment is OK tonight and the boys put on a great show. One guy tells me he'd buy 'Radios In Motion' on the spot if it was put out as a single. Among the crowd (and I mean crowd, 'coz the place is packed) is Ultravox's keyboard player. He has seen the band before but wants a better look at them. Andy King floats around after the gig and tries to get the band into the studio over the weekend, but they are all against it.

 Thursday June 30: The Hope and Anchor, Islington. Colin and Barry arrive after gear is set up. They had been to Virgin to ponce a few drinks and look at the studio. Band take to the stage and one can tell from the word go that tonight is going to be great. Andy's new number ('New Town Animal') is tried tonight. Colin's ('Dance Band') is not done due to Barry's organ going wrong. But the crowd goes mad all the way through the set. XTC's reputation has spread across London and tonight they are showing their skills to a hooked audience. XTC ARE HERE TO STAY.

Thursday July 7: Pioneer Club, Cymmer. Typical Welsh pub gig. Long room with tables along the walls. I play tapes to the crowd (a packed sell out) to try and create some atmosphere. The band has to do two 40 minute sets. In this heat it was pretty hard to do. They dug up some old numbers such as 'Monkey Woman' and 'Boogie Woogie City'. All goes well in the first set. Terry plays with just his underpants on. The second set is where it all happens. Terry chucks a drumstick out into the crowd and smashes some guy's drink. Heavy scenes follow when the guy tries to get at Terry and cut him up. The band retreat to the dressing room and with the help of the bouncers the situation calms down. Andy's voice is pretty gone by the end of the night, and I don't think Terry wants to come back here again in a hurry!

Friday July 8: The Red Cow, Hammersmith. Back in London again. Tonight XTC pack the place out solid and the reaction is great. On this very warm night The Red Cow feels like a sauna bath. Terry plays in his underpants again. Andy had lost his voice this morning but he just about comes through the gig after much honey and the usual tin of melloids. Island and Virgin are here tonight and they virtually have a punch up over who is going to sign up XTC.

Tuesday July 12: The Rochester Castle, Stoke Newington. Tonight's gig was not the best by a long way. Andy's guitar was out of tune for the first three numbers and Colin forgot the words to the second verse of 'Crosswires'. Even so, each number gets more applause than the last, and they finish up with 'Saturn Boy'. Jeff and I take the gear to pieces then I set out to take Terry, Colin and his wife to Finsbury Park so they can get back home on the train. When I get back to the venue Reid gives me an almighty bollocking for the "abysmal sound" tonight. I almost tell him where to go - he wouldn't know a good sound from a bad sound. Anyway, signing with Virgin records is IMMINENT!

(Author's note: 'Jeff' refers to Jeff Fitches, one of Steve Warren's mates, who also became an integral part of XTC's early road crew. He became a tour manager later on until being dropped by Reid after contracting pneumonia on a European tour.)

Wednesday July 13: The Greyhound, Fulham. After Reid going on at us about last night's gig we come up with one of the best stunts yet. The band mimed to the first number. Apart from the slightly different sound, and the fact that Terry was not always on cue with his cymbal smashes, you couldn't really tell they were miming. *Top Of The Pops* eat your heart out. The Greyhound isn't the best place to get a crowd going. Andy King comes along as usual. So does Tim Lott of *Sounds*, Fred Cantrell, and two Virgin staff.

By mid July it had become obvious that XTC was going to sign to either Virgin or Island. CBS had failed to better their class 'C' offer and any other interested companies had by now dropped away. "Actually we nearly ended up with Harvest as well at one point," Andy remembers, "but they were pushed out of the running when their A&R man got into a pissed-up stupor in a London pub and insulted Ian Reid's wife!"

Representatives from both companies were regularly turning up to gigs and were well aware of each others' presence. It put Ian Reid in a strong position, especially as he had appointed Steven Fisher, a solicitor who specialised in the music business, to advise him on the optimum level of royalties and advances to demand. Of the two labels, the band preferred Virgin because they had the right kind of 'underground' identity, but for a while Virgin seemed to be hedging on details.

Towards the end of July, Reid took his wife and two small daughters on holiday to Sidmouth in Devon. While he was away Virgin finally agreed to all the band's terms. So keen were they to close the deal with Ian Reid that they sent a motorbike courier all the way from London to Sidmouth (some 200 miles) with a copy of the contract. A few days later, on August 9, the formalities were completed in Steven Fisher's office just off Oxford Street. (The complexity of the situation meant that in fact only Ian Reid was signing with Virgin and the band had a separate deal with Allydor - the company they thought they owned.) It was an event that Dennis Detheridge has particular cause not to forget.

"I'd been dashing all over the bloody place for weeks, plus I'd had all the responsibility of sorting out the Island/Virgin business while Ian was away on holiday, so by then I was exhausted," says Dennis. "I can remember sitting in Steven Fisher's office and suddenly this incredible wave of nausea coming over me. Moments later I collapsed on the floor. I now know that I'd only fainted, but of course everyone thought I'd had a heart attack so they called an ambulance. The meeting proceeded as if nothing had happened! Andy later told me that Ian Reid put his brief case under my head as a sort of pillow and every time he needed to get some papers out of it he'd shove my head to one side! The ambulance arrived and I was taken away to the Middlesex hospital for all sorts of tests - meanwhile the rest of them carried on signing. I mean, I could've flaked out permanently for all they cared!"

Although the Virgin deal was fairly generous by 1977 standards - £250,000 covering a six album period - the initial £25,000 advance (£15,000 from Virgin Records and £10,000 from the publishers Virgin Music) paid to Allydor was nothing to shout about. Even more modest was the £25 weekly wage Ian Reid advanced each member of the band. But in the euphoria immediately following their signing to Virgin the only thing that really seemed to matter was that they could at long last give up their day jobs (actually Andy had given his up four months earlier) and concentrate on making a living doing what they loved.

Andy: "As soon as we'd signed our record deal we naïvely thought 'This is it. We're finally going to be rich and famous. This is the moment we've been waiting for.' We thought that we were going to go straight to number one with our first record and then we'd all be able to retire. Of course it doesn't really happen like that."

6

ARE YOU RECEIVING ME?

I n the event, signing a record deal was less glamorous than the band
expected but Dennis Detheridge could be relied upon to make sure
a bit of showbiz sparkle entered the proceedings. Back in Swindon
he'd arranged a "mock" signing session between the band and
Virgin for the benefit of the local press, attended by the Mayor of
Thamesdown and Virgin's high profile chairman Richard Branson. It
was followed by a party at The Affair where the band played a one/off
celebratory gig as The Psychedelic Hawaiians. Wearing gruesomely
loud Hawaiian shirts, they blasted through a set of well trodden
standards like 'Wild Thing' and 'Hippy Hippy Shake' with Barry on
Stylophone, Andy on ukelele, Colin on fuzzbox bass and Terry on
buckets! Major record deals may have been two a penny in the big
city, but in provincial Swindon it was big news.

Virgin were keen to get XTC into the studio as soon as possible,
and suggested the band work with John Leckie, who had been an
engineer at Abbey Road for the previous seven years and was under
direct contract to EMI. As a producer he was virtually an unknown
quantity, but Virgin's managing director (and XTC's A&R man)
Simon Draper thought he would be well suited to the task because of
his previous studio work with Be Bop De Luxe, an innovative, eclectic
band that had much in common with XTC.

"The first time I saw XTC was at a gig at The Nashville," recalls
Leckie. "They were supporting a punk band called London and were
getting a torrent of gob at them. They looked pretty menacing and I
was a bit wary of meeting them, but when I did there was an instant
rapport between us.

"They were so funny to be around because you had these anarchic,
very witty characters in the band - and then you had Dennis Detheridge and Ian Reid. Detheridge was this very straight-laced press man,
always looking for a corny headline and a good angle. Reid was this
clean cut character with a very militaristic presence, and the band
seemed to do everything he said."

This last comment is confirmed by Dennis Detheridge: "Ian was a typical product of his military background (his father was a high ranking army officer). He was very much a disciplinarian with the regimental manner, and he had the flair - the Oxford accent, the smart clothes and the Jensen Interceptor - to go with it. But when it came to rapport with the band, you couldn't say they were friends. I think they regarded it very much as a business relationship.

"Ian knew very little about the technical side of the music business in those early days, and he would often say things that would give his ignorance away. I remember one day we were sitting in his office talking about the band's equipment. The question Ian asked was 'What do you mean, backline? What's backline?' I think that says it all!"

John Leckie's first task was to mix a live set that had been recorded at Liverpool Eric's Club with a view to having live versions of some songs on the first album. This idea was subsequently abandoned, however, and XTC and Leckie went into Abbey Road studios in London on August 28 to record and mix a batch of songs for their first single. Although they'd been in recording studios before, this time was different. This time they were actually making a record! "It was quite intimidating," Andy recalls. "I felt wound up and hyper-elated. I couldn't eat, couldn't sleep, couldn't think . . . I could barely play I was so excited."

Colin, too, found the occasion a little overwhelming. "It was one of the most frightening things I've ever experienced. There I was in a professional studio - a studio that The Beatles had recorded in! - thinking 'Am I good enough for the job? When that red light goes on I've got to be fantastic.' Because this was our first commitment to vinyl the sense of occasion was really special."

In three days they recorded two original Partridge compositions - 'Science Friction' and 'She's So Square' - and Colin Moulding's 'Dance Band'. This was to become known as the 3D EP, a title that once again reflected Andy's infatuation with science fiction comics.

During the sessions at Abbey Road the XTC party learned that former Prime Minister Edward Heath - a keen organist - was recording an LP of Christmas carols in an adjacent studio. Detheridge immediately seized on this as an opportunity to squeeze some column inches out of Fleet Street and went to ask Heath's personal secretary if he'd like to meet a punk rock group. The message came back that he'd been wondering where the noise pervading the church-like ambience of his studio was coming from and he'd like to meet XTC on the condition that no photographs were taken.

"Detheridge and Reid were really excited about this," John Leckie remembers. "Much more so than the band. He came up to our studio a bit later in the day with a small entourage of security men and complained nicely about the noise. He asked if it could be turned down a bit - it wasn't loud either! I just remember Barry Andrews sitting cross-legged on a flight case breaking match sticks in half and talking to Ted Heath. He looked as if he couldn't give a toss. We had microphones placed in all the plant pots in the studio and I was recording their good natured banter. The idea was that we'd use this in the run-off groove on the record, but the sound quality wasn't good enough."

It may have been a brief encounter but it was enough for Dennis Detheridge to get XTC their first mention in the tabloid press. *The Daily Express* covered the story in their William Hickey diary, and *The Sunday People* ran the corny headline 'This Is One Ted The Punks Do Like' (which referred to the notorious on-going rivalry between Punks and Teddy Boys).

The release of the 3D EP on October 7 was an exciting time for the band. Well received by music critics, it perfectly encapsulated what XTC were about at that moment in time: bright, breezy pop peppered with unexpected twists and a rhythmic itch. Even the song title seemed to say it all: in 1977 XTC looked like the future direction of rock.

After a week of trying to promote 'Science Friction', mostly on hopelessly inappropriate kids' TV shows like *Magpie* and *Tiswas*, but also with an appearance on the 'serious' late evening rock show *The Old Grey Whistle Test*, the band were put back into the studio on October 15 to record their first album. In just two weeks - with frequent interruptions for their 3D EP TV promotional appearances - they recorded 17 songs at The Manor, the Virgin owned studio in the Oxfordshire countryside.

Essentially they were recording what they considered to be the best of their live set with songs ranging from the old - the oldest being 'Neon Shuffle', a less manic version of which had been performed by The Helium Kidz as early as 1974 - to the brand new. Colin had by this time been writing songs for about six months and his 'Set Myself On Fire', which he'd only just completed, was added to the set at the last minute.

70

"They were very quick," says John Leckie. "It was almost like recording their stage show. We'd do four or five songs a day and then tart them up a bit. It was all very fiery and speedy. You didn't sit around in the studio programming and trying out different routes like you do now. You just went ahead and did it.

"There was a very creative mood floating between them. They'd have these energetic discussions about how everything should be done. But it wasn't argumentative, it was stimulating. Andy just wanted everything stripped away. He was in a very 'zen' mood. Because of punk he had kind of 'zenned' himself of his musical knowledge and was taking a very minimalistic approach."

"It was so rushed," says Andy. "Besides we didn't really have much of a concept of overdubbing. We didn't really know how to make records, full stop. Before we started making records I literally thought that on an LP a band got quieter and quieter at the end of a song, were as quiet as possible during the little gap between tracks, and then started up the next song! That's how I thought you did it!"

During the sessions the prospective LP was given the name 'Black Music'. Andy thought it would be a fitting title because, just as black humour is funny because it's not, XTC's music was a challenging combination of melody, jumpy rhythms and gratuitous noise; music, but not music. But the idea was rejected by Simon Draper at Virgin who was worried that the uninitiated would think XTC were a soul band!

"One day Ian Reid said jokingly, 'Well, why don't you call it 'White Music'?" says Andy. "I thought 'Wow! White Music as in white noise, as in white boys making it. Yeah, that'll do!'"

Virgin were somewhat taken aback by the speed at which the album had been completed and asked John Leckie to re-mix it. After four more days' work the final result wasn't much changed from the original, but met with everyone's approval.

When their 3D EP failed to gain a chart placing, everyone connected with XTC was understandably disappointed. Part of the problem was that in 1977 12 inch EP's were a difficult commodity to market and although a standard seven inch version (missing out 'Dance Band') was also released simultaneously, very few copies were put on sale. It seemed that Virgin's efforts to cash in with a gimmick had largely backfired. Even so, with some TV and radio exposure sales of 'Science Friction' reached a respectable 30,000.

Typically self-effacing, Andy now looks back and cringes: "It was

71

pretty awful," he says. "I don't have any fond regard for 'Science Friction' at all. It's one of the few things that we've ever done that I find immensely embarrassing. I felt as if I had to get it out of my system and move on straight away."

The build-up to the album's release was punctuated by a relentless barrage of live work towards the end of the year. On December 3 XTC took part in The Hope And Anchor Front Row Festival in London, alongside bands like The Stranglers, The Pirates, X Ray Spex - and an unknown group called Dire Straits. Described by Andy as "a misconceived Woodstock in a cellar" - but actually an attempt to raise funds to prevent the venue closing - the festival was recorded over several days and highlights were later released on a double album on WEA which included XTC's 'Science Friction' and 'I'm Bugged'.

On January 6 the single 'Statue Of Liberty' - the first fruit of the October sessions at The Manor - was released. Three days later, XTC made four very rushed videos - for 'Statue Of Liberty', 'She's So Square', 'Dance Band' and 'Hang Onto The Night' - with the Keefco Film Company in the studios of ITN in London. That same evening they departed for Holland for the start of a mini European tour. It was the first trip abroad for XTC and passports had to be hurriedly obtained for Colin, Andy and Terry.

Journalist Tony Mitchell, who followed XTC in Europe and went on to become one of their staunchest allies in the music press, later wrote in *Sounds* of this tour, where they were supporting Talking Heads: "Both bands got on like a house on fire, and although they're both headlining separate UK tours, XTC hope very much that they might tour the States with the Heads in the not-too-distant future. 'They're a bit quiet,' said XTC stixman Terry Chambers, 'but they say they like us because we make them laugh.' Later over dinner Tina Weymouth confirmed that XTC's non-stop antics had somewhat revitalised the Heads, who by then had been on the road for four months solid.

"It's not just XTC's music which is bright, zany and full of unexpected twists. This trait is also reflected in a kind of group humour which has grown to proportions such that it dominates everyone and everything they encounter. At the end of a long weekend which I, Virgin Records press officer Al Clarke and international manager Laurie Dunn spent with XTC in Hamburg and Amsterdam, everyone - even their manager - was snapping at each other in the high pitched staccato tones of Laurence Olivier's famous Richard III portrayal which the band drop into as if it were a second language."

Hardly an article was written about XTC without some mention of the unique chemistry between them. When the four were together their humour set the air alight. Ordinary conversation was a pinball jangle of comedy and absurdity. Andy, with the kind of verve that a comedy script writer would kill for, had an answer for everything and was impossible to upstage. Barry was his sounding board, capable of being sharp witted and caustic in equal degrees. Terry was Terry - the drummer, the drinker, the animal, a walking, talking Troggs tape! The most Wiltshire sounding of them all, he often spoke in a flood of West Country expletives. Colin, the quiet one, was a constant enigma. Sometimes he hardly said a word, but when he did speak he was capable of matching the others' wit and presence.

But they had their downside too: Terry could often be quite abusive and threatening, especially when he'd had a few drinks, and sometimes the tension between Andy and Barry was almost tangible. "We were always having arguments," says Andy. "We'd be constantly playing verbal tennis with each other. Barry had this thing where he'd have to stick up for the underdog. Because Colin was further down the chain of command to me in some respects, Barry would always support him against me - which I found intensely annoying. If Colin had written a new song, Colin's would always be better than mine and all that sort of thing." The tension would get much worse . . .

The head of Virgin International, Lisa Anderson, also accompanied the band around Europe and, in a move which he'd live to regret, Andy ended up having a brief affair with her. "Everything was going to my head at once," says Andy. "The fact that it was my first time abroad and we were 'famous'. I was rather distracted. But I was immediately racked with guilt. I owned up to Marianne as soon as I could - I felt terrible. Actually Marianne met Lisa at a gig in Reading on a later tour. When she realised who she was she punched Lisa in the face. That seemed to solve it!"

When the band returned to Britain from their short European tour they were greeted with the news that their new single 'Statue Of Liberty' had been banned from daytime airplay by the BBC for the ostensibly 'provocative' lyric "and in my fantasy I sail beneath your skirt"! With only John Peel prepared to champion the record on his late evening show on Radio One the single, not surprisingly, flopped.

Their début album 'White Music' fared better when it was released on January 20. With generous music press coverage - which included getting on the cover of three of the four rock weeklies - and a further splash of TV appearances (mainly kids shows again), it reached the Top 40 in the UK.

For a record that had been recorded in such little time, 'White Music' was an unexpectedly good album, dominated - naturally enough - by Andy who contributed eight of his songs against three by Colin. The only outsider was an energetic version of Bob Dylan's 'All Along The Watchtower' - already an established part of XTC's live set - which gave Andy an opportunity to show off his skills on the harmonica.

Among the band's original compositions there were several highlights: 'Radios In Motion', 'This Is Pop', 'Statue Of Liberty' and 'Atom Age' between them exemplified Andy's exceptional knack for fusing clever pop melodies and those ever-present sci-fi themes with provocative musical shapes. Like the best thriller stories, his songs were neither predictable, nor unresolved. An exhilarating balance between the conventional and the experimental.

But ironically, for someone who was still taking his first steps as a songwriter, it was Colin who came up with the album's most challenging moment. 'X Wires' - a song that unashamedly borrowed from Andy at his most audacious - was simultaneously the most inventive and least accessible moment on the album.

'White Music' could hardly have been better received by the music press - all four of the principle music papers gave the LP the thumbs up.

Melody Maker: 'Warm, angular, intelligent and enthusiastic are XTC'.

Sounds: 'This is a truly FAB album'.

NME: 'If Power Pop is this year's 'new thing', XTC have to be 1978's superstars. No frills, nothing wasted, rocks like a bitch'.

Record Mirror: 'XTC have summed up 1978 in less than 40 minutes'.

'White Music' was keeping very select company. Very few other new wave records could touch its eccentric style and sparkling wit. Not everyone understood what XTC were about, but that was half their appeal. Even Andy confessed that many of his (and Colin's) early songs were nonsensical. They could be disjointed and discordant, but never clichéd. The Swindon mavericks had succeeded in forcing rock's avant garde hierarchy to sit up and take note. Theirs wasn't always an easy cup to swallow, but XTC had a sharp definition and distinctive sound. There was no mistaking them for any other band in the world. As the record's producer, John Leckie was credited with having taken a photograph of the band as they were at the time. "Basically I got down the best recording of the best performance of them as they were," he says.

With barely enough time for their feet to touch the ground the band were off on another extensive UK tour to promote 'White Music' on January 20. The seven week club tour took in many small towns like St Albans and Barnstaple - places not normally visited by nationally known groups. On the whole music press reviews were very favourable. On stage XTC were a force to behold - the constant gigging had welded their disjointed rhythms together so neatly you could almost set your watch to them. Usually the songs were played at twice the speed of the records, and by the end of the night everyone, even the crowd, would be exhausted.

"I remember a time when XTC could justly be described as fairly restrained on stage," wrote Kim Davis in the *NME*. "After all, they look and dress normal, they don't swing from the rafters or scale the PA. Andy Partridge, however, has turned into a rivetting, robotic mover, eyes staring, head jerking, mouth strained in an unbreakable grin. He points, waves, chops at his guitar, all sudden, sharp motions, only relaxing the tautness of his slender frame as the last chords die."

Ian Reid and Dennis Detheridge took it in turns to visit the band at various venues along the way. Travelling back from a gig in Reid's Jensen interceptor one night, Barry Andrews asked how much was in Allydor's account. "I don't ask you how much you've got in your account Barry," had been Reid's curt reply. "So why do you ask me?"

On another occasion, Terry got a similar response for asking the same question one night. "We'd just come off stage," Terry explains, "and Reid was waiting backstage. I'd just opened my first can of beer of the night, looked at Reid and said 'So how much money's in Allydor then Ian?' Reid looked at me and the can of beer and said 'Talk to me when you're sober, Terry'. I'd barely had a sip of the stuff!"

On the whole the tour went very smoothly. The problems that other leading new wave bands were experiencing on their tours - council paranoia, bannings, gang fights etc - weren't affecting XTC. At some venues they played special matinée performances to under 16 year olds (because of their frequent appearances on children's TV shows they'd built up a sizeable pre-16 following!) which was a source of much amusement to the street-cred obsessed music press.

Modest as it was, XTC enjoyed their success to the full. Groupies - those much prized trophies of rock'n'roll stardom - were in evidence everywhere, and only Andy, who had learned his lesson, managed to resist their temptations. Though married, Colin succumbed. Some of these early fans were legendary. 'Rats and Delicious', for instance, were a couple of girls from Leeds who followed the band around the north of England religiously for a while. 'Rats' was a mortician who had a rather macabre interest in the after life. 'Delicious' lived up to her name and was the most sought after of the pair, often wearing a fetching line of skintight leopard skin leotards.

On the 'White Music' tour the band's lighting man George, nicknamed The Dogcatcher, was despatched into the audience each night to invite some of the best looking girls back to the band's hotel after gigs. The scenes of revelry that followed sometimes resembled the most debauched Roman orgies. The band shared hotel rooms so there wasn't much chance of discretion or privacy. Girls were passed around; so too were diseases. Steve Warren can recall at least a couple of occasions when VD clinics were visited mid-tour and the relevant inoculations administered. "It got to the point where Barry would have his injections before the tours to keep him going till the end!" he says.

In 1978 XTC worked staggeringly hard. They were on the road, either in Europe or the UK, for a solid eight months of the year, and in various recording studios for a further two months. Much of the remainder of the year was set aside for rehearsals and promotional work. Actual days off could be counted on the fingers of one hand. Small wonder, then, that tensions were rising.

A constant gripe on these early tours was an apparent haphazardness of planning. In February 78, NME's Phil McNeil wrote: "When I first meet XTC in the bar of their Edinburgh hotel, it's the second time they've visited Scotland in a week. In between times they've been right down to Cardiff, and come back via Yorkshire. The jokes, inevitably, concerned the method by which the tour route had been chosen; the conclusion is that a map of the country was pinned to the wall and used as a dartboard."

In an effort to net the elusive hit single, Virgin suggested that the band re-record 'This Is Pop?' - without doubt one of the more accessible songs on 'White Music' - feeling it had been overlooked first time around. So on February 26 and 27 they teamed up, on Virgin's recommendation, with producer Mutt Lange at Utopia Studios in north London. Lange, who had produced other acts like The Boomtown Rats and Graham Parker, had a reputation for extreme fastidiousness and perfectionism in the studio.

The new version of the song was discernibly tighter, tougher and more commercial. With a light hearted lyric that castigated élitist pop bands who tried to deny they were making pop music, it was XTC's best chance of a hit from the album, but the best evidently wasn't good enough. Andy was puzzled and disillusioned. "I had high hopes for everything we did at that point," he says. "I wasn't aware of the reality of how hit singles came about. I just thought you did the best you could, and if you did your best it became a hit. We now know that it's got very little to do with the musical content. With that first album we went from being the band that was going to change the world, to realising we weren't in a very short space of time. We soon had the naïvety knocked out of us."

With almost indecent haste XTC were back in the studio to start work on their second LP in August, less than a year since they'd recorded their début. For a while Brian Eno was a strong contender for the role of producer. The former *enfant terrible* of Roxy Music had since carved out a solo career of exceptional individuality, releasing albums of 'ambient' music to be played as an accompaniment to other activities, his unique antidote to the dreadful Muzak often played in public buildings. He had also proved himself as an imaginative record producer with his critically acclaimed 'Berlin' collaborations with David Bowie in recent years, and he would go on to achieve stunning success by merging 'ambience' into the music of U2, the most successful young rock group of the Eighties.

Eno had seen XTC play live a couple of times and was reported to have told friends later that they were the only band he'd felt tempted to join in a long time.

This compliment reached the ears of Andy and his cohorts who were duly flattered and sent Eno demos of their new songs. During a meeting at Virgin's old offices at Vernons Yard, off Portobello Road, Eno - then busy with his 'Before And After Science' project - told them in all sincerity that he didn't think they needed a producer because they obviously had plenty of original ideas of their own. Nevertheless, both Virgin and the group still believed XTC needed a strong hand in the studio and so John Leckie was once again enlisted as producer.

It had become evident to the more perceptive of those involved that the band's strong democratic ideals had created a situation where too many cooks might spoil the broth. Until now Andy, and to a lesser extent Colin, had been XTC's songwriters, but in the short gap between albums Barry had come up with several songs which he insisted should be recorded. Strangely, two of his better songs which were rehearsed - 'Mousetrap' and what was later to become 'Rossmore Road' - never found their way on to tape. Andy felt at the time that Barry might have been saving them for a project of his own.

A growing tension between Barry and Andy dominated the 'Go 2' sessions. They were both forceful characters, outspoken in their views. Barry felt Andy was controlling him too much, while Andy thought Barry was trying to whip the carpet from beneath him. The atmosphere grew very unpleasant and eventually it became difficult for the two of them to be in the studio at the same time. Barry would demand Andy leave while he was recording his parts, and vice versa. It was a marked change from the 'White Music' sessions, when everyone enthusiastically pitched in.

To make matters worse, the band were living communally in a rented flat in Belsize Park for the duration of the 'Go 2' sessions. Disagreements in the studio continued after hours. "We'd constantly argue because I thought Barry's first foray into songwriting wasn't in keeping with the direction we were going in," says Andy. "It was a dual concern of mine that the band was really struggling to get an identity over to Mr and Mrs Public and suddenly here he was trying to make us veer off in a wildly different direction. Certainly for first efforts his songs were very good, but at the time I thought they weren't as good as some of the things Colin and I were doing. I thought he was taking us into a kamikaze nose dive before we'd even established full flight."

The result was that they emerged after five weeks in Abbey Road studio with 19 tracks, not all of which could be used. When it came to making a final track selection, five of Barry's seven songs were dropped, while virtually all Andy's and Colin's were used either on the album or on subsequent B sides. "I remember I had to phone Barry and tell him his songs had been dropped," says John Leckie. "He wasn't at all happy about it and in fact he didn't come to any of the mixing sessions after that."

When Virgin heard the completed album, they listened through each track individually, trying to select a single to act as a trailer for the forthcoming LP. 'Are You Receiving Me?' was the noisiest, most exhilarating wall of sound the band had yet delivered. It was unmistakably XTC - the anguished vocals, the angular texture and the clever hookline - yet it was melodic too. Simon Draper decided it was a strong contender for a single but wanted the band to record it afresh with a different producer. He suggested Martin Rushent, who at that time had enjoyed the most success in getting hits for new wave bands like The Buzzcocks, The Stranglers and Generation X.

Rushent persuaded the band to record a version that was still punchy, but also neat and crisp enough to be radio friendly. 'Are You Receiving Me?' was released as a single on September 22 but failed to excite those who compile radio playlists around the country. As a result, it failed to reach even the Top 75 in the UK.

'Go 2', on the other hand, had quite the opposite impact. Released on October 6, it received rapturous reviews in the music press. *NME* wrote "'Go 2' is a gem. It establishes XTC firmly among the best groups in the country, yet it bears no relation to anything else around. In particular, Andy Partridge emerges as a truly brilliant writer and performer." *Melody Maker* commented: "The massive achievements of XTC's second album are best realised when placed alongside the failed attempts of their contemporaries to succeed in similar areas." Meanwhile Tony Mitchell in *Sounds* questioned: "Could this album have been any better if the much vaunted link-up with Brian Eno on production had taken place? I doubt it."

Coming less than nine months after 'White Music', 'Go 2' was indeed a triumph over back room adversity. The minimalism and harshness of the first album had now been replaced by a superior melodic strength and a greater willingness to experiment. On the album itself, songs like 'Battery Brides' - which Andy dedicated to Eno in his absence, adding (Andy Paints Brian) to the title - and 'Life Is Good In The Greenhouse' showed they were quickly getting to grips with more imaginative production methods and John Leckie freely admitted that this was as much due to the band themselves as it was to him. A free EP issued with the first 15,000 copies of the album proved that in many ways XTC's thinking was years ahead of its time. The appropriately titled 'Go +' featured five tracks of radically re-mixed and re-titled songs from the album. It was a brave and innovative leap which anticipated the upcoming trend for re-mixing tracks by several years.

'Go 2' - a title borrowed from a Japanese strategy game - reached

No 21 in the UK, a chart placing made all the more impressive by the fact that no singles were culled from the album (UK pressings of 'Go 2' didn't include 'Are You Receiving Me?' because the Martin Rushent production wasn't ready in time). The only sour note for XTC in what appeared to be a glittering triumph was the extent of the problems they'd experienced while making the record.

In retrospect Andy now says it's the album of which he's least proud. "I think everyone contributed their worst songs to 'Go 2'. I'd written a lot of rubbish because we were constantly touring and I couldn't find the time to write. Colin was groping for an identity after the initial shock tactics of things like 'X Wires' - which I think was him trying to write a piece of fake Andy Partridge. And then there was Barry steering the band off too quickly with things like 'My Weapon' and 'Super Tuff . . .'"

With teeth clenched and brave smiles all around, the band set off on another exhaustive tour of the UK, including for the first time gigs in Ireland and the Continent to promote 'Go 2'. Barry pushed aside his keyboards on many of these dates and just played saxophone - a move that baffled audiences! - and while in Ireland he introduced Terry to the delights of magic mushrooms after a gig one night.

"Terry flipped," Andy recalls. "When the mushrooms took effect he became intensely petrified of Barry for some reason. He was convinced that this was all a plot to kill him. Barry was going to get him out of it - which he did successfully - and then he was going to chop him up! Terry is not the sort of person you should give drugs to. He can take his beer, but forget anything else. He barricaded himself in his room, he couldn't handle it at all."

NME journalist Steve Clarke caught up with XTC in Ireland that autumn and wrote the following prophetic report: "As we talk it becomes increasingly obvious that Barry for one isn't over enamoured with the lifestyle and status of a rock musician.

"There are already murmurs that XTC will be splitting up soon. One of the problems is that old faithful, 'ego clashes'. There's too much material around to keep everybody satisfied; 'Go 2' was originally going to be a double album, but the idea was scotched because of financial considerations. But the other reasons for the dissatisfaction in the ranks stems from the group's attitudes towards XTC. 'I don't see it lasting a hell of a lot longer,' says Barry. 'I think it'll explode pretty soon. Maybe one more album. I think we're soon going to exhaust the rock band format'."

When the band returned from the European leg of their tour - a rather demoralising three weeks of playing to largely disinterested audiences - they learned to their delight that they'd been personally invited to support Talking Heads in New York that New Year's eve. Since they'd toured together earlier in the year the two bands had kept in touch, and considerable mutual respect had developed between them. Andy and David Byrne maintained a lively correspondence, sending each other notes and telegrams from time to time. In fact, Andy kept in touch with several like minded musicians including Thomas Dolby.

In order to make the most of their first trip to America, Ian Reid fixed up a dozen additional dates in small clubs in the north eastern states. They were often greeted, somewhat ominously, with the question: "You boys ain't punk rock are ya?" Totally unknown in the States, XTC found it difficult to muster much of a reaction, although in New York itself they were favourably received at the legendary CBGB's down on the Bowery where audiences were more likely to appreciate the more imaginative strands of the New Wave. The main event of the trip - a gig at the prestigious Beacon Theatre supporting the Heads - also went well, and acted as a useful introduction to the American music business.

"David Byrne actually came out on stage and introduced us to the audience," says Andy. "I thought . . . 'Don't do this, you're blowing your cool'. But I don't think he realised he had any cool to blow!" Robert Fripp, the West Country avant garde guitarist temporarily transplanted to New York, saw the show and was so impressed with Barry's wild, rebellious keyboard playing that he invited him, on his one day off, to collaborate with him on his current 'League Of Gentlemen' project.

Rumours concerning Barry's future in XTC had been flying around for weeks and it was while they were in Boston on the US tour that the fragile thread finally broke. No one was surprised by Barry's formal announcement and no one tried to make him change his mind. When they returned to England in the middle of January 1979 a big question mark hung over XTC's future.

A couple of days after they returned home a meeting was held in Ian Reid's office during which Barry confirmed he was leaving. It was an immense relief to everyone but, ironically, it was Andy who would miss their anarchic keyboard player the most.

"I felt a terrible vacuum when he left," he admits. "If ever I went out with Barry socially we'd gravitate towards drinking, but you could sit down and chat to him about literature or European films. I couldn't talk to Terry about anything other than the price of a pint. And I couldn't talk to Colin because Colin wouldn't talk. So Barry Andrews was my conversational lifeline with the world. But looking back it was inevitable he'd have to go from the minute he joined and was given permission to just be himself."

7

LIFE BEGINS AT THE HOP

News of Barry Andrews' departure from XTC soon circulated around the music business and the assumption was that the group would be looking for a new keyboard player. There was no shortage of prospective replacements. XTC may not have been setting the world alight in the commercial sense but they were highly respected in musicians' circles.

Initially both band and Virgin were concerned that much of the identity they had worked so hard to establish had walked out the door with Barry. His scientific 'split-the-atom' keyboard style had become a major component of their sound which would be very difficult to replace. Virgin immediately honoured Barry's contribution to XTC by giving him a solo deal.

Andrews recorded only one single and an EP for Virgin before his contract was terminated. He went on to do session work with people like Robert Fripp and Iggy Pop, and eventually formed his own band Restaurant For Dogs, and later Shriekback, who signed with Arista.

For a while XTC went through the motions of auditioning a series of keyboard players but they were either unsuitable or incapable or both. One of the first applicants for the as yet unadvertised vacancy was Thomas Dolby who had kept a close and admiring eye on the band's career since the release of 'White Music'. He sent Andy copious letters and copies of demo tapes - most of which were impressive.

"The last thing we wanted when Barry left was Barry 2," says Andy. "That's really why I reluctantly fought off all the attention from Thomas Dolby. His material was really good, but I thought 'No, this is going to be trouble. I'm going to be making a rod for my own back if we take on another songwriting keyboard player who's going to take us off on another course'."

It was in any case a farcical scenario because Barry's replacement had already been earmarked as long ago as that night in Boston when the situation came out into the open for the first time. Moments after Barry announced he was leaving, Andy made a panic transatlantic call to a long-time musician acquaintance in Swindon to tell him he was in the band if he so wished. There were three surprises: he was predominantly a guitarist; no one, not even Andy, knew he could play keyboards as well; and he'd already failed an audition for the pre-XTC Helium Kidz!

He was, of course, Dave Gregory.

"I don't know why we went through the stupid pretence of auditioning other people - we all knew we wanted Gregsy. We all knew how he played and that we'd get on with him all right. Plus he was from Swindon which was very important."

Dave Gregory was born on September 21, 1952, at the Cheriton nursing home on Westlecott Road, Swindon, where Terry Chambers was also born. At that time his parents Roy and Margaret lived in a small cottage in Purton, a village about five miles outside the town. Because of Swindon's alarming expansion rate - at one point in the Eighties it was reputed to be the fastest growing town in western Europe - Purton is now desperately trying to hold on to its green belt, but back then it was a caring go-ahead little village favoured by many of Swindon's well-to-do.

In 1959 the Gregorys moved to a bigger house in Hyde Lane, Purton, to accommodate their swelling ranks, who would soon include Dave's younger brothers Ian and Robert, and they have lived at that address ever since. Roy was a clerk with the railways and it was this that sparked off Dave's early fascination with steam locomotives. The bright, single-minded kid liked nothing better than an afternoon of train spotting, or - if he was really lucky - a visit to a signal box, whose interior he would pencil sketch in scrupulous detail back at home.

The Gregorys were a fairly musical family. When Dave was nine they installed a piano in the house, and there was always a wide selection of 'serious' classical music 78s playing on their radiogram. Dave was persuaded to take piano and 'cello lessons. At the Commonweal school in Swindon he excelled in all the arts subjects and his parents had visions of him one day sawing away at the back of an orchestra. One of his friends in Purton was Tony Climpson (later a member of Stiff Beach with Andy and Spud Taylor) who came from quite a well off family.

"Tony's sister had loads and loads of records," Dave remembers. "I used to go around to his house and he'd always get the Dansette out and we'd play her records. They'd be things like 'Let There Be Drums' by Sandy Nelson, 'Forget Me Not' by Eden Kane, and she had a load of Cliff Richard and The Shadows records. I remember this Shadows EP - I think it was from the film 'The Young Ones' - and there was a photograph of them on the front wearing bright red jackets and holding these brand sparkling new pink Fender guitars. I thought 'Give me some of that!' At the time it was just an amazing image."

But it was 'Please Please Me' by The Beatles that tipped Dave, all of 12 years old, over the edge. Suddenly he was hooked. He asked his parents if they could get him an electric guitar but, both very disapproving of pop music, they declined in the hope that it was just a passing phase. But it wasn't. During school holidays Dave would tune the radiogram into the BBC's *Housewife's Choice* on the off chance that a Beatles record might be played. The minute one came on he'd dive down and press his ear to the speaker, trying to coax more Beatles out of it. It was total obsession.

The pestering continued until eventually his parents relented and let him have an electric guitar - on the condition that he paid for it himself. The grey/silver Rosetti - with three pick-ups and a tremolo arm - cost 14 guineas (nearly £15). It was bought on hire purchase from Kempster's in December 1966. "I worked out that if I kept my paper rounds going, I could pay for it over 12 months," says Dave.

"I can always remember the smell in Kempster's. It had a magical smell upstairs. I don't know if it was the polish on the lino, or whether it was just all those guitars reeking of quality. I'll never forget that aroma."

Dave's first proper group The Four Aces - which featured a drummer who played on a set of toy drums! - swung into action shortly afterwards, playing their first live gig at The Silver Threads Hut in Purton in March 1967. A week or so later came another great turning point when the Gregory family got their first television set.

"One of the first things I saw on it was Jimi Hendrix miming to 'Purple Haze' on *Top Of The Pops*," says Dave. "I didn't believe what I was seeing and hearing! For weeks I went around besotted with this Hendrix guy and trying to turn everyone onto him. Even Eric Clapton hadn't had this effect. I dedicated my life to being just like Jimi Hendrix, except I knew my mum wouldn't stand for me having a hair-do like his."

Dave's obsession with the guitar, and guitarists, grew to the exclusion of everything else. After refusing to practise "stodgy pieces of classical music", he was dropped by his piano tutor and school work became an unfortunate daily interruption to guitar playing. "Every spare second I had I'd be practising. I didn't do any homework. I always used to lie to the teachers the next day that I'd left it at home."

But there was also another reason for Dave's poor exam results. The run up to taking his 'O' Levels coincided with the sudden discovery that he had diabetes - a disease which made itself known via an abnormal increase in his appetite and an insatiable thirst. It was a worrying time for his family. "I can still see him heading off for an exam one morning," says Margaret Gregory, "walking away from the house as though he didn't know how to put one foot in front of the other. I jumped every time the phone rang because I thought . . . 'They're ringing from school to say he's collapsed'. Instead of which he came home as bright as a button. The sugar had worked off during the day and he was okay. It was all quite alarming."

He struggled through the rest of his time at school, eventually leaving at 16 with few qualifications because "my head was just full of guitars. There wasn't anything else I wanted to do."

Dave learned to live with his diabetes - in particular the self-administered daily shots of insulin - which had a severe curbing effect on his rock'n'roll lifestyle in the years ahead and which would lead to some interesting confrontations with customs officers as XTC returned home from a tour equipped with needles and syringes for Dave's injections.

Of all its members past and present, Dave Gregory had by far the most colourful pre-XTC musical career, and probably the most frustrating as well. After The Four Aces his next group was Pink Warmth (named after a brand of Paraffin!) which he formed with his best friend from school Richard 'Tich' Adams in 1968. Pink Warmth's psychedelic offerings captured the admiration of the 15 year-old Andy Partridge at a regular booking, the St Peter's Church Hall 'hop' at Penhill.

"We began to see familiar faces returning to those ramshackle evenings," says Dave. "Not least of which was a skinny little kid with a deathly white pallor, tassled suede jacket and a hair cut just like Peter Tork's from The Monkees. He was fascinated by all the equipment and seemed to be running on a severe overload of adrenalin. He'd come backstage and plunk the guitars even though he couldn't play a note. We never knew his name - he was just 'that weird kid'."

After Pink Warmth came Catfish (featuring Tony Climpson on drums) a 'heavy blues band' influenced by such luminaries as Taste, Led Zeppelin and Free. Catfish played several gigs in the Swindon area

- most notably at McIlroy's ballroom - coming into contact with other contemporary local bands like Stray Blues. "I kept bumping into that crazy kid I'd met at Penhill the previous year, who I now knew simply as Rocky," says Dave. "Every time we met in a music shop we'd have a guitar off the wall apiece and would exchange chords and 'licks'."

With the loss of one member, Catfish became Orange late 1969, and worked hard to consolidate their reputation as Swindon's very first heavy rock band. But in October 1970 Orange collapsed, and so did Dave's dreams. He sought psychiatric help after becoming very depressed. As well as receiving psychiatric treatment for a year, he was prescribed Valium and Librium which he took for a while. His whole life seemed to be a disaster - his group had split up, he was an 18 year-old diabetic who had fallen hopelessly in love for the first time, and he hated his job, working full-time as a trainee manager at a television manufacturing company. The vicious circle dragged him down until he'd just about lost interest in life, even turning his back on music which had been the centre of his universe until then.

For two years he hardly touched his guitar, until one day in March 1972, he walked into the record department at Bon Marche in Swindon. "Who should be serving behind the counter, but Rocky Partridge with whom I was now quite friendly," he explains. "'What d'you reckon to this?' he said, despatching me to one of the listening booths and placing a disc on the turntable. What I heard changed my life once again - a guitarist, a drummer, a keyboard player and a violinist playing the most incredibly complex, virtuosic and spiritually uplifting music I had ever encountered. It was the Mahavishnu Orchestra and the album was called 'The Inner Mounting Flame'. I bought it and played it and played it and played it. The depression began to lift, but slowly."

In August 1972 it dawned on Dave that if he sold his guitar and all his equipment he could probably afford something better than the rusty old Austin car he shared with his mother. On the point of advertising the lot for sale, Margaret suggested that maybe it would be better to join a working band and make some money back on his investment. It wouldn't matter what sort of music he played as long as it was paid, she reasoned; besides it would stop him moping around the house at weekends.

A few days later an ad appeared in the local *Evening Advertiser*: "Lead guitarist wanted, work waiting. Call Eric." As a result of calling Eric he auditioned, got the job and played his first gig with the band, New Country Roads, the following evening. "Taking that job was probably the most important move I made career wise," says Dave. "Eric Dus, the drummer and leader of the group, was the first person to actually tell me I was any good! At the audition he positively overflowed with enthusiasm at my efforts to the extent that I could hardly refuse his invitation to join the group."

As the name implied they were a Country and Western band and Dave found playing with them was musically unrewarding, but being a member of a gigging band heralded a new lease of life for him. Work came at the rate of two or three gigs a week and the money, coupled with the wages he earned from his day job, put him in the best financial position he'd ever known. More importantly, Eric Dus's continued enthusiasm and encouragement gave Dave the renewed confidence he needed to pull himself out of the doldrums and stick at it.

The regular gigs with New Country Roads went on for about two years, interspersed with work with other groups and musicians. Although Dave and Eric eventually went their own ways, they remained in touch for several years.

By the summer of 1974, Dave had joined an old friend called Tony Green in Alehouse, a pub band which leaned on the Heavy Metal side of R'n'B. Returning home from a rehearsal in Calne one evening via the village of Hook, he noticed The Helium Kidz battered van in the village hall car park. "I pulled up and sneaked a crafty listen to them rehearsing and was amazed at how good they'd become," he remembers. "The songs had an irresistible catchy quality to them. They were happy, snappy, good-time slices of nonsensical pop, with rhythms and melodies that made you want to dance and lyrics that made you want to laugh - all products of the ludicrously wired brain of Andy Partridge. It struck me how much more vital and original their music was compared to the deadly serious power-rock I'd just left behind. I walked in, said hello, sat and listened awhile and later jammed on a couple of tunes with them. I left very impressed."

Not long afterwards Dave Cartner was sacked from The Helium Kidz and Andy rang Dave and asked him if he'd like to join. "I thought there was no harm in going along for a blow so I agreed to go to one of their rehearsals at Jennings Street School in Rodbourne, Swindon. I guess I failed the audition because I never heard from them after."

Dave stayed with Alehouse and in early 1975 came the big break he'd been working for - or so he thought. As a result of sending off numerous demo tapes, EMI despatched an A&R man down to Calne to check them out for possible inclusion on a special pub rock compilation album to be released on their Harvest label. On November 30 Alehouse went up to London to record two songs - 'Magic Moon' and 'Funky Junk' (both co-written by Dave) - at the BBC's Maida Vale studios. "The session was ruined by nerves", says Dave. "It was our first time in the studio and we blew it. We never heard the finished mixes and the album was never released." Alehouse's fortunes went into dramatic decline thereafter and the band played their last gig in February 1976.

The following May, Dave was made redundant from his day job after seven years but by a divine stroke of luck, or so it seemed, he received a phone call from a friend called Dave Fitchett who worked at John Holmes Music Centre in Swindon. He told Dave that he'd heard a band called Profile, who were based in Coleford in The Forest Of Dean, were looking for a guitarist and wanted to know if he'd care to chance it and 'go pro'. Dave jumped at the opportunity even though it meant leaving home and uprooting to the Gloucestershire country-side. He had seen Profile supporting Be Bop DeLuxe at the Brunel Rooms some months earlier and had been very impressed.

In reality 'going pro' meant signing on at the Monmouth dole office and it soon became clear that things were not going to be as easy and straightforward as Dave had been led to believe. As time passed it got progressively harder for the band to get work. The type of music they played, pompous, symphonic material favoured at the unfashion-able end of the progressive rock spectrum, was completely out of sync with the punk revolution which was now in full swing. No one wanted a band that sounded like a third rate Yes.

In 1977 Profile changed their name to Gogmagog which, if anything, exacerbated their declining fortunes. Dave's final gig with them was in February 77 at The Affair in Swindon when they appeared as a short notice substitute for a band that hadn't turned up called Siouxsie and The Banshees. As they did their thing to a dozen or so unreceptive and abusive punks, Dave realised it was time to get out. So after one year, a great deal of wasted time and money and just five gigs he left Gogmagog and went home to his parents in Purton with a heavy heart and £1.37 in his bank account.

After two months on the dole he found a job delivering parcels for the local White Arrow mail order service. During his time in The

Forest of Dean he'd kept in touch with Andy Partridge and the fortunes of XTC and watched enviously as they developed into a dynamic, punchy and energetic outfit. Andy and Dave would still get together from time to time and jam. "He'd teach me some new weird chords he'd found or run through some of his new songs." Envious as he was, Dave was proud of Andy's achievements. The newly signed XTC were obviously going places, and he wasn't.

His next band, though, managed to create a bit of a stir, even if it was restricted to a tiny pocket of north Wiltshire. Dean Gabber and his Gaberdines, which he formed with an old friend called Tony Green who'd previously been in Alehouse, were a fast'n'dirty pub rock group closely modelled on Dr Feelgood and The Pirates. They had no trouble in winning over tanked-up pub audiences with their good time R'n'B and were a popular draw on the Swindon circuit; so much so that in July 1978 they were invited, along with a few other bands, to audition for Virgin Records at The Affair.

Following the success of XTC someone had suggested to Virgin that maybe little old Swindon was a hot bed of untapped talent. The result was a ludicrous pageant of local bands strutting their stuff one after another on the tiny stage of The Affair in front of record company executives. Although the Gaberdines went down well and received a rave review in the local paper, after two nights of auditions Virgin signed no one.

Dean Gabber and his Gaberdines - so named because they had decided on a 'dirty old man in his mac' image! - continued to be a useful diversion for Dave from his day job until, one evening early in January 1979, the phone rang at his parents' house in Purton. His brother Robert answered it. "Is Dave there?" said a voice. He wasn't - he'd just left to play a one/off gig with a local Country and Western singer called Mike Hawkins. "This is Andy Partridge," continued the voice, "I'm phoning from Boston. Tell Dave I'll get in touch with him the minute we get home."

Dave was bowled over by Andy's subsequent offer. Like everyone else, he had assumed that XTC would be looking for a new keyboard player and he was worried that if he joined it would alienate their rapidly growing following. But Andy was adamant that they all wanted to start again from scratch and gave Dave a list of XTC songs he wanted him to have learned by the end of January.

A get together was arranged for January 27, to take place in the band's 'rehearsal barn' in a small village called Shaw. As Dave drove through the snow from Purton he was pessimistic about his chances. He had tried to learn all Barry's keyboard parts on the guitar (!) and it wasn't sounding right. But he needn't have worried. "We were amazed by Dave's playing," Andy remembers. "We'd say things like 'Shall we do 'This Is Pop?' and he'd say 'Which do you want - the single or the LP version?' Most of the other people we'd auditioned didn't even know how to play in the right key!"

Things happened quickly. Dave officially became a full member of XTC on March 5, 1979, quit his job with the White Arrow Parcels Delivery Service, left home and moved into a house of his own in Stanier Street, Swindon (where he still lives today). He could hardly believe it: eleven years after leaving school, at the age of 26, he was at last a professional musician.

Almost from the moment Dave Gregory joined the band a sense of purposeful calm returned to XTC. The wired tension that had pervaded the 'Go 2' sessions and the subsequent tours evaporated, replaced by a positive, creative atmosphere once again. Dave wasn't as idiosyncratic a musician as Barry Andrews, but all those years spent with other bands adapting to a whole range of musical styles had honed him into an adaptable and highly experienced instrumentalist.

If there had been one uncertainty about John Leckie it was that the band felt he didn't capture the full dynamism of their live sound. Although they acknowledged that he was restricted by the technology of the time, they thought the drums in particular sounded a bit weak on the first two albums.

When Andy put this to an A&R meeting at Virgin someone played him a copy of Siouxsie and The Banshee's début LP 'The Scream' and asked "Is this what you're after?" The cinemascope percussive sound that boomed from the speakers was exactly what he wanted. When Andy asked who the producer was he was told it was the young, and then fairly unknown, Steve Lillywhite. "Let's have him," said Andy.

So at the beginning of April XTC reconvened at the newly built Townhouse Studio on Goldhawk Road in West London, with Lilly-white and engineer Hugh Padgham. The Townhouse had a specially built ambient stone room designed to record full bodied acoustic sounds. Terry set his drums up in there while microphones were positioned in each corner of the roof.

"I remember Andy saying to Hugh Padgham during that session 'I want the drums to really knock your head off! They've got to be bigger than everything else'," says Dave. "That really was the start of the big XTC drum sound which has since become an industry standard." Hugh Padgham, who orchestrated the drum sound, would go on to produce multi-million selling albums like 'Face Value' and 'Hello I Must Be Going' by Phil Collins and 'Ghost In The Machine' and 'Synchronicity' by The Police - all records that put successful emphasis on the big drum sound.

The autobiographical 'Life Begins At The Hop', with its up-tempo Sixties flavour, was the first of Colin's songs to be chosen as a single and the first XTC record to feature Dave Gregory. It was released on May 4, 1979 - midway through another low key British tour which had started at Exeter Routes club on April 18.

'Life Begins At The Hop', the first XTC single to chart, reached No 54, high enough to secure a spot on *Top Of The Pops*. Although, disappointingly, the record dropped a week later, the excitement of appearing on the show was felt particularly strongly by Dave. Two months earlier he'd been driving a van around Swindon. Now he was appearing in front of an audience of 11 million people.

'Life Begins At The Hop' was also the first XTC record to be produced by Steve Lillywhite, who would be instrumental in transforming the band's fortunes over the next two years. Pleased with the overall sound of 'Life Begins At The Hop', and the fact that it had been their most successful single to date, the band agreed to work with Steve Lillywhite on their third album which they started to record at The Townhouse on June 25. Working at the usual frenetic pace, they had three weeks for recording and two weeks for mixing.

"We were still very excited about being in the studio," says Andy. "You'd get red light fever - as soon as the little red light went on you'd go into this nervy panic and think 'Jesus, this is forever!'"

The album was to be a major step forward for the band artistically. Although it was inevitable that their sound would change with Dave instead of Barry and with the extra emphasis on production, there was another, less obvious, reason. "For obvious reasons Dave was especially nervy," remembers Andy. "I think that was evident in his playing, a lot of which was very grabbed and sparky. The music suddenly took on a more wiry nature."

"I seriously didn't think I'd last more than one album," counters Dave. "I'd convinced myself that this was going to be my 15 minutes of fame."

Having discovered the 'big' drum sound they'd been searching for,

Terry's role became more crucial. Always a very adept drummer, he was now encouraged to be more flamboyant and stylised. On one occasion Andy stood over Terry trying to get him to play a certain drum pattern the way he could hear it in his head. Terry misinterpreted the instructions and played the odd combination of hi-hat, bass drum and tom-toms in reverse. The result was an imaginative, complex sounding drum pattern for one of Colin's new songs called 'Making Plans For Nigel'.

Ironically Andy had genuine doubts about how the new material would be received by the public. After the failure of the first two albums to attain mass acceptance he felt this one was less likely to break through than either of its predecessors. Yet contained in the twisted pop-flippancy of 'Scissor Man' and 'Helicopter', and the denser textures of songs like 'Millions', 'Roads Girdle The Globe' and 'Complicated Game', was all the proof needed to sustain Andy's reputation as a wonderfully innovative songwriter. His ability to colour great tunes with lyrical wit and musical agility gave his songs an irresistible charm as well as substance.

Surprisingly, the biggest step forward was taken by Colin. In the past he had looked upon Andy as a back-seat driver - being guided by the off-beat structures and themes of Andy's songs. Now he had come into his own as a songwriter. While Andy would always remain the most prolific, and perhaps more inventive, songwriter of the two, Colin's soft, melodic approach complemented Andy's occasional abrasiveness. But this was not to say that the shifting emphasis didn't cause petty rivalries from time to time.

"Quite early on it had been decided that 'Making Plans For Nigel' was going to be 'the single'," recalls Andy. "We spent five times longer messing with that song than any of my tracks. At one point I was fuming because my songs were being ignored." Eventually Andy realised that what was important was the band's overall output and once he agreed that 'Nigel' was the obvious choice as a single the atmosphere in the studio became much more relaxed and confident than before.

Originally the album's working title of 'Boom-Dada-Boom', inspired by a phrase appearing over Gnasher (Dennis the Menace's dog) in one edition of *Beano* as he attempted to drum, was now dropped. The record was retitled 'Drums And Wires' - a title, suggested by Andy, that more appropriately reflected XTC's discovery of the 'big' drum sound offset by the 'wireyness' created by having two guitarists in the group.

93

While XTC were in the studio, plans were laid for their first-ever Australian tour, to commence on July 20. Suddenly a spate of air crashes involving DC 10 aircraft was being reported in the media and the band were very concerned. They were terrified at the thought of a journey to the other side of the world, especially since flying was a relatively new experience for all of them. "We told Ian Reid that none of us were prepared to fly to Australia in a DC 10," Dave recalls, "so he had to make sure that we were on a 'proper' plane! It was really silly, but I think we still had that small town mentality."

XTC arrived unscathed in Sydney (on a Quantas Boeing 747!) on July 16 - Terry's birthday, which he celebrated in his own way by drinking from dawn to dusk - four days before the tour was due to begin.

Although practically unknown down under, XTC were propelled into the limelight almost just by turning up. At the time very few British bands bothered to tour Australia - even fewer New Wave bands. Punk rock in all its guises had been a phenomenon that most Australians had only been able to read about in the pages of imported British music papers, and had to some extent re-created for themselves. The real thing rarely came to town. Virgin saw untapped potential for XTC in Australia. The video to 'Are You Receiving Me?' had enjoyed some exposure on Australian TV, and there was the new single 'Life Begins At The Hop' to promote.

Literally from the moment they'd cleared customs at Sydney airport, already without sleep for 26 hours, the band were thrust in front of the media. As they were ferried between radio stations they frequently fell asleep in the backs of cars. Virgin press officer Al Clark distinguished himself by falling asleep, beer in one hand, cigarette in the other, live on air in one Sydney radio station. Among the first journalists to interview the group was Debra Robertson of the *Sydney Sun*, who immediately struck up a lasting rapport with Colin. A gradual infatuation developed.

It was hard work but the group's Australian record company - Festival Records - made every effort to make XTC and their guests feel like kings. As well as the group and their road crew, headed by Steve Warren, the tour party included the hard-working Al Clark and Allan Jones, a journalist from *Melody Maker* who travelled extensively with the band in these early years and wrote several definitive accounts of life on the road with them. The entourage was completed by the Sydney based support band The Flowers, who some time later changed their name to Icehouse.

94

Each member of the band was presented with a silver plaque, featuring a silhouette of the country, commemorating XTC's first Australian tour. These were taken away from them and presented back every time they made a TV appearance. One occasion Allan Jones wrote about in his subsequent report was when the band appeared on Australia's equivalent of *Top Of The Pops* - a show called *Countdown* on the ABC channel:

"Neon lighting strips flank the stage. An XTC backdrop, provided by ABC, rises behind them. Five takes of 'Life Begins At The Hop' and the television crew are still arguing with the director. The floor manager paces the studio, asks for another take. *Countdown*, and Ian Meldrum, is the focus for considerable criticism in Australia. That very week there had been a vitriolic attack on its format, content and presenter in the magazine *Nation Review*. Meldrum was described as the show's 'resident buffoon'.

"Molly they call him in Australia, for reasons that become obvious when you meet him. He counts Rod Stewart, Elton John and John Reid amongst his "close personal friends". We watch him in action when the show is broadcast. He seems incapable of putting together a coherent sentence. His conversation consists of so much small talk you'd be forgiven for thinking he was being manipulated by a midget ventriloquist.

"Molly attempted to interview XTC. He kept referring to 'White Music' as 'The White Album'. 'Paul is not dead,' said Partridge. 'I was the walrus.' Molly was bemused. The man had all the wit of a small brick. He presented Andy Partridge with a plaque of Australia. 'Just what I've always wanted,' said Partridge. 'A map of Portugal'."

Overall the five week tour was a bitter-sweet experience. Part of the problem was that the Australian music scene lagged well behind Europe's, and facilities for presenting bands were sorely lacking in some places. The venues were a bizarre combination of large theatres with a seating capacity of two or three thousand, and tiny clubs, some hundreds of miles from major urban centres. The tour was arranged so that days off were kept to an absolute minimum in order to reduce financial wastage. The promoter's philosophy seemed to be that a gig in the middle of nowhere was better than a night of inactivity.

The tour got off to a promising start at the Bossley Park Marconi Club in Sydney on July 20 - a gig that was broadcast live to air on local radio - and progressed well for the first few days. Generally speaking the venues were bigger, and the reaction warmer, than they'd been used to at home.

One week into the tour, XTC hit Brisbane, playing the Cloudland Ballroom. "It was a massive old Thirties ballroom, built out of wood," recalls Dave. "The place was packed out, it was heaving. We went down really well, in fact it was one of the most enjoyable gigs on the tour for us. Afterwards we thought 'Yeah! Brisbane likes us!'.".

When Ray Hearn, the tour manager, said 'Well boys, we've got another little gig to play here tomorrow night', they were perfectly happy. The Windsor Zillmere Football Club was indeed 'little'. Located in an industrialised suburb of the city, it was a watering hole where workers from nearby factories came to refresh themselves between shifts, and where the landlord occasionally put on a little light entertainment to keep the punters happy.

XTC gave a collective groan when they saw they'd been billed as 'Cabaret from England'! Their protests grew louder when they saw the tiny makeshift stage on which they were expected to perform and the house PA, which doubled as an announcement system for the food bar, through which they were expected to sing.

"The dressing room was just this tiny area by the stage that was partitioned off by a curtain," Andy explains. "I remember some old bloke sticking his head round this curtain and saying 'I've got some second hand furniture to sell mate. Would you mind reading this out between songs?' He handed me a list of the furniture he was trying to sell!"

There was no choice but to enter into the spirit of the occasion. Andy introduced the band that night saying "Hi! We're the beef-burgers that Bruce ordered." No one laughed. A wall of stony silence greeted their first song and as they performed the usual eclectic XTC set to several dozen disinterested shift workers, with frequent inter-ruptions from the food bar announcing the orders that were ready, they couldn't help wondering if this had really been worth coming 13,000 miles for. "We were pretty much ignored," admits Andy. "We were these noisy punk rockers who were stopping them from hearing their food orders!"

If there was one thing that was never in short supply in Australia, it was girls. The Stranglers had recently toured the continent and XTC played at many of the same venues and stayed in many of the same hotels. The posse of girls that had followed The Stranglers everywhere now latched onto XTC. "A couple of them were exceptionally beautiful," Andy recalls. "It was very difficult to restrain yourself, but I had to because I'd just proposed to Marianne over the phone - we'd fixed the wedding day for the end of the tour - and I wanted to be a good boy! This one girl, a very gorgeous blonde, kept pestering me. I'd come down to breakfast each morning and Ray Hearn would say 'I see that girl was hanging around your room again last night, Andy'. He and the rest of the band would then start to giggle. This went on for a few days and I couldn't understand why everyone was giggling until someone told me that this girl - apart from being stunningly good looking - had a colostomy bag. They were all dying for me to get her into bed so I could find out the hard way, the bastards!"

A separate bunch of less well-seasoned hangers-on would also turn up at venues from time to time and keep talking about their boyfriends, who they said, were in a band called The Farriss Brothers. One of the girls told Andy that their boyfriends were all really into XTC - so much so that they were going to re-christen their band with a similar sounding name. That was the first time Andy had ever heard of INXS.

"To be truthful we were having to fight their girlfriends off," says Andy. "They'd be turning up at half a dozen gigs and you'd think 'Christ, it's not that lot again'." Not everyone showed Andy's self-restraint around the Australian women. For Terry and Colin, in particular, there were going to be far reaching repercussions as a consequence of their liaisons with the opposite sex. At the Ambassador night club in Newcastle, New South Wales, Terry met a bubbly blonde waitress called Donna Blanchard. Although at first it looked like being a casual affair, it precipitated the end of Terry's seven year relationship with his girlfriend Lynn Fowler, and would prove to be very significant to the future course of events. Meanwhile, blinded by his infatuation with Debra Robertson, Colin admitted to his wife Carol that he was having an affair. In an act of extreme imprudence he later invited Debra over to England. This was obviously more than just a fling . . .

The tour ended where it had started, in Sydney, on August 17. If it hadn't been a wild success, it had at least demonstrated their tenacity and determination. Whatever XTC's thoughts about some of the gigs, Festival Records were delighted with the overall response to the tour.

When XTC - accompanied once again by their Australian tour manager Ray Hearn - arrived in Tokyo on August 18, the temperature was an unusually sultry 104 degrees Fahrenheit in the shade, with a staggering 90% humidity. In this debilitating heat it was impossible to go anywhere or do anything outside an air-conditioned environment without feeling totally exhausted. Yet for all the discomfort the band were swept along in a heady whirl of fan frenzy and media attention - the likes of which they'd never experienced before. For seven brief days XTC found themselves at the centre of an irresistible media circus.

Until the tour's pre-publicity machine had swung into action, XTC were hardly known in Japan. Both 'White Music' and 'Go 2' had been released on their Japanese label RCA/Victor, but sales had been negligible. It took a promoter brave enough to anticipate their crowd pulling potential to bring them over. So successfully had the media machine been manipulated, the band could be forgiven for thinking they had been sold as the new Beatles.

"For the first couple of days in Japan we were doing endless press conferences all day," says Andy. "You'd be taken into these vast, sterile, wood-panelled hotel conference rooms and there'd be 20 or so journalists waiting for you. Most of the questions would be passed through an interpreter, but some of them would attempt to ask questions in English. It would be surreal gibberish: 'You many much wind come here with guitar, yes?' You'd be thinking 'What was all that about?' Obviously they meant well but it was very difficult. After an hour they'd clear one lot out and bring another 20 in."

XTC were also approached by several up-market glossy magazines who wanted to arrange fashion photo-spreads of their guitars and clothes. "You'd take them up to your hotel room and hand them a pair of jeans and a shabby T shirt," recalls a bemused Andy. "They'd photograph them in porno detail!"

This was the closest the band had come to experiencing all-out teen hysteria. "We could hardly go anywhere without being screamed at," says Andy. "You'd walk into the hotel lobby and there'd be a crowd of girls sitting around waiting for you. As soon as they saw you they'd start screaming and you'd have to run for the lift. After a while you'd be entering and leaving the hotel by the back stairs to avoid them."

Some of the girls had booked rooms in the hotel to have easier access to their idols. They'd call band members on the internal phone system at all hours of the day or night inviting them up to their rooms. "They all seemed to use this funny little phrase: 'Please, you come to our room. No make love - only want to know you.' You'd think 'Wait a minute! It's four in the morning and you've just woken me up . . . because you want to know me!'"

The band stayed at one of Tokyo's most opulent hotels - the Sun Route in the centre of town. Although the hotel management was able to tolerate the extraordinary scenes that the fans of their English rock star guests created, they were less willing to accept the occasional behavioural excesses of the rock stars themselves.

Hotel regulations strictly forbade non-residents being in the rooms at night, but this didn't stop Terry inviting a dozen or so girls up to his room. Although the management knew he had several girls with him, it was past midnight when uniformed hotel staff eventually decided to break up his little party. They knocked on his door and asked politely if his guests could now leave. But Terry was in his element. As usual, he'd had several drinks and - with a room full of attentive and attractive young Japanese fans - he was in no mood for an early night. The more insistent the hotel staff were, the more belligerent Terry became. The scene that followed woke an entire floor of the Sun Route hotel.

Colin had just got off to sleep. Suddenly he was awakened by agitated shouting. Opening his room door, he saw Terry and a group of hotel officials yelling at each other. All along the corridor the other guests were poking their heads round their doors. "Terry was giving this drunken sermon about the war," recalls Colin. "He was shouting things like 'We fought a war to get rid of you zipper mouthed bastards! Come on, I'll take you all on!'"

Andy was also woken up by what he describes as . . . "a God Almighty row. At first I thought I was dreaming it, but as I came round I thought 'Oh no, that's Terry's voice. Oh no, that's Ray's voice. What's happening?'"

Ray Hearn was in his kimono shouting "Calm dahn Terry or they'll all do the bloody Judo on yer mate!" By now, the staff were really irate, but their natural politeness made them hesitate from entering Terry's room. Inside, the girls had been given strict instructions to hide in Terry's bathroom and be quiet!

Steve Warren still remembers the occasion well. "My room was next door to Terry's so I was right on the frontline of it all. I was so convinced we were going to be turfed out of the hotel I had started to pack my bags. Someone had to back down and luckily the hotel staff did. They could obviously see they were on to a loser.

"Dave won't like me for saying this, but he also had a few girls in his room. What did he do? He got out his guitars, played to them and talked to the girls about how good his guitars were and then sent them on their way! He had his chance but he didn't take it. He's the real gentleman of the team, a great man. I could always respect Dave for the way he treated people."

Terry's party ended but not everyone went home. The following morning the parents and relatives of one girl who'd spent the whole night in Terry's room turned up at the hotel accusing Terry of taking advantage of their daughter. Not until Terry married her would their family's honour be restored, they said.

When Terry made it clear that he had no intention of marrying their daughter, a brief fight broke out in the hotel foyer between Terry and the girl's relatives, with Ray Hearn trying to act as mediator. Although Terry managed to extricate himself from his marital obligations his behaviour had shocked the hotel management who'd never seen such a display before. The band were asked to leave immediately and after packing their bags they moved to the Tokyo Hilton a few blocks away. For once, Terry remained very sheepish for the rest of the tour.

On August 23 the band played the last of their four Japanese gigs in Osaka in a big theatre called the Midou Kaikan. The show was like all the others - an energetic XTC set performed to a far from typical XTC audience. The incongruous sound of screaming fans sometimes made the band feel like intruders on someone else's stage. Was all this fuss really being made over a bunch of hit-less British New Wavers?

A day later, Andy flew home to give himself time to recover before his wedding day. The rest of the band stayed on in Tokyo for a few more days. They had stumbled upon a fantasy world, after all, so why hurry back to reality?

Andy and Marianne's wedding took place at the Registry Office in Swindon on August 28, 1979, three years to the day after they had got together. It was a low key affair. The guests amounted to a few relatives and close friends. Because the couple had very little money - Andy was on a fixed wage of only £40 a week - everything was done on the cheap. Marianne had bought the silver plated wedding ring for £2 in a local market and a cut price dress. The reception was held at their new home 46, Kings Hill Road, in Swindon's old town - a house owned by Marianne's family's business, Wyborn Signs, into which they'd just moved and which was rent free.

While Andy and Marianne's father had not been on speaking terms for the first year of their relationship, their differences were eventually patched up, and they had become firm friends. Sadly he died 18 months before the wedding, so her younger brother Rob - who now ran Wyborn Signs - gave her away. Also absent from the wedding were the other three members of XTC. They were still having far too much fun in Tokyo to make a special journey back.

Carol Moulding went on Colin's behalf, but it was a painful experience for her at a time when her own marriage was falling apart. Colin arrived back from Japan with just a few days to spare before XTC were off on another tour, and stopped off merely to collect some clothes. A few weeks later Debra Robertson arrived in England and moved into a rented flat with Colin in London.

If Colin's personal life was in a state of disarray, at least XTC's career prospects were looking healthier. Their third album 'Drums and Wires' was released on August 17 while the band were still in Japan. Although it only managed to reach No 34 in the charts, it had got there with very little promotion. There was initially no single to help it along - 'Life Begins At The Hop' wasn't included on UK versions of the album. The band weren't even in the country for the first two weeks of its release. The Top 40 chart position was achieved on the strength of XTC's name and, once again, a spate of excellent reviews in the UK music press.

In *NME* Paul Morley wrote: "XTC are doing all sorts of things they've never done before and never hinted that they would . . . They're pushing forward and sideways with enough subtlety and imagination to connect with any listener whose demands are for the unusual, accessible and enlivening. They have moved many steps closer to making a rock classic."

The twelve new songs had surpassed expectations. XTC were sounding more self-assured than ever before. As an overall achievement 'Drums and Wires' was widely acknowledged in the music business. Bill Nelson - the ex-Be Bop De Luxe frontman with whom Andy kept up an irregular correspondence - wrote to Andy congratulating him on "making the record (he'd) always wanted to make". And to this day it remains a landmark album. Whereas 'White Music' and 'Go 2' were both very much products of their time, this was an album that would stand the test of time.

On September 5, Colin's 'Making Plans For Nigel' - an insidious, quirky, tongue-in-cheek song about dominating parents - was released as a single. Lifted from the 'Drums and Wires' album, it received good reviews but no immediate radio play.

The obligatory 'Drums and Wires' British tour began on September 11 at Manchester Apollo, a venue that proved oversized for XTC. Although venue capacities overall had been stepped up, XTC's popularity hadn't increased proportionately. They were still essentially a critically acclaimed cult band who hadn't yet outgrown the club circuit. As the tour progressed the picture looked depressingly familiar. Everywhere they were playing to half filled theatres. After the thrill of Japan it was very much an anti-climax.

The breakthrough was waiting just around the corner, however. 'Making Plans For Nigel' began to pick up airplay around the country, most importantly on Radio One. Slowly, very slowly, it began to climb up the charts. By the time the British tour had ended on October 5 the record had penetrated the Top 40 and was climbing steadily.

By the end of October, after appearances on *Top Of The Pops* and continued heavy airplay, 'Making Plans For Nigel' peaked at No 17 in the charts. At long last XTC had their first Top 20 hit, although it was later learned that a computer error by the chart compilers had forced the record downwards when it had in fact gone up. The 11 week chart run gave them renewed hope that there was indeed a much wider audience for their music.

(Author's note: The week that 'Nigel' peaked at No. 17, Dave also contributed guitar to two songs - 'I Don't Remember' and 'Family Snapshot' - for Peter Gabriel's third album, recorded at The Townhouse with Steve Lillywhite.)

Having missed the boat with the 'Drums and Wires' tour, Ian Reid hurriedly organised a second leg built around a previously arranged European tour. The band weren't too happy about being put on the road again so soon, but at least they would be able to measure their new popularity first hand.

The 'Drums and Wires' tour resumed on November 23 at Nottingham University and instantly it was clear that the success of 'Making Plans For Nigel' had propelled the band out of cult obscurity. "The venues were a similar size to the ones we'd been playing in on the previous tour, only this time they were packed," Dave explains. "The audience seemed to change overnight from the punky, spitting crowd to mainly ordinary members of the public. Suddenly people of all ages were coming to the gigs."

Accompanying the band for much of the tour was Debra Robertson, Colin's controversial new girlfriend. Although the success of 'Nigel' might logically have gone to anyone's head, especially as it was his song, Colin remained calm and unaffected by it all. In truth his mind was elsewhere. On the one hand he was besotted by Debra, and on the other hand he hated himself for what he was putting his family through. It was a dream that was rapidly turning into a nightmare.

"My thoughts really weren't on what we were doing at the time," Colin admits. "That whole period of my life is just a haze. It was all go - we were making videos, touring, appearances on *Top Of The Pops*, interviews . . . it was all prolonging the nightmare. If we'd come back to England and been on our own for a month I think I would probably have realised what I'd done earlier, and what a bloody fool I'd been. But I didn't have time to think."

"The 'Drums and Wires' tour took us up to Christmas time and it was then that the family thing really hit me. I came to my senses and thought 'Oh my God, what have I done? How can I undo the damage?'"

Colin decided to break with Debra and told her that the affair was over shortly after the end of the tour. He was re-united with Carol the day after Boxing Day 1979. For Colin it had all been a mistake - one he was determined never to repeat again.

8

WAIT TILL YOUR BOAT GOES DOWN

After the success of 'Making Plans For Nigel' there was an overriding sense of optimism and confidence in the XTC camp. Now they had broken the spell of commercial disinterest there was no going back and they were convinced that with recognition would come substantial financial rewards.

Unfortunately, in true XTC style, things were never that simple. Aware of the extraordinary fickleness of the industry they immediately got down to the task of rooting out a new single before the momentum was lost. Thus began the saga of 'The Desperate Search For A Follow-Up'.

Although the 'Drums and Wires' album was loaded with potential singles, neither the band nor Simon Draper could agree on what should be released next. Choices considered were 'Real By Reel', 'When You're Near Me', 'Helicopter' and 'Outside World', but Virgin insisted on Steve Lillywhite remixing them. When none of these remixes met with unanimous approval - even though everyone agreed they now sounded much tougher and sharper - the band decided to demo some new songs back in Swindon. Andy was particularly excited about a song he'd just written called 'Wait Till Your Boat Goes Down'.

"I wrote it sat up in bed at about three o'clock one morning," he explains. "I got my guitar and the song came pouring out - the melody, the lyrics, everything. Of course the Missus was moaning at me because I'd woken her up, but I said 'I've got a great idea for a song. I can't get the melody out of my head.' Marianne got up, made a cup of coffee and sat with me. I was really excited. I honestly thought it would be a huge hit. It was really singalong-able."

Borrowing some recording equipment, the band installed themselves in a large garage owned by a plumber friend of Terry's known simply as 'Toots'. In this makeshift studio they recorded rough versions of 'Wait Till Your Boat Goes Down', another song of Andy's called 'Don't Lose Your Temper' plus two new Moulding compositions 'I Overheard' and 'Officer Blue'.

Virgin weren't exactly bowled over by any of the new demos, but after much gentle persuasion from Andy, Simon Draper agreed to let them record 'Wait Till Your Boat Goes Down' on condition that they worked with a producer with a strong hit-making pedigree. The band conceded, not realising how inappropriate Virgin's choice would be.

Phil Wainman had a pop pedigree all right, but it wasn't the sort XTC were likely to appreciate. His production credits spanned the heyday of sugar-coated seventies teen idols like Sweet and The Bay City Rollers. But Virgin were certain that if XTC put themselves in Wainman's experienced, but expensive, hands he would make their song a hit.

The session took place early in the new year at the DJM studios off London's Theobald's Road. Almost immediately Wainman - himself a capable drummer - offended Terry by suggesting that he took care of some of the drumming himself. "Phil would keep chipping in with all these ideas," says Andy. "They were just a way of trying to get on our record. He'd say 'You want to overdub some timbals here. Remember that Sweet record "Coco" with the timbale breaks on? Well I did that!' We were saying 'No, no, we don't want that. It'll sound ridiculous!' In the end, though, he let Terry do all the drumming."

As well as 'Wait Till Your Boat Goes Down', a brand new electric version of the semi-acoustic 'Ten Feet Tall' - one of the most accessible tracks on 'Drums and Wires' - was recorded for release as a single in America. XTC were due to start their first proper tour of the States on January 14, and Virgin thought it was their best chance of a hit there.

On March 17 the band returned from their gargantuan American tour - two months of uninterrupted travelling around the States interspersed with seven Canadian gigs. Most of the concerts were small club dates where XTC headlined, but there were also three dates on the east coast, supporting The Police. "At that time I'd only heard 'Roxanne' and thought it was very average," says Dave. "I just saw these three good looking guys with their blond hair and thought 'They're welcome to all that'. I hadn't paid them any attention at all."

But once XTC met The Police and saw their show, they realised how approachable and talented they were. "We got on really well with them considering we were rivals and were having to share the same stage," recalls Dave. "They were trying to crack America as well. They were by no means superstars at that time."

Canada, where XTC enjoyed a big burst of success, was the most rewarding part of the tour. The shows - all big theatres and universities - were packed with ebullient crowds. 'Making Plans For Nigel' had been a Top 20 hit in Canada and had propelled 'Drums and Wires' to number two in the nation's album charts. Before leaving the country the band were presented with gold discs for the album.

But in the States there was no consistency. Generally the gigs were low-key affairs, separated by punishingly long overland journeys in a rented Dodge minibus. The band was popular in small pockets around the country, mostly in big cities, but these were a long way apart. Among the highlights were six consecutive sold out shows at the legendary Whiskey A Go Go club in Los Angeles, where they were told they'd broken the house record.

XTC was nearly two weeks into the US tour when a representative from Virgin America brought them a tape of the finished mix of 'Wait Till Your Boat Goes Down'. As they listened to a very loud playback over the PA at that night's venue - the Emerald City in Philadelphia - it sounded nothing like the hit that Virgin hoped for. "My first reaction was 'God, this is so weird'," Andy recalls. "Phil Wainman had put all these strange echoes and effects on it. I found it quite exciting, but I thought if anything he'd made it less commercial. We thought the exercise was to make it more acceptable to the public, but he'd actually made it weirder." Puzzled by the whole situation, the band was nevertheless reasonably happy with what Phil Wainman had done and approved the mix.

One memorable low point of the American tour was a 1,800 mile drive across the desert from Austin in Texas to San Diego in California. After the exhausting two day drive the band arrived in San Diego only to discover that the venue, the Lion's Park Club, was the size of a Scout hut! By the end of the tour they'd clocked up over 13,000 miles in their minibus and were physically and emotionally at the point of collapse.

According to Dave it had been "stupidly hard work", but mixed in with their exhaustion was a feeling of pride that they'd actually managed to complete the tour. For Colin and Andy it had helped that they'd had their wives with them to keep up morale. But there were still times when everyone thought they were going to burn out or become very sick.

For Andy, the tour marked the end of his Valium addiction. While the party was in LA Marianne decided to flush his tablets down the toilet and when Andy discovered what she had done he went berserk, almost destroying their hotel room. As a petulant reprisal, he threw all Marianne's make-up away and tore up a pair of Disneyworld tickets. But after a couple of weeks the unpleasant withdrawal symptoms had subsided, and Andy got used to coping without the Valium after 13 years.

"When we got back we thought we'd broken the back of America," Dave says. "We thought it was just a case, from then on, of going back there a couple more times and then we'd be superstars. Easy."

In February 1980 - while XTC were touring America - an Andy Partridge solo album of sorts was issued by Virgin. 'Take Away (The Lure Of Salvage)' was a collection of 11 dub cuts in much the same genre as the previously successful 'Go +' freebie. Although 'Take Away' was the aural equivalent of a Jackson Pollock painting - a spontaneous, some would say pretentious, splurge of modernism - it was only intended as a bit of fun.

Andy and John Leckie were the conspirators responsible for 'Take Away'. They took the tapes of the first three albums and all the B sides into the studio and came away seven days later with eleven completely re-worked versions. "Every morning we'd put a tape on," explained John Leckie, "it might get put on backwards or something - whatever inspired us to go further we'd work on. It might just be one of Terry Chambers' tom-toms, or maybe a guitar overdub that came up every twelve bars. We overdubbed some Korg synth and some guitar in places - but a few of the tracks ended up being straight remixes of the original."

Andy wrote new lyrics, usually on the spot, throwing in bits of poetry and always bearing in mind that it wasn't meant to be taken too seriously. Fortunately the band had a supportive record company in Virgin who were prepared to give the album a commercial release.

On the whole the reviews of 'Take Away' were unfavourable. Whereas 'Go +' had been lauded as an inspired breakaway from convention, this time the music press accused John Leckie and Andy of being charlatans who should've left the sacred art of dub well alone. Except in Japan, where it did surprisingly well, 'Take Away' sold only to fans who had enjoyed unravelling the 'spot-the-XTC-song' puzzle of 'Go +'. There were never any serious ambitions of reaching beyond XTC's hard core following.

The same could not be said of 'Wait Till Your Boat Goes Down', however. The long-awaited follow-up to 'Making Plans For Nigel' was finally released a full six months after its predecessor, in March, just as the band returned from America. As fully conversant as XTC fans were with the band's habit of almost perversely subverting the straightforward appeal of their songs, 'Wait Till Your Boat Goes Down' still managed to raise a few eyebrows. Under no stretch of the imagination could it be described as an obvious single. Its mid-paced white-reggae structure, combined with a typically audacious Partridge melody, totally failed to have any immediate impact. At a stroke it seemed to destroy the fragile hit making momentum they had worked so hard to achieve. The record was given the cold shoulder by radio stations everywhere and it sank faster than the ship pictured on its sleeve, eventually registering as the worst selling XTC single to date. While disappointed by this setback, the band had almost expected it.

"After the mix, and the way the song had been perceived, I wasn't surprised it didn't happen," says Andy. "I thought the melody might've carried it through, but that wasn't enough. Very soon after we'd recorded it I thought maybe we should've been really banal with it. Maybe we should've gone the whole hog and given it a great big disco beat and a huge chanting chorus."

"It was probably the most uncommercial single we've ever released," Dave agrees, "but we had no idea how to make a hit record. I thought 'Wait Till Your Boat Goes Down' was a good song and the fact that it wasn't a hit didn't matter. The important thing was we'd put something out that we considered to be worthwhile."

The band spent the two months after their American tour writing a new album. As usual the relentless barrage of live work meant that very little new material had been written since 'Drums and Wires' and at this stage in their career everyone in the XTC camp thought it was important to get at least one album out a year if they were going to progress towards big success before the public forgot who they were.

After Colin's coming of age as a songwriter on 'Drums And Wires' and the commercial success that emerged from it, the scales now tipped back in Andy's favour. It was only to be expected that his songs would dominate the new album, but their melodic consistency was a surprise. Often Andy seemed to deliberately taint the commercial potential of his songs by subjecting the melodies to strange, occasionally unpalatable, twists and turns. This was a constant source of contention between XTC and Virgin, who would try to get him to re-write songs they had earmarked as possible singles, in a more commercial vein. Andy would refuse. But with the new songs, Virgin had no need to ask for re-writes: the songs were wonderful first time round.

Because 'Wait Till Your Boat Goes Down' was such a disappointment, the record company were keen for a single to bridge the gap leading up to the next album. So between May 10 and 12 two new songs, 'Love At First Sight' and 'Rocket From A Bottle', were recorded as a potential double 'A' side (Virgin's way of appeasing the songwriting rivalry between Andy and Colin) at the Townhouse with Hugh Padgham. Both songs were subsequently scrapped and re-recorded at a later date. Also recorded was 'Take This Town' for the forthcoming 'Times Square' movie soundtrack.

After the US tour, Virgin had pressured Ian Reid to get Dave to sign to Allydor. Although it had been a year since Dave had joined XTC, he wasn't contractually committed to Allydor like the rest of the band. His refusal to sign would cause contractual complications with Virgin that Ian Reid would rather avoid, as Virgin would not advance any more money to XTC until Dave signed - which would mean jeopardising the imminent recording sessions. XTC's accountant and solicitor were promised that accounts would be prepared and on their advice Dave signed the Allydor contract.

There had been several changes to Allydor and the management set-up. Ian Reid had come a long way in the music business for someone who'd known almost nothing about it four years earlier. He had sold The Affair in 1979 for a handsome profit and was now managing the band from his new house in Highworth. Dennis Detheridge stayed on at The Affair, handling PR for its new owners under its new name SAKS, but was still available to undertake any assignments for Allydor.

In fact since selling The Affair, Reid had taken over sole responsibility for XTC, as well as promoting concerts under the name Sounds Promotion. Dennis Detheridge had been given other duties within Allydor, such as looking after the affairs of Dozy Beaky Mick and Tich - the Sixties hit band minus singer Dave Dee, who were attempting to make a comeback - and a Bristol based band Vitus Dance. None of the other bands Allydor managed seemed able to get record deals, and Detheridge had less and less to do until Ian Reid took over completely.

Work began on the new album on June 8 at the Polygram studios near London's Marble Arch, second choice because The Townhouse was occupied by Yes who were behind schedule. The sessions were disastrous. 'Drums and Wires' had set a standard that they were determined to match, but the sound was disappointingly lack lustre. The studio was also plagued with irritating little technical problems - like mysterious buzzing noises that couldn't be located for hours. So after a week the sessions were aborted for resumption on June 23 when The Townhouse became available.

Back in their favourite studio, work progressed smoothly with the formidable team of producer Steve Lillywhite and engineer Hugh Padgham at the helm. "The band had all the songs written and rehearsed. We'd do two weeks recording, two weeks over-dubbing and two weeks mixing," says Steve Lillywhite, who subsequently went on to produce many huge international acts including Simple Minds and U2. "The great thing about XTC was they didn't overdub for the sake of it like a lot of groups do, especially today. There was no spare flesh on those songs. Every note that everyone played was intrinsic to the make up of the songs."

Part of the reason for this was Andy's insistence that they record only arrangements that could be duplicated in concert. For instance, any keyboard overdubs - to be played by Dave - would be at the expense of an extra guitar track. This self-imposed restriction tended to work in the band's favour, inevitably speeding up the pace of their work in the studio.

The working title of the new album was 'Terry & The Lovemen' and some foreign magazines even advertised it with that name later. It was based on the whimsical concept that Terry Chambers was the band's leader, and seemed a fun way of acknowledging the humble anchor man - especially as XTC's drum sound was now such a major component of their music. The sleeve concept had been carefully thought out and everyone, bar Terry, thought it was a great idea.

"We were going to dress Terry in a gold lamé suit," Andy explains, "ponce his hair up a bit and stick him at the front with a really swish looking drum set. It would be like a Las Vegas version of The Dave Clark Five. The rest of us - The Lovemen obviously - would be right in the background with our guitars."

Terry was horrified when he heard about this. "I ain't fuckin' 'avin anything to do with that!" he stormed. "You ain't putting me at the front in daft clothes!"

"He really got spooked about the idea that we were putting him forward as this mythical band leader," recalls Andy. "I don't know why, but I think he found it insulting."

"Get it down before I get 'em down," was Terry's familiar studio expression (meaning he'd do his drum parts before getting down to his customary serious drinking). Indeed, Terry and a crate of beer were never far apart. Once he'd fulfilled his studio obligations he'd work his way through the beer until he'd drunk himself into a near stupor. Occasionally after closing time, if other members of the band fancied a beer and didn't have any of their own, Terry would offer to sell them one of his at an inflated price! "He could be a bit mercenary at times," says Andy. "I remember Colin arguing with him about that once. He was desperate for a bottle of his beer and Terry was trying to charge him night club prices!"

In the studio, Terry would often get very drunk, sit on the settee at the back of the control room and suggest unusual things. While recording 'Love At First Sight', Andy suggested to Terry that Steve put an echo on the word 'sight' and catch the tempo of the track and Terry thought it was a great idea. Every now and again he'd splutter "Ay Schteeve! Don't forsget ssight ssight ssight ssight. Alright!" Steve Lillywhite would say, "Okay Terry, we'll get around to that in a minute."

"The next time the tape stopped," laughs Andy, "you'd hear 'Ay, what about ssite ssite sssite?' - like Terry had thought it up! This would go on all evening as he got more and more drunk. Eventually he'd be lying there with bubbles coming out of his mouth going 'sssite . . ssite . . sssite'."

After 'Terry & The Lovemen' was rejected, the next prospective album title was 'Work Under Pressure' - an aptly sardonic reference to the constant tour-album-tour cycle in which they found themselves trapped. This, too, was eventually dropped because it upset too many people - Ian Reid for one! But the sleeve concept for 'Work Under Pressure' lingered on. A photo session featuring XTC in deep sea diving suits went ahead anyway and the album was given the throwaway nautical title 'Black Sea' instead.

The album was completed by the end of July. While Virgin were delighted with it, not everyone had been happy making it. For Dave, still struggling to establish his own identity within the band, it was a time of insecurity. No longer the starry-eyed new boy, he wanted to have more of a creative say and felt he was being controlled too tightly by Andy. "Andy wasn't really interested in anything I was contributing," Dave explains. "He was having everything his own way and the band wasn't really getting a look in. He was telling Terry exactly what drums to hit, he was telling Colin what notes to play. If there was any room left I might get a couple of notes on the guitar in. There were times when I seriously questioned the point of my even being in the band."

Colin was also dissatisfied, but for different reasons. He was unhappy about the number of songs he'd been able to contribute to the record, and agreed with Dave that Andy had dominated proceedings. Such suppressed wranglings weren't noticed by Steve Lillywhite, who was later to remark that the two albums he did with XTC were probably the easiest he'd ever been involved with.

With a surplus of original songs left over, Colin persuaded Virgin to let him do something on his own, and immediately after the 'Black Sea' sessions, aided by Terry Chambers and a small group of session musicians and backing singers, he headed into the studio with producer Mick Glossop to record three songs: 'Too Many Cooks', 'I Need Protection' and 'Cheap Perfume'. "Virgin figured it was a good way of satisfying the bass player's appetite for wandering, I think," says Colin. "I felt I had to do something with the songs I had hanging around, and they weren't really right for XTC. On reflection I don't think they're as good as I thought at the time. 'Too Many Cooks' turned out very 'Jonathan King', I thought! Still, it was fun to do, and I thought that by some fluke it might be a hit."

In fact 'Too Many Cooks' - a flippant piece of pop candyfloss - was given a low key release the following autumn under the pseudonym The Colonel. With minimal promotion, it sank without trace and was soon deleted. It remains one of the most collectable items in the XTC catalogue.

On August 8 they joined The Police, The Beat and UB40 as part of a Miles Copeland package touring France, Belgium and Spain in a circus tent. By now Dave Gregory was an integral part of the group and XTC had become a sharp, aggressive live attraction. The band had to break away from the tour, briefly, half way through to fly home and re-create a recording session for a BBC film crew who were making a documentary on the group. Although they still had only one hit single to their name, there was a growing expectation that XTC was about to break big. Their close association with The Police - who were now international superstars - helped to compound everyone's hopes.

While XTC were in Europe, a new single was released on August 28. The Moulding-penned 'Generals & Majors' had been saved from the studio dustbin by Andy, who suggested adding a chiming guitar phrase and boisterous disco style drumming to colour what was otherwise just Colin's basic melody. When the recording worked out better than expected, it replaced 'Towers Of London' - for which a video had already been made - as the first single from 'Black Sea'. With its infectious Beatle-esque melody, 'Generals & Majors' looked set to return XTC to the charts in a big way. Surprisingly it only reached No 32.

The arrival of 'Black Sea' a month later made up for the disappointment by reaching No 16 within two weeks of release. It was a tremendous album - a testament to the huge amount of musical ground XTC had covered in under three years. Polished and slick, it was the closest they would ever come to making a mainstream pop album, and the closest XTC would get to capturing their live sound on vinyl. While 'Drums and Wires' had caught the band between their old, angular style and a more melodic approach, 'Black Sea' was a more definite statement by the new line-up.

Critically 'Black Sea' was adored. Although XTC were not entirely without their detractors - some found their complex musical nuts and bolts too arty or too clever for their own good - there was a general feeling that 'Black Sea' was the peak of the band's output to date. For the first time, the individual songwriting skills of Colin Moulding and Andy Partridge were being compared to Lennon & McCartney.

Although in retrospect the notion sounds faintly absurd, their respective songs on 'Black Sea' measured up to that comparison quite well. Colin contributed two of the sweetest tunes with 'Love At First Sight' and 'Generals and Majors'. Andy's songs were the most brash and incisive - 'Respectable Street', 'Sgt Rock (Is Going To Help Me)' and 'Rocket From A Bottle' in particular. But it was the album's denser moments - of which Andy himself was typically most proud - that provided the album's greatest reward.

"I was very proud of 'No Language In Our Lungs'," he says. "I thought it conveyed a message of hopeless non-communication between people. Language is the best thing we've got and it's useless. I thought the whole thing fitted together really well. Also I think 'Travels In Nihilon' came out well in a depressing sort of way. I wanted to write a song about feeling disappointed and trapped on a hopeless cycle of fashion and expectation."

"'Black Sea' is probably the closest any of our records have come to what we sounded like live - it was almost a xerox of our stage show. It has a kind of well oiled aggression. Whereas 'Drums and Wires' is a bit fragmented style-wise, 'Black Sea' has one sound all the way through - very loud drums and cranked up guitars. It caught us at the pinnacle of being a performing machine, which is what we'd become."

XTC's career seems to undulate wildly from the sublime to the ridiculous with their popularity level careering along corresponding lines; fervid excitement greets one album only for the next to sink without trace. This can be explained by the volatile nature of the unpredictable and irrational music industry but fortunately for XTC, just as one door has closed on them another has opened. Such turns of good fortune have seen them through highs and lows for 15 years. Fame is a fickle mistress. Sometimes they would discover how fickle . . .

XTC - plus their support band Magazine - reluctantly found themselves back in Australia for the start of another tour on September 5, 1980. The inconsistency of the previous year's tour made the band question the value of another visit, but Ian Reid swung it by promising each of them a £600 bonus. 'Life Begins At The Hop' and 'Making Plans For Nigel' had been sizeable hits for them Down Under ('Drums and Wires' had sold well too) and it seemed churlish to throw those gains away. Besides there was another reason for going: as an adjunct to the tour they were to play a handful of dates in New Zealand. With its population of only three and a half million people (against 30 million sheep!) New Zealand was a market of negligible world importance, but there was a feeling of 'test it and see'.

The second Australian tour, as the band themselves had expected, was much like the first. Although Festival Records had come up with the bizarre and embarrassing promotional slogan "XTC. Music to rip seats by" as a way of trying to provoke more interest, it didn't work. More people knew who they were, but they were still returning to many of the same venues (the Windsor Zillmere Football Club was one merciful exception). This time, though, Marianne Partridge and Carol Moulding came along too for a holiday.

At the Ambassador nightclub in Newcastle, bachelor Terry Chambers renewed his acquaintance with Donna Blanchard, the bubbly blonde waitress he had met a year earlier. They had barely kept in touch during their time apart, but their relationship was soon re-kindled. From now on, they vowed, they would be with each other whenever tour and recording schedules permitted.

The band arrived in New Zealand on September 11, the day before they were due to play their first concert in Christchurch Town Hall. XTC had no idea of what to expect in New Zealand and were mildly surprised to find themselves immediately thrust in front of TV cameras. They all wanted to go straight to the hotel, but the record company had arranged a press conference at the airport. Someone told them 'Black Sea' was at number six in the charts. "When we landed at Christchurch airport we thought 'What the hell's going on here?'," Colin recalls. "We were big stars in New Zealand and knew nothing about it!"

The head of XTC's New Zealand record company, R.T.C., had come to meet them and was determined to wring as much publicity out of them as he could. "I remember him baiting us to make a comment about the local record industry," says Colin. "The government had just added some sort of tax to records and this bloke was telling us to go on live TV and say how bad we thought it was, and how damaging it would be for the industry. We thought, 'Hang on a minute. We've only just got here and we know nothing about this. We're not going to get involved in your politics!'

"When we eventually got back to our hotel I turned the telly on and there we bloody were on the news! After the news came this old black and white episode of *Coronation Street*, it was bizarre! That was my lasting impression of New Zealand - like England in the Sixties. It reminded me of back home a lot. The gigs were great. We went down a storm. And we seemed to be on TV all the time!"

XTC were in New Zealand less than a week to play four shows: one apiece in Christchurch and Wellington and two in Auckland. By the time it came to leave they had built up such a high profile that 'Black Sea' was on its way to No 1. When the band arrived at Auckland airport, about to fly back to Australia, someone phoned up from the record company to announce they'd done it - 'Black Sea' was at number one! "We'd sold seven and a half thousand copies, or something," laughs Andy, "and we had a number one album! You only have to think about making an album in New Zealand and you go straight in at 99. I think it's the only time we've been number one anywhere! A couple of albums later all our records bombed in New Zealand."

After Australia, the 'Black Sea' world tour continued in the UK. Coinciding with these dates, on October 10, the BBC2 documentary *XTC At The Manor* was shown on prime time television. The hour long special took a broad look at XTC's career and Richard Branson's snowballing Virgin empire, and featured the group falsely going through the motions of recording their new single 'Towers Of London'.

(Author's note: In fact two versions of 'Towers Of London' were recorded during the 'Black Sea' sessions. At Polygram studios they'd completed a much slower version that Andy describes as 'very pedestrian'.)

Despite all the exposure, and the fact that it bore the hallmarks of a classic pop single, 'Towers Of London' peaked at No 31. The short British tour culminated at the Lyceum in London on October 12 - a gig that was to be Steve Warren's last as XTC's long-running sound man. "The touring was getting too much," Steve explains. "You'd be working an 18 hour day and getting paid, at most £70 a week."

The band were just about to start another exhausting American tour, coast to coast over eight weeks, and they'd already been on the road for two months. A couple of days before the US tour, manager Ian Reid told Warren he couldn't travel with the band. "I'd have to sleep in the road crew's coach the whole tour - no hotel rooms at all," said an astonished Warren. "I'm six foot six and the berths on those things are barely five feet long. How was I expected to do my job properly if I couldn't get a proper night's sleep?

"Reid expected so much from everyone. There were times on that last British tour I did when some of the crew were on the point of quitting. I had to beg them to stay. Nobody knew it, but I kept that tour on the road while I was being treated like rubbish."

It wasn't as if the band were unaware of Steve's complaints. "Steve was always bringing his complaints to us. After a while we wanted to stay out of it and let Steve have it out with Reid himself," says Colin.

After the Lyceum gig, Warren gave Reid an ultimatum: "Either I get hotel rooms, or I'm not doing the tour." Reid tried to avoid the subject, saying "We'll talk about it tomorrow," but Warren was not to be fudged. "Tomorrow we're flying to America. We'll sort it out now."

Reid paused a moment and replied, "Okay then, you're fired."

"The following morning the band flew off to America," recalls Steve. "I packed my bags and went home to Swindon."

"Admittedly Steve was treated badly a lot of the time, but we weren't very happy that he decided to make his stand on the eve of an American tour," says Colin. "We didn't know Steve had left until we got to the airport!"

Gary Bradshaw, who'd previously been the band's guitar roadie, took over from Steve Warren and proved a very capable sound man. XTC were returning to north America principally as guests of The Police, although they also had some headlining gigs of their own. The Police were now having phenomenal American success with their third album 'Zenyatta Mondatta' - and its accompanying Top 10 hit 'Don't Stand So Close To Me' - and were playing in huge sports stadia. For XTC this was an inspiring example of how it could be done, and they didn't doubt that they would shortly be hitting the big time themselves. After all, just a few months earlier The Police were playing in the same small theatres and clubs.

For most of the tour the two groups shared a luxury coach together. It made a pleasant change from the uncomfortable vans XTC had been used to travelling in. "It proved an expensive exercise because we were staying in the same hotels as The Police, and they were staying at the best," says Colin.

As the tour went on XTC's own fortunes seemed to be improving. Their previous three month slog around north America had brought them cult status, and sales of 'Drums and Wires' of around 100,000 in the States. The band was now with Australian entrepreneur Robert Stigwood's RSO label. As the manager of The Bee Gees and owner of their record label, Stigwood had considerable influence within the American music industry and he had vowed to put plenty of promotional muscle into making 'Black Sea' a success.

"We met Robert Stigwood and got on well with him," says Colin. "He told us we were the most exciting band he'd seen live since The Who, although every time we saw him he was pissed out of his brain. After one gig he introduced himself to Andy about six times in an hour! Everywhere we went there seemed to be an RSO representative to meet the band and take us out to dinner. We really felt we could be doing it this time."

"From a playing point of view that particular tour was as hot as we ever got," says Dave. "It was the one I enjoyed the most. We were running like clockwork and the fact that we weren't headlining, most of the time, but still playing on a full sized stage in front of a decent crowd took a lot of the pressure off. Although a lot of people were telling us they'd come specifically to see us, we were still just the warm up act so we could have some fun."

RSO's hard sell tactics seemed to be working. 'Generals and Majors' picked up considerable airplay around the States and became what is euphemistically known as an airplay hit. A little later 'Black Sea' entered the American Top 50, a breakthrough that almost certainly reflected Robert Stigwood's standing in the industry since actual sales weren't much of an improvement on 'Drums and Wires'.

At the end of the tour on December 3 and 4, the band played what would be the biggest gigs of their career, supporting The Cars at Madison Square Garden. XTC were superb and appeared to win over many new admirers in the partisan crowd. They flew back to England immediately afterwards feeling very optimistic about their future prospects in America.

On December 5, Virgin released 'Sgt Rock (Is Going To Help Me)' - the third single from 'Black Sea'. Its robust singalong melody and comic lyrics made it an obvious single pick. As XTC went straight into a British tour, 'Sgt Rock' began to attract airplay. By mid-January 1981 it had peaked at No 16 - one place above 'Making Plans for Nigel'. While Andy could at last lay to rest his frustration at not having a hit, perversely he wasn't pleased that it had come about with his least favourite song on the album.

"'Sgt Rock' was just a piece of candyfloss really," he says, "one of the most disposable songs I'd ever written. It doesn't actually mean anything - it was a throwback to the old Helium Kidz cartoon lyrics. To be truthful I was a bit embarrassed when it became a hit, but I just had to bite my tongue. The ridiculous thing was we got letters from feminist groups complaining that it was encouraging violence towards women!"

Another past project Andy lived to regret also emerged in January. Andy and Colin flew to New York for the première of the Robert Stigwood teen-movie 'Times Square', to which XTC had contributed the specially written song 'Take This Town'. "When we first saw the script we thought it was pretty lousy," Andy admits, "but we thought 'Well, they're obviously going to make it better than this.' During the première Colin and I gradually slid down our seats. If we'd known how wretched the film would've turned out we wouldn't have got involved. During the première Andy Warhol was sitting right in front of us. We were both restraining ourselves from putting our legs up on his shoulders - the sort of thing we'd have done if we'd been at the Swindon Odeon!"

On March 13 'Respectable Street' - a song which Andy had said was 'inspired by my neighbour who spends half her life banging on the wall should I so much as sneeze' - became the fourth and final single to be lifted from 'Black Sea'. Despite an impressive video and re-recorded lyrics, this established stage favourite flopped after failing to pick up sufficient airplay.

But by now Colin and Andy had come up with a batch of new songs, two of which - 'Ball and Chain' and 'Punch and Judy' - Virgin thought should be recorded as a potential double A sided single. It was suggested that, as an experiment, the band work with Clive Langer and Alan Winstanley who were having great success at the time with Madness. XTC agreed, but when work began at The Townhouse the sessions went awry almost immediately.

Clive Langer wanted to make drastic changes to the songs, and Andy didn't like any of his ideas. "I thought 'Woah! Hang on a minute! Surely we should be checking the songs out naturally before we go tearing them apart?' I told Clive I wanted to record the songs the way they were, and that any changes were going to be minimal." Langer sat quietly for a couple of hours, then suddenly leapt up and announced "Right! I can see you don't need me here!" He left the studio and refused to return.

"I take my hat off to Clive for having the balls to be honest enough to admit he didn't stand a chance with Andy," says Dave. "Clive could see he was up against a brick wall and he was happy enough to let us get on with it and let Alan Winstanley do the engineering." Despite some misgivings, the tracks were subsequently delivered to Virgin who decided, on reflection, they weren't singles material after all, and the session was scrapped.

On April 2 XTC headlined another American tour. The shows were generally well attended, and it seemed to the band that they were starting to get their message across in the States. As stage managed as their 'Black Sea' success had been, it had got their music over to a much wider audience. In general, the venues were larger, the crowds wilder, the hotels better and - the real test of rock'n'roll stardom - the transport less cramped and more stylish. By now XTC had graduated to a luxury mini-bus just for band personnel, while all the equipment travelled with the road crew. No longer would Terry have to sleep on top of his drums!

(Author's note: In Athens, Georgia, the band was supported by a new local group called REM, who played XTC songs as part of their set!)

As a brief side-step to the tour XTC played two of the most dramatic concerts of their career - in Venezuela. The previous December The Police had made their first visit to South America, playing concerts in Brazil and Argentina. They were due to play a gig in the Venezuelan capital, Caracas, too, but illness forced them to cancel the show. Tony DeLuca, the local promoter, wasn't willing to accept disappointment. Somehow he would introduce Venezuela to new wave music.

DeLuca contacted Ian Copeland, the younger brother of The Police's manager Miles, whose New York based FBI agency had organised the previous year's Police/XTC tour of North America, and asked for his suggestions. Copeland offered DeLuca a new package: XTC and Jools Holland and his Millionaires, saying he was convinced that XTC were on the verge of a major breakthrough. He also sold the idea to Virgin and XTC.

On August 26 Ian Reid and press officer Al Clark arrived in Caracas ahead of the main tour party, determined to alert the local media to the imminent arrival of XTC. After all, they were almost totally unknown in Venezuela. Both Reid and Clark were alarmed at what they discovered: very ambitiously and somewhat imprudently, Tony DeLuca had booked XTC to play at the Poliedro, a huge venue with the dimensions of an American baseball stadium. It was a mistake that would cost the promoter his shirt.

XTC and their tour party - which included *Melody Maker* journalist Allan Jones - arrived in Caracas on April 28, a day before the first gig at the Poliedro. Despite cramming in as much press and radio promotion as was physically possible in one day, it was obvious that XTC weren't going to be able to get anywhere near filling the Poliedro.

The local police, however, thought otherwise. They responded to the event with incredible officiousness, turning up in the sort of numbers that would have been more suited to a subversive political rally. Armed with automatic weapons, handguns and machetes, they looked more like stormtroopers preparing to go into battle than officers policing a rock'n'roll gig. By the time XTC took the stage, the atmosphere in the Poliedro had become highly charged.

"Something curious was happening but we couldn't put our finger on it," wrote Allan Jones in his subsequent report. "XTC had a more immediately clear view, and it was obviously affecting them. They'd opened promisingly enough, with a vivid 'Real By Reel'; 'Life Begins

120

At The Hop' had sucked everyone into its irresistible orbit; everyone had swooned to the languid sensuality of 'When You're Near Me I Have Difficulty'. Then XTC started to lose their grip. The long stretch of songs from 'Black Sea' that currently occupies the important middle ground of their set started to drag and meander.

"The group struggled to lift themselves, but 'Sgt Rock' seemed tired; 'No Language In Our Lungs' carried none of its original poignant weight; 'Love At First Sight' was flat and listless. A bright new song, 'Ball and Chain', lifted our spirits momentarily, but there was no continuity of impact.

"What XTC could see and watch helplessly, we gradually became aware of. The police were gradually moving into sections of the audience, machetes drawn for action and expelling large numbers of the crowd. Slapping anyone who looked like they were remotely enjoying themselves with the flats of their machete blades, the police were bullying the audience into scarpering. The audience was retreating faster than a regiment of Italians.

"With the concert over-running, the cops had decided to bring it to an end: XTC weren't even consulted. The police had had enough; that was that. XTC had just pitched into a momentous version of 'Making Plans For Nigel', were preparing for the final twin thrust of 'Living Through Another Cuba' and 'Generals And Majors' when the houselights went up with a sudden, blazing flash. XTC stood dumbfounded; the audience looked at the police who were descending on them. What was left of the audience was off. They knew better than to stay and argue.

"Partridge watched them go, curiously exposed on the stage. In the dressing room the group's mood was bleak and deflated. 'You could just feel the indifference,' Colin Moulding complained. Al Clark tried to reassure them; the police had been an intimidating distraction, he reasoned. XTC wouldn't listen; they blamed themselves for not being able to get through to the audience. 'It was like trying to get your old dear to listen to Captain Beefheart,' Moulding said, dejected. 'Yeah,' Partridge agreed, 'it was exactly like that . . . like trying to get your mum to listen to "Dachau Blues" while she's doing the dusting'."

Back once more at the Poliedro the following evening, the audience indifference of the previous night was turned around completely. Word of the chaotic event had circulated around Caracas, attracting a larger crowd for the second night. While the police had been the intimidators before, the crowd were now the aggressors - taunting and provoking the machete wielding police like fearless matadors.

"By the time XTC hit the planks, the audience was courting hysteria," wrote Allan Jones. "As the chaps tipped full tilt into 'Real By Reel', the more zonked out members of the crowd started building fires, burning rolled up newspapers. The bonfires were burning everywhere, crazed zombie dances were performed around them; drunk, stoned, coked to the roots, the more frenzied locals dived into the flames, emerging with shirts and trousers burning.

" 'Lively bunch aren't they?' Al Clark remarked, as a conga line of dancers threatened to bowl us over into a bonfire. They were: and so were XTC, the lethargy of the previous evening comprehensively bowled out of play. Confident, happy, determined, XTC were on vintage form. Chambers' buckshot drumming carried everything with a mighty crack. The music bristled with majestic zest."

After a few more American dates, the band returned home unscathed by this latest, fatuous, experience. If nothing else DeLuca and XTC had proved between them that there was an audience for this kind of music in Venezuela. But in the process of making that point, DeLuca had paid a considerably higher price than XTC.

"Venezuela was typical of the kind of touring that the band did," says Al Clark. "When you consider that until 1978 none of XTC, except Barry Andrews, had been out of the country, they had become - along with The Police - the most widely toured group during that period. They would play anywhere, to anyone. I'd never come across such resilience before."

The final leg of the 'Black Sea' world tour culminated, on June 2, with a gig at the Cardiff Top Rank. Although they weren't to know it at the time, the audience was the last to witness XTC live in Britain . . .

XTC spent the summer of '81 writing, demo-ing and rehearsing new material at Tudor rehearsal studios in Swindon, eventually teaming up with Hugh Padgham at The Manor to start work on what would become 'English Settlement' on October 5. With four albums under their belts, they now felt more confident in the studio and decided to cut out the middle-man by co-producing the record with the best engineer they knew.

The mood as work got under way was almost tangibly optimistic. Terry, whose Australian girlfriend Donna had spent part of the summer in Swindon, had just discovered he was to become a father.

Dave was much happier with his contributions to the record, and Colin and Andy were satisfied with the way their songs were shaping up.

Having had four months respite from touring - the longest break since they'd become a recording group - they'd had time to develop more than one album's worth of songs. The twenty on offer, some of which would go on to make B sides, formed a kaleidoscope of style and colour. As always Andy's songs were the more dominant. These varied from melancholic pastoral ballads like 'All Of A Sudden (It's Too Late)' and 'Yacht Dance' to the clamorous 'No Thugs In Our House' and 'Melt The Guns'. They touched new ground on 'It's Nearly Africa', a jaunty ethnic funk outing that brought world music into XTC's orbit before the term had even been coined and, of course, the anthemic 'Senses Working Overtime'.

Colin's contributions, although fewer, were no less impressive. 'Ball and Chain' - a re-recording of the track they'd recorded earlier in the year with Alan Winstanley - 'Fly On The Wall' and the reggae-tinged 'English Roundabout' were all bright effusive pop songs. But Colin's most outstanding contribution was 'Runaways', which went on to become the album's opener. With its warm, insidious, melody it proved that the quiet member of the group still had something to shout about.

Lyrically the songs formed a broad observation of modern life; a questioning of modern issues such as the futility of the arms race ('Melt The Guns'), racial hatred ('Knuckle Down' and 'No Thugs'), unemployment ('Leisure'), the rat race ('English Roundabout') and buried emotions ('All Of A Sudden' and 'Snowman'). It was as if XTC were discovering for the very first time how to work with a full palette after having restricted themselves to bold, primary colours all their recording career.

Several new instruments had arrived on the scene: Dave had a new 12 string Rickenbacker guitar that, offset against Colin's fretless bass, helped give certain songs a round folk-influenced feel. Terry had a new drum synthesizer and Andy - who would also play alto sax on a couple of songs - had a new acoustic guitar. The band had also acquired a Prophet V synthesizer which was state-of-the-art in 1981. All these instruments combined to diversify XTC's sound significantly.

Mixing was completed by mid November and on the last night of the month the band sat around to hear the finished songs arranged in their preferred running order for the first time. "This is going to sound awfully pompous," says Andy. "But after six weeks I felt we'd made a big friendly giant of a record. I remember thinking 'My God, this is really good!' I was very, very happy with it. It was somehow bigger, grander than anything we'd ever done before.

"Until 'English Settlement' I'd felt like a child in a sweet shop wanting to try a bit of everything, but only being allowed to choose licorice allsorts. I'd broken free from this moral chastity belt that told me it was wrong to put anything on our records that we couldn't reproduce live.

"Even on 'Black Sea' we'd arranged all the songs so that when we got to play them live they wouldn't sound so different. But I'd got a lot more realistic with myself about what I wanted to do, and that included different textures, styles and different instruments. I was no longer afraid to let the songs develop naturally, the way they were written. If it had been written on an acoustic guitar and it went 'plink' then that was okay. It was obviously a 'plinky' kind of song, so why make it sound like anything else?"

It was XTC's masterpiece. Now titled 'English Settlement', this was an album of immense accomplishment, not only artistically but technically as was reflected in the sound fidelity awards it ultimately won. The fifteen songs - spread over two discs to prevent the sound suffering from 'groove cramming' - elevated the band to new heights. XTC were no longer just a quirky eccentric pop group, hitching a lift on the back of the new wave movement. They had found a maturity that would do full justice to their sparkling inventiveness. They had found a balance between accessibility and their tendency to wander up obscure musical avenues that, uniquely, would satisfy them, their record company, the critics and the public.

'English Settlement', with its evocative, shifting moods, was an album to discover and re-discover. Above all, it was the work of a single-minded, uncompromising, quintessentially English band; a band whose ideas and influences seemed to be little affected by their travels across five continents.

"I felt more English in the face of travelling the world," says Andy, "and seeing how some groups were rootless - their music didn't seem to be grounded in any one country. A band like The Police weren't obviously American, or British, or Caribbean. They had this 'everywhere' kind of sound. But I felt decidedly English in all its connotations. It took going around the world a few times to get an idea of what it meant, and how to get it across."

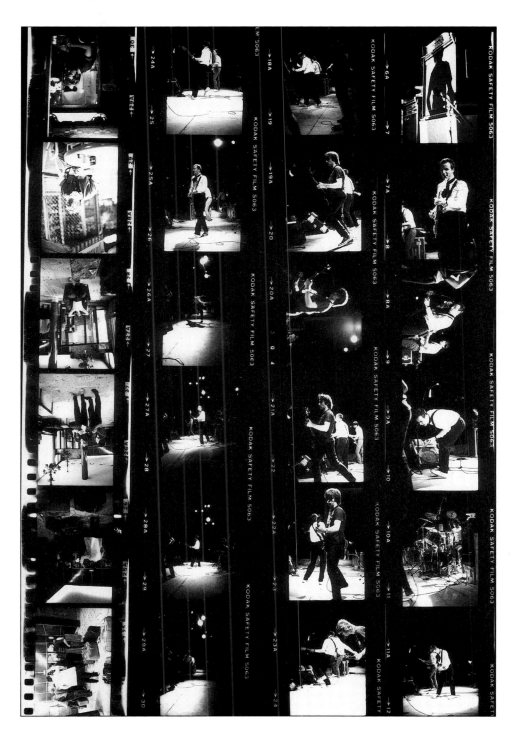

XTC on tour in Spain, 1980. (*Pennie Smith*)

Right: The U.S. tour
1980/81. Partridge,
Moulding and
Dave Gregory.
(Adrian Boot)

Below Right and
Left: Andy in full
flow. *(Adrian Boot)*

XTC on tour with The Police in the U.S during early 1980: Andy with Sting and
Stewart Copeland. *(Andy Partridge Collection)*

XTC during their last American tour, 1981. Left to Right: Colin Moulding, Dave Gregory, Andy Partridge, Terry Chambers. *(Peter Noble/S.I.N.)*

The Dukes Of Stratosphear, with Ian Gregory (left), aka 'El El Owen', August 1987. *(L.F.I.)*

Marianne Partridge with six-week old daughter, Holly, in 1985. *(Andy Partridge Collection)*

Joanne, Carol, Colin and Lee Moulding in 1986. *(Colin Moulding Collection)*

Dave Gregory, Andy Partridge and Todd Rundgren, doing backing vocals to 'Grass'. June, 1986. *(Colin Moulding)*

Dave Gregory circa 'Oranges and Lemons', early 1989. *(Renaud Monfourny)*

XTC, U.S. acoustic radio tour, May 1989. (Gary Gershoff/Retna)

XTC with Dave Mattacks, rehearsing at First Play Records, Gorse Hill, Swindon, 8th March 1991.
(Dave Gregory Collection)

XTC with Terry Chambers, Chipping Norton Studios, 16th October 1991. *(Gus Dudgeon/Dave Gregory Collection)*

The photo session for 'Nonsuch', February 1992. *(Kevin Westenberg)*

'Senses Working Overtime' - a song that would shortly have ironic reference to Andy's life - was released on January 8 1982. It became XTC's first Top Ten hit. A month later, on February 12, 'English Settlement' was released. "XTC have made the first indispensable record of 1982," said *Record Mirror*. Meanwhile in *Melody Maker*, Adam Sweeting wrote: "Not so much of an album, more of A Work".

'English Settlement' reached No 5 in the UK and sold over 60,000 copies within the first two months of release. Moreover it started to pick up healthy sales overseas. This seemed to be the turning point everyone had been waiting for. "'English Settlement' was an absolutely critical record," says Simon Draper. "All those years of touring around the world were just paying off. XTC were at the point where they would start to make big money on the road, and they would sell records in bigger and bigger quantities. It was gathering momentum in such a way that the next record would've - should've! - been another big leap forward."

Despite Andy's protests - "I was petrified at the thought that we'd now have to go on the road with the album . . ." - the 'English Settlement' world tour loomed. A glossy colour tour programme had been produced. In its foreword it said "XTC have already begun 1982 with a vengeance, and the activity threatens to continue into the year. They tour a number of European countries over the next couple of months and follow that with a British tour. Meanwhile, America awaits, and no doubt XTC will be there before the year is six months old . . ."

On March 7 XTC left for Europe . . .

9

TRAIN RUNNING LOW ON SOUL COAL

In the period immediately following Andy's breakdown and the subsequently aborted British and American tours, XTC's career took a startling nosedive - precipitated by the chaos and confusion around them. As far as most people were concerned they were doing the unthinkable: on the brink of a major breakthrough they were sabotaging their own career. It was a criticism they would hear over and over again in the coming months.

At Virgin, Simon Draper treated the news that XTC weren't going to tour again with a degree of disbelief. "I understood Andy's reasons for not wanting to tour at the time of the announcement. But like everyone else I thought, 'Just give him a little while and he'll feel more positive about it again.' I don't think anyone really believed that he really meant never."

By cancelling a sold-out British tour at the eleventh hour, the band had alienated a sizeable part of their British following and this was already having an effect. Two more singles were released from 'English Settlement' - 'Ball and Chain' and 'No Thugs In Our House' - but they both flopped. It seemed to reflect a growing disenchantment with XTC.

Within the ranks of the band themselves, matters were equally dispiriting. Terry was still in Australia with Donna, who was about to give birth to their first child. Colin had begun writing and demoing some new songs at home, but with little enthusiasm. Dave was waiting to see what would happen and whether he'd end up back on the dole.

Everything depended on Andy. Although safely back on home turf, his mental health problems persisted for several weeks. In June 1982 he and Marianne moved out of the rent free flat on King's Hill Road and bought their first home, a modest Edwardian terraced house in Swindon's Old Town. Here Andy shut himself away for days on end, unable to come to terms with his obsessive fear about being on display. The thought of venturing out to do something as innocuous as the food shopping filled him with dread. "I'm becoming like Howard Hughes without the money," said Andy.

Marianne suggested introducing themselves to their new neighbours, but even this was too much for him to handle. "I put it off for days and days," he says. "When I eventually tried I'd get to the front door and freeze. It became totally irrational but I couldn't do anything about it. I didn't want anyone connected with the outside world seeing me. I felt trapped like a monkey on a barrel organ. Everything I did was some sort of performance."

The hypnotherapy sessions were resumed, but recovery was slow. That summer Andy sat in the back garden for most of the time, an acoustic guitar on his knee and a bunch of new songs that almost wrote themselves. These songs - 'Ladybird', 'Love On A Farmboy's Wages', 'Desert Island' - all had a light summery feel and Andy demoed them with sparse, simple arrangements of just acoustic guitar and vocal. "I was in a strange frame of mind, but I couldn't stop these songs tumbling out," he says.

As Andy exiled himself in his own garden, the cancelled American tour left a line of creditors and debts totalling £20,000. The most pressing of these was money owed to Entec who supplied the tour PA as well as pre-tour rehearsal space in a warehouse on the Shepperton Film Studios complex near London. Because they hadn't been paid, Entec impounded XTC's instruments and back line amplification.

Unable to rehearse the new songs, the band decided to concentrate on restructuring their financial affairs. Reid advised that XTC was already £75,000 in debt to Allydor and refused to advance further money to pay Entec. This situation forced the band to seek specialist advice elsewhere. They engaged a firm of London based accountants, Wilkinson & Mellor, who recommended a well-known music business lawyer called Alexis Grower, whose previous clients included Mick Jagger and David Bowie. Grower advised them that their main priority should be to renegotiate their recording contract with Virgin in order to raise enough money to pay off their debts.

The gist of the renegotiation was that XTC would sign up for another six albums ('English Settlement' was the penultimate album under their existing deal), plus a 'Best Of' package, in return for which Virgin would alter the terms of their contract and advance the band enough money to take care of their immmediate financial problems.

XTC took advantage of the renegotiations by insisting that from now on they were to have direct control over their finances. Any advances or royalties owed by Virgin would be paid into a deposit account from which they would pay themselves a monthly wage of £650. It wasn't a fortune, even by 1982 standards, but it was the most any of them had ever earned.

As the months passed, and Terry Chambers still hadn't returned from Australia, his absence started to cause some concern. The band wanted to get on with the next album but Terry was too busy having a good time to hurry back to Swindon. In June he and Donna had become the proud parents of a son Kai and Terry enjoyed being a family man almost as much as the Australian lifestyle. Obviously he was going to have to return to England at some point to fulfil his XTC duties, but his apathy was telling.

By the end of July Terry had finally been talked into coming back to start rehearsals by Ian Reid. In the past Terry had always lived at home with his parents and now he was obliged to set himself and his new family up in a tiny starter home on a new Swindon housing estate called Kingsdown Park. Predictably, Donna hated her new surroundings. She was the active outdoor sort and she missed the sun, sea and surf. The muddy, unfinished estate - thousands of miles from family and friends - was a miserable start to a new life.

Privately Terry was less than ecstatic himself. He did little to hide his disgust at Andy's decision to quit touring. While the rest of the band had grown to dislike touring in varying degrees, Terry positively thrived on it. To him it was his main justification for being in a band. "I never resented touring," Terry Chambers admits. "I always enjoyed playing live. Generally speaking that was what it was about - recording always came second to me. I didn't like recording much, although we got better at it as we went on. I found the process of going over and over and over the same thing too monotonous."

Nevertheless XTC began rehearsals that August in the prop store of the Mechanics Institute theatre - a dilapidated old Victorian railway workers social club complex - to plough through the new material. Virgin had selected two songs from their demos, 'Beating Of Hearts' and 'Wonderland', which they wanted the band to record as a double A sided single.

The session took place, early September, at Martin Rushent's Genetic studios, near Reading, with producer Steve Nye at the helm. Nye had been chosen by Andy because he was impressed simply by the sharpness and clarity he had achieved on 'Tin Drum', an album by

Japan. But when work was completed on the single (a third track 'Toys' was also recorded in the same session) Virgin decided the songs weren't strong enough to be hits, and told XTC to press on with their plans to record the next album. With the recording date fixed for mid October, rehearsals immediately resumed at the Mechanics Institute.

Almost inevitably, Terry wasn't keen on the new songs Andy and Colin had written. He was unable to get to grips with the gentle, pastoral textures which didn't suit his no-nonsense style of drumming. With the pressure of his unsatisfactory domestic situation adding to his worries, Terry had good reason to question his decision to return to England and XTC.

"Terry's mind wasn't on the job," says Andy. "He was bashing the drums and not really concentrating. You could see his mind was elsewhere. For some reason he had a lot of difficulty trying to grasp my ideas."

This dissatisfaction reached a head when the band was rehearsing a song called 'Love On A Farmboy's Wages'. Andy was pushing Terry to get the drum track right and both were close to losing their patience. Suddenly Terry put his drumsticks down and said calmly, "Hang on a minute, I'm not really enjoying this. I don't think the new songs are much good. I'm sorry chaps, I'm leaving the band." With that, he got up from behind his drumkit, grabbed his jacket and went out the door.

"That was it!" recalls Colin in disbelief. "There was no 'What shall I do about my drum kit?' Or 'Are there any outstanding debts?' Or 'Does anyone not want me to leave?' There was no talk about it. He just went."

"There was this amazing silence for ages afterwards," remembers Andy. "Cymbals were still swinging where they'd been struck. We just looked at each other. We'd sensed it coming - I think he'd already made up his mind to leave, only he was trying to find a way of saying it. But it was still quite shocking. We thought he'd be the last of us to give in because he was the toughest, the meanest, the biggest drinker and all that."

The day Terry Chambers quit XTC was the last Andy, Colin or Dave saw of him for nearly a decade. There were no second thoughts, no tearful recriminations, no looking back. Within a month Terry had sold the house on Kingsdown Park and emigrated to Australia with Donna and Kai, leaving his drums behind.

Yet again, XTC were in the dumper. With only 11 days to go

129

before they were due to start recording their new album at The Manor, they were drummerless, not to mention low on morale after the departure of an original member. For all Terry's brash and acerbic nature, he had always been a dependable and practical influence, a fully paid up member of the anti-bullshit brigade whose down to earth mentality often kept XTC's more outrageous flights of fantasy on an even keel. He would be sorely missed.

Determined not to let the situation ruin their plans, the band looked around for a suitable temporary replacement. One name immediately suggested by Dave was Pete Phipps, a session drummer of some note. He'd been in a band called Random Hold who supported XTC on their 'Drums and Wires' tour in 1979 and although Random Hold's sub-Genesis/Soft Machine fare hadn't been much to XTC's liking, they thought Phipps was a good drummer and had got on well with him. Besides, he was a former member of The Glitter Band so he had to be all right!

"We rang Pete up and asked him if he wanted to do the album and he agreed," Andy recalls. "It literally happened overnight. He brought his drum kit down, set it up in the Mechanics Institute and we had about a week's rehearsal before we started the album in October."

The mood at The Manor, a year after the recording of 'English Settlement', had changed surprisingly little, despite Terry Chambers' departure. On the downside Steve Nye, an unusually dry character, certainly wasn't on the same wavelength as the band in the way that previous album producers Steve Lillywhite, Hugh Padgham and John Leckie had been. But on the plus side they were very happy with their new - albeit temporary - choice of drummer.

"Pete Phipps was a very different sort of drummer," says Andy. "Although he'd been in The Glitter Band, and you'd think he would have had Terry's heavy style of drumming, he was much lighter and deft of touch. He brought a jazzy edge to the music immediately, which was very exciting and suited a lot of the material. I think the excitement of having a different style of music put around us made up for the fact that Terry wasn't there."

On November 5 Virgin attempted to revive the flagging momentum of XTC's career by releasing a definitive 'Best Of' compilation called 'Waxworks' (in the UK the first 50,000 copies of 'Waxworks' came with a free LP, 'Beeswax' a collection of B sides and extra tracks). Although this formed part of the renegotiation agreement, there was ample justification for releasing such a compilation as many of XTC's singles had either never been on album before, or had been completely re-recorded versions. Virgin was hoping that 'Waxworks' would do as well as, if not better than, 'English Settlement'. In the event it struggled to reach No 54 in the UK charts, and disappeared after only three weeks.

"We were expecting 'Waxworks' to sell very well," says Simon Draper. "So many of their singles had gone on to become mini-classics. If you saw the band live, you'd be forgiven for thinking that 'Statue Of Liberty', for example, had been a major No 1 hit from the way the audience responded to it. And yet it hadn't even made the Top 75. There were so many tracks like that. I thought finally putting them all on one record would help establish their credibility as singles writers. In fact it was one of the most incredible disappointments. Whether we handled it wrongly, or whether it was packaged wrongly . . . I don't know. But it didn't do them any good."

Recording of the basic album tracks lasted two months, after which they had a short break for Christmas and New Year. Everyone took home rough copies of the mixes to live with over the break, and everyone came to the same conclusion. The songs had gone down onto tape okay, but they sounded dull and lifeless. They were going to need a big shake up in the final mix.

Following the contract renegotiation with Virgin, Ian Reid knew the writing was on the wall. He knew XTC was trying to get rid of him, and he'd become an increasingly remote figure. The band wouldn't see him for weeks on end and when they did it would only be fleetingly. During the mixing of the album at Air Studios in London in January 1983, Ian Reid stuck his head round the door briefly to see how things were going. By then the band was virtually running its own affairs. With no tours to arrange and no financial control over XTC, Reid quickly fell out of the picture. The visit to Air Studios was the last they'd ever see of their manager.

By the end of January, mixing at Air had been completed and some life breathed back into the disappointingly flat songs on the new album - enough to satisfy XTC at least. Although they instinctively knew they weren't delivering an album that was in the same league as 'English Settlement', they were still confident it was a good album. Besides, 'English Settlement' was a hard act to follow, they reasoned.

At Virgin - of whom, Andy once said "Virgin without XTC would be like The Tower of London without the ravens" - big changes were afoot. Simon Draper had relinquished much of his A&R control over XTC and they were now chiefly in the hands of Jeremy Lascelles, an aristocratic young executive, with whom they would always have an uneasy relationship. Added to that Al Clark, their industrious press officer - and probably their greatest ally at Virgin - had now left the company.

In their years with Virgin, XTC had witnessed the record company grow dramatically. From being one on a modest roster of about 25 acts in 1977, the band now found themselves overtaken by a host of more successful recent signings like Phil Collins, Culture Club, OMD, Simple Minds and The Human League. XTC felt they were being pushed down the pecking order by a record label that had lost interest in them. The initial reaction of the new album did nothing to allay their insecurity.

"If there is such a thing as a pecking order, it rides entirely on sales," says Jeremy Lascelles. "Clearly acts that are selling many millions are going to take up more of the company's time than an act that is selling in the tens of thousands. At the other end of the scale are the brand new groups. You're going to pay them a lot of attention because you're excited about them and you're convinced that every time you sign a group they're going to be the next Beatles.

"XTC came somewhere in the middle so they probably had a legitimate complaint. But they weren't helping themselves by deciding to take a much more low-key approach to their career by not touring."

Indeed, XTC had all but admitted this by their approach to the album's title and sleeve artwork. The title 'Mummer' referred to traditional West Country performers in a play staged by members of the community. The mummers would appear in disguise so that the audience could not tell if the lead character was portrayed by the local baker or butcher and would concentrate more on the actual performance rather than the performer.

Andy thought this approach suited XTC now that they had ceased to be a touring outfit, and the band designed their own mummer suits made from newspapers for the album sleeve. The photo session was rejected by Virgin, who complained the suits obscured the band's faces and "you couldn't tell who they were!" Andy remarked that this was the whole point of 'Mummer' but band and label were obviously now on divergent paths.

Both Jeremy Lascelles and Simon Draper felt that the first batch of recordings for 'Mummer' weren't up to standard, and Lascelles turned them down. "No one heard a hit single," he complained. "We were still at a point where we were desperately trying to get XTC to write and record hit singles. We thought 'Mummer' was a little lacking and felt the need for them to do more work."

Demoralised by having the album rejected, XTC returned to Swindon. But within a few days Andy had come up with a couple of new songs, 'Great Fire' and 'Gold'. When Virgin heard the demos they called Andy to tell him that 'Great Fire' was the single they'd been waiting for.

By then Steve Nye had gone off to work with another band in Canada, so Virgin hunted around for an alternative producer. XTC were prepared to produce the tracks themselves, but Jeremy Lascelles wasn't having it. He put the band in touch with Bob Sargeant, who'd worked successfully with bands like Haircut 100 and The Beat. The two parties got together towards the end of February at Odyssey studios in London.

The sessions went well and 'Great Fire' - an impassioned, up-tempo love song - had the record company's full approval as a single. Plans were made to release the album with 'Great Fire' added to the running order, and Virgin announced the imminent arrival of 'Mummer' to the major retail outlets.

'Great Fire', the first new single from XTC for almost a year, was eventually unleashed in the UK on April 22. Apart from one play on Radio One 'Saturday Live' show, and a Single Of The Week review in *Melody Maker*, it was virtually ignored. Virgin immediately suspended their plans to release 'Mummer' and told the band they'd have to write more songs. XTC refused. Virgin backed down but told the band they'd have to re-mix four tracks on the album - the four most likely to become singles - with another producer.

One day Jeremy Lascelles phoned the band to say that top producer Alex Sadkin - who had worked with Duran Duran, Grace Jones, Bob Marley and the Thompson Twins - was in town, and suggested he do the re-mixing. The band's reaction was, "Alex Sadkin! How the hell can we afford him? We've already spent a fortune on this album." "Don't worry," says Lascelles. "We'll sort something out."

A deal was agreed with Sadkin and XTC went into RAK studios with him and his engineer Phil Thornally to re-mix 'Wonderland', 'Funk Pop A Roll', 'Deliver Us From The Elements' and 'Human

Alchemy'. "They sounded a little more exciting than the Steve Nye mixes," says Dave, "but not much."

At the end of June 'Wonderland' came out and XTC filmed a video for it at Hatfield House, a stately home near Luton. On the back of this Virgin re-scheduled the album for the end of July. "Everything looked good at last," says Dave. "Until the single stiffed. Virgin said 'No album, sorry chaps. We want more songs.' We said 'No! You're not having any more songs. You're putting the album out. We're sick to death of it. We want it out of our lives so we can look to the future. We're fed up with this'."

'Mummer' was finally released, with some reluctance on Virgin's part, on August 31. With no tour and minimal record company promotion, it reached No 51 and quickly disappeared. The pattern was frustratingly echoed everywhere else in the world.

In truth 'Mummer' was a big disappointment for all but the most dedicated and persevering of fans. For the first time in XTC's career they sounded listless and unsure of themselves. It seemed to reflect the growing confusion and lack of confidence in the band. Sure, there were still occasional moments of brilliance: 'Beating of Hearts', 'Love On A Farmboy's Wages', 'Human Alchemy' and 'Funk Pop A Roll', for instance - but much of the record's impact was diluted by sentiments that were too oblique and melodies that were too opaque. Also, the fact that three producers had been involved meant that the overall continuity of the album suffered.

Critically, 'Mummer' was damned with faint praise. XTC had gone from being great pop innovators to endearingly unfashionable country eccentrics in the space of one album. Almost every reviewer pointed out how hopelessly at odds they were with the contemporary music scene. It was a situation XTC acknowledged themselves. In 'Funk Pop A Roll', a stabbing rebuke of the ephemeral music industry, Andy emotively expressed his indignation:

> "Funk pop a roll beats up my soul
> Oozing like napalm from the speakers and grille
> Of your radio
> Into the mouths of babes
> And across the backs of its willing slaves
>
> Funk pop a roll consumes you whole
> Gulping in your opium so copiously from a disco

Everything you eat is waste
But swallowing is easy when it has no taste

They can fix you rabbits up
With your musical feed
They can fix you rabbits up
Big money selling you stuff that you really
Do not need

Funk pop a roll for fish in shoals
Music by the yard for the children they keep
Like poseable dolls
The young to them are mistakes
Who only want bread but they're force-fed cake

Funk pop a roll the only goal
The music business is a hammer to keep
You pegs in your holes
But please don't listen to me
I've already been poisoned by this industry
'Funk Pop A Roll'

With initial UK sales of 'Mummer' trailing around the 20,000 mark, the September release of 'Love On A Farmboy's Wages' - a song which amiably reflected the folkier element now present in XTC's music - briefly revived hopes of an elusive hit. The single enjoyed considerable radio exposure and support from DJ's, before peaking at No 50, and led to the band being asked to appear on the BBC TV daytime show *Pebble Mill At One*. It was Andy's first live appearance since his breakdown nearly 18 months earlier, and he was still in a fragile state of mind. Although the band were only required to mime before a small (and elderly!) studio audience, Andy tried to back out of doing the show minutes before it was due to go out live. He eventually agreed, under duress, to go through with it in the knowledge that if he couldn't even promote his own records XTC were finished.

As XTC's career hit an all time low, there was some comfort for Andy in the fact that he now seemed to have a burgeoning career as a producer. He had taken the first tentative steps in this direction in 1980, when he co-produced Thomas Dolby's self-financed single 'Urges' b/w 'Leipzig', on which he also played drums and sang backing vocals! But in October 1983 Andy's first major production -

Peter Blegvad's album 'The Naked Shakespeare' - was released, and picked up great reviews.

Peter Blegvad was a New Yorker who'd been a member of the Seventies avant garde band Slapp Happy, one of Virgin's first signings, and who had at one time worked as an illustrator for various cartoon strips such as Charles Shultz's *Peanuts* and the bubblegum strip *Bazooka Joe*. He was now a solo artist on Virgin and he'd requested a producer who wouldn't attempt to iron out the idiosyncrasies in his songs, so Jeremy Lascelles suggested working with the most idiosyncratic songwriter he knew, Andy Partridge.

Information surrounding XTC's mysteriously aborted American tour the previous year had been grossly exaggerated in some quarters, and when Blegvad mentioned the probability of teaming up with Andy to a friend he was told, "Didn't you know? Andy Partridge is dead - he died last year." Virgin assured Blegvad that Andy was very much alive, and after a meeting and exchange of ideas in Jeremy Lascelles' office, sessions for 'The Naked Shakespeare' began at Crescent studio in Bath in June 1983.

"I liked the idea of working with a dead producer!" Peter Blegvad explains. "And although I didn't know much about Andy or XTC before we worked together, we were very compatible. Andy very economically and imaginatively transformed my songs just by suggesting an alternative rhythm or changing a chorus a bit. He was a master of song structure."

Andy enjoyed working at Crescent studio and was impressed by the studio's resident owner/engineer/adviser David Lord who had produced mainly classical musicians in the past. As a former Director of Music at Bath University, he'd once declined a request from Paul McCartney to score the strings for The Beatles classic 'She's Leaving Home'! XTC decided to try the studio out, with a view to recording their next album at Crescent, and recorded a Christmas single there under the pseudonym The Three Wise Men.

" 'Thanks for Christmas' was just a fun song," says Andy. "I had it lying around on this cassette for a long time. It wasn't doing anything and I thought that people might want to buy it and be cheered up. We had good fun making it. It was just a laugh. The original idea was to do it with us backing some office girls from Virgin Records and calling them The Virgin Marys, but the record company thought it was in bad taste!'"

The Spector-esque 'Thanks For Christmas' - produced, appropriately enough, by the Good Lord - was released on November 21. With some radio play and a lot of unfounded rumours about who was really on the record (one theory being that Phil Collins was singing and drumming), the single still managed to sink without trace. However, the band were sufficiently happy with the recording to agree to go back to Crescent for the next album with drummer Pete Phipps in March 1984 for what would turn out to be their most protracted recording session to date. A special deal had been worked out with the Crescent Studio's owner David Lord, so they could spend longer working on the album - the idea being that it would give XTC a chance to make the most meticulous, sonically impressive record of their career.

The session began with good news from Virgin. Jeremy Lascelles phoned to congratulate them on excellent record sales which had wiped out their existing debt. Recording royalties for 'English Settlement' had been audited and they were about to be sent a cheque for £13,000

The following month XTC received a nasty shock in the shape of a huge VAT bill for the period when Reid was presiding over the group's financial affairs.

The band summoned their solicitor Alexis Grower down to the studio in Bath and he advised them to take legal proceedings against Reid. Within days of a writ being issued, Reid made a counter claim for unpaid commission on royalties. The litigation had begun . . .

Away from the legal world, XTC still had music to make. At a cost of only £350 a day - compared to the £1000 a day The Manor charged - Crescent Studio was, at least, a bargain. On their recording budget of £75,000 the band could afford to spend more time in the studio exploring a myriad of musical avenues. Andy, who enjoyed experimenting in the studio, was in his element. But as the days became weeks, and then months, Colin and Dave began to get bored and impatient.

"I went into it with a good attitude," Dave says, "but we were in the studio too long, dicking around with ridiculous, totally self-indulgent ideas. Because we got Crescent for a real knock-down price, along with David Lord, we were thinking 'What else can we put on this track' - even if it didn't need anything adding. David Lord was as bad as Andy for tarting things up when they didn't need tarting up."

Colin, who had only two songs on the album - 'Wake Up' and 'I Remember The Sun' - was even more dispirited. "I didn't enjoy it at all. It was just too analytical. Andy tends to analyse down to the minutest detail. We'd be listening to bass drums all fuckin' day to see if they had any feel! David Lord loved to go in that direction as well. There wasn't any performance about that record, it became very sterile to work on."

By early August mixing of the album, now entitled 'The Big Express', had been completed. Most of the mixing was done by Phil Thornalley at RAK studios in London because David Lord had to abandon the project in July to fulfil a contract working for The Europeans. The first single from the new album, 'All You Pretty Girls', was released soon afterwards on September 3. A boisterous pop song-meets-sea shanty with an infectious chorus and probably XTC's best chance of a hit from the album, Virgin gave it their biggest push for a long time with a £33,000 video budget and aggressive radio promotion. But frustratingly 'All You Pretty Girls' peaked at No 55. A month later 'The Big Express' was released.

Although a marked improvement on its predecessor, 'The Big Express' was never destined to achieve mainstream success. Its hard-edged bluesier sound had turned parts of the album into a multi-layered impervious wall of sound that only true XTC converts could get around. The five month conception period had left much of it overworked and overproduced. On almost every song there were tantalising snatches of XTC at their most melodically potent, but the group was suffocated by heavy handed production and cumbersome arrangements. "By the time 'The Big Express' came out," admits Dave, "I was so fed up with it I never wanted to hear it again."

Conversely, 'The Big Express' was a magical album lyrically. Whether dealing with the futility of the nuclear arms race ('This World Over'), the hypocrisy of world leaders ('Reign Of Blows'), the nostalgia of childhood ('I Remember The Sun'), bad managers ('I Bought Myself A Liarbird'), the mediocrity of day to day life ('The Everyday Story Of Smalltown') or a sailor's fantasy ('All You Pretty Girls'), both Andy and Colin occasionally displayed a dexterity of expression which bordered on poetic.

> "I think about your pale arms waving
> When I see the caps upon the green
> And the rocking roller coaster ocean
> Think about you every night when I'm fathoms asleep
> And in my dreams

We are rocking in a similar motion"
'All You Pretty Girls'

'The Big Express' reached No 38 in the UK and sold as poorly as 'Mummer'. The band were disappointed but not entirely surprised. "I was becoming undentable," says Andy. "I felt more armoured against the disappointment. I knew I was right, which you've got to feel to keep at it. If you ever had doubts about what you were doing, you might as well stop. I was, and still am, immensely proud of 'The Big Express'. Songs like 'This World Over', 'Train Running Low' and 'Seagulls Screaming' I'm more proud of than virtually everything on the albums either side of it."

Andy's enthusiasm for 'The Big Express' was shared, if not surpassed, by an effusive full-page review in *The Spectator*. In an imaginative departure from the norm the review's author, Rick Miller, transported himself to the year 2084, and talked hypothetically of the posthumous acclaim XTC were enjoying - an acclaim matched only by The Beatles. The review concluded: "'The Big Express' is the most exciting record I've heard in years, and I don't recommend it to everyone. Most popular music forces us to lower our demands on artists. Bands who give us something either catchy, sexy, fast or fun often get a portion of our support because the bottom line of acceptance has reached a level just above terrible. XTC has nothing to do with that kind of pitiful acceptance. Andy Partridge, Colin Moulding and David Gregory have raised the stakes back to where they belong - to nothing less than excellence."

Purveyors of excellence XTC may have been, but it wasn't doing much for their financial state. In November 84 the money in XTC's account dried up and because litigation against Ian Reid was in full swing Virgin Records put a hold on all further payments of advances and royalties - as much to protect the band as anything else. Meanwhile, publishing royalties - due from Virgin Music Publishing - were paid into a frozen deposit account. The only money XTC had was in the form of short term loans granted by Virgin.

As the debt to Virgin spiralled ever upwards, the situation seemed hopeless and worries over the group's future grew. Temporary relief, however, was waiting just around the corner from a totally unexpected quarter . . .

In November 1984 Andy took himself off to Monmouth, Wales, to produce an album for a newly signed Virgin artist Mary Margaret

O'Hara. Virgin suggested the pairing, hoping that Andy would treat the Canadian singer's sparse, enigmatic songs with an empathy they deserved. Since Andy liked the demos, and had got on well with O'Hara on the one occasion they'd met briefly, it seemed like a good idea. Andy asked John Leckie if he'd like to co-produce the record with him, and Leckie agreed.

Mary Margaret O'Hara arrived in Britain, complete with band, for a week of rehearsals at Rockfield Studios near Monmouth, prior to recording the album. Because John Leckie was still tied up with a job in London, Andy supervised pre-production on his own. The rehearsals got off to a bad start. Andy didn't think much of O'Hara's band - he felt their lumpen old-fashioned approach didn't do justice to the subtlety of the songs - and the band didn't much care for Andy. They had immediately taken offence at his attempts to program some of the drum tracks on his Linn Drum ("The drummer was crap," says Andy) and resented his radical restructuring of their song arrangements.

There was another problem: O'Hara herself was hardly to be seen. She spent hours locked away in her room every day with her sewing machine which she'd had shipped over! Andy would only get to see her in the evenings at dinner time. The singer's boyfriend/manager Jody Colero placed a protective shroud around her and her eccentric little ways. No-one, he insisted, not even Andy, could disturb her during these sewing marathons.

Mary Margaret O'Hara was also a devout Catholic. One of her first demands was a list of all the Catholic churches in the vicinity of the studio, and if she did venture out of her room during the day, it was usually to visit one of these churches. During dinner one evening the conversation inevitably gravitated towards religion. When O'Hara asked Andy what religion he followed, he told her that he had been brought up an Anglican, but that he now considered himself to be an atheist. "Oh!" O'Hara exclaimed, evidently a little concerned. "And John Leckie? What about him?"

At the time John Leckie was a follower of Bhagwan Shree Rajneesh - a controversial Indian guru whose followers were popularly known as the Orange People after the colour of their clothes. The movement frequently found itself under the scrutiny of the more salacious tabloid rags because of its open approval of 'free love', and was generally abhorred by the established churches. "Oh, you'll like John," Andy pitched in enthusiastically. "He's very religious. He follows this Indian guru and is really into spiritual things." From the look Mary Margaret O'Hara gave Andy, he knew he'd said the wrong thing.

The following day Jody Colero took Andy aside and told him he'd been fired because, he said, Mary thought his "vibes weren't right". John Leckie had also been fired because they didn't think Mary should be involved "with someone who belonged to a religion that promoted free love". Angry and upset, Andy phoned John to tell him the news.

"I was pissed off," John explains, "because they'd booked us for two months and we hadn't been paid anything."

Andy was inclined to just forget the whole episode, but Leckie was indignant at being hired to do a job for two months, then being fired just hours before work was due to begin. He told Andy, "We've got to get something out of this" and phoned Simon Draper with the demand: "I need some compensation, and Andy does as well."

During recent conversations, Andy had enthusiastically told Leckie about a bunch of psychedelic songs he and Colin had written which were totally over the top and not right for XTC. "I was desperate to work with XTC again, and said, 'Well we've got some spare time now. Why don't we find a cheap studio and record them?' All the band thought it was a great idea."

Leckie approached Virgin with the project. "They weren't terribly enthusiastic initially. I said 'Just give us £5000 - which is pretty much what you owe us for the Mary Margaret O'Hara gig - and we'll make a record for you. Eventually they agreed and gave us the money."

Andy had wanted to make a psychedelic record for many years. He'd long wanted to record some kind of tribute to the music that dominated his youth, and had been inspired by overt forgeries like Reuben and The Jets (a thinly-disguised Frank Zappa and The Mothers of Invention performing a convincing doo-wop pastiche) and, more recently, the psychedelic 'Hilly Fields 1892' by Nick Nicely released in 1982. But until now there had been neither sufficient time nor the justification to indulge in such a venture. From an unfortunate sacking came a fortuitous break.

The original idea was to record on a four track machine belonging to Edgar Broughton for authenticity. When this fell through, John Leckie said he knew of a cheap 24-track studio - Chapel Lane Studio at Hampton Bishop, near Hereford - that, ironically, was owned by a Christian organisation and was usually used by Gospel singers. He booked the studio for two weeks in December. With as much vintage gear as they could find, Andy, Colin, Dave and his brother Ian Gregory (a drummer who had played with many amateur groups in Swindon) recorded a mini album as their psychedelic alter-egos Sir John Johns, The Red Curtain, Lord Cornelius Plum and E.I.E.I.Owen - collectively known as The Dukes of Stratosphear. It was the most fun XTC had enjoyed in ages.

"Everyone got into the spirit of it," says John Leckie. "We all wore our Paisley shirts, burnt incense, read Oz magazine - all that sort of stuff. It was the most fun I've ever had in a studio. No one knew if Virgin were going to release this thing - we just did it for ourselves."

Nearly everything was recorded in one take. If mistakes were made they were left on and smoothed over with a bit of phasing or blurred with effects. Five songs - 'Your Gold Dress', 'What In The World', 'Bike Ride To The Moon', 'My Love Explodes' and '25 O'Clock' - were written before going into the studio. A sixth, 'The Mole From The Ministry', Andy wrote at the piano one morning.

"It was this strong desire to copy the bands we always wanted to be in when we were kids," explained Andy. "Groups like The Beatles, The Small Faces and Pink Floyd - bands that had singles out in 1967/68. Because they were what we were spending our pocket money on at the time, they were enormously influential."

Wherever possible the band stayed faithful to the limited studio trickery that had been available to groups in the Sixties. "We took our forgery very seriously," says Andy. "We're really the Tom Keatings of the pop world. We tried to stay away from synthesizers and modern effects, because if you're going to re-create the feel of that music you've got to use the techniques they used. There was no sampling or anything like that. We tried to do everything to sound as authentic as possible."

Dave Gregory was already an accomplished musical forger. During time off he was known to record his own versions of classics on his home studio under the pseudonym Arch Marble and the Hallmarks. Dave's version of The Beatles' 'Strawberry Fields Forever', featuring Andy on lead vocals, was later included on Imaginary Record's 1990 release '1967 - Through The Looking Glass'.

"Despite the fact that I don't write songs I have this insatiable need to make music," Dave explains. "If there's a song that I've particularly loved in the past my immediate instinct is to see if I can do a version on my own, and see what it would've sounded like if I'd written it myself. I like analysing things in detail. Every time I buy a guitar, for example, the first thing I do is take it to pieces. I have to know exactly how it works. It's the same with music."

On December 20 recording of the already christened '25 O'Clock' was completed. The next day, John Leckie drove straight back to London to take the finished master, plus £1000 change, to Virgin. "Andy was frightened to play the tape to them," Leckie recalls. "I think he thought they'd just dismiss it as a bit of pointless messing around. But when Simon Draper heard it he was in hysterics. He was calling people into his office and playing it to them. He thought it was wonderful!"

Virgin agreed to go along with the joke and release '25 O'Clock' with a look, and a budget, that was consistent with the period. Andy designed a sleeve, loosely based on Cream's 'Disraeli Gears' album, on his kitchen table with the aid of a pair of scissors and some photocopied book illustrations. Everything else about the packaging, right down to the specially resurrected old-style Virgin labels, was designed to fit in with the ruse that these were in fact a bunch of 'lost' sixties EP's that had recently been discovered at the back of a warehouse!

'25 O'Clock' - a title that parodied the daft, nonsensical nature of English psychedelia - was finally released on April Fool's Day 1985. It was a wonderfully tongue in cheek, and surprisingly authentic pastiche of Sixties pop psychedelia, and shamed recent attempts by others - most notably The Damned with their Naz Nomad and The Nightmares alter-egos -to do the same. With no reference to XTC anywhere on the record The Dukes managed to fool a surprising number of people.

"Virgin passed on quite a few letters to us saying things like 'They're fantastic! They're great! Where can I buy a T shirt? Signed Clive Shirk, Pontefract'," says Andy. "You could tell they were serious because most of them were written on that apologetic note paper, with a flowery border and a bear in one corner!"

On April 15 'The Mole From The Ministry', a blatant musical reference to The Beatles 'I Am The Walrus', was issued as a single. A budget video of the song, itself a cliché riddled pastiche of the era, was shown on *The Old Grey Whistle Test* and the BBC West programme *RPM*. '25 O'Clock' started to sell by the bucket load and within a few weeks it had, rather embarrassingly, outsold 'The Big Express' in the UK with initial sales of around 50,000. It helped to rekindle some of the flagging interest in XTC and earned them some badly needed money to pay off the Virgin debt. More importantly, it injected some much needed zest back into the band.

"With XTC we'd lost sight of how to enjoy ourselves making a record," admits Colin. "It had become an assault course. We spent a lot of time and money on our records and they weren't necessarily any better for it. The Dukes taught us how to have fun again."

Aside from The Dukes, XTC remained out of public sight for much of 1985. The Partridges swelled ranks when, on June 9, Andy and Marianne became parents to a daughter, Holly. During the year Andy also produced a single, 'The Miracle Of The Age', for Doctor and The Medics' who hired Andy because they were all big Dukes fans, and six songs for The Woodentops, which included the subsequent singles 'Well Well Well' and 'Move Me'.

Having sold their house in Ferndale Road, the Mouldings moved to the positively rural surrounds of Lower Wanborough, near Swindon, where Colin put most of his energy into renovating the cottage they'd bought.

Dave was known to Arch Marble his way through many a night. He also played guitar on a single for The Big Dish called 'Big New Beginning' and on a few tracks on ex-Orange Juice drummer Zeke Manyika's album 'Call And Response'. Meanwhile, despite initial promises by Alexis Grower to the contrary, the litigation against Ian Reid dragged on . . .

With no manager to goad them back into action and a record company that, by their own admission, now saw XTC as part of the furniture, they had become the epitome of the reclusive cult group. Months passed by with no mention of them in the music press which had by now abandoned its supportive attitude and treated XTC as a spent force. As far as the great majority of the public knew, or cared, they had been buried in the annals of rock history.

At the beginning of 1986, with almost enough tracks for a new album written and demoed, Virgin summoned the band to London. XTC thought it was a routine meeting to discuss plans for the forthcoming LP, but Simon Draper and Jeremy Lascelles had a potentially more decisive agenda up their sleeves.

Both were extremely concerned that Virgin's relationship with XTC had become stale and was in danger of stagnating altogether. "We had reached a point where I genuinely felt that we'd come to the end of an era," says Simon Draper. "I felt maybe they should go with another record company. They were constantly complaining about Virgin so I said 'Okay then, if you want to go, go. Alternatively, if you want to stay, we'll spend a bit more money than we're contractually obliged to spend, bring in a producer who's going to take a radical approach, and let's have a real shot at getting you some significant success. The choice is yours'."

"After they'd gone away and thought about it a while they decided they wanted to stay. I smiled to myself because I knew that - despite everything - they'd got used to us."

With a sincere joint commitment to proceed, a shortlist of producers was drawn up and given to Jeremy Lascelles. A few days later Lascelles got back to the band with a suggestion of his own. He had been talking to someone at Geffen, who, since 'Mummer', had handled XTC in America and they'd put forward the name of Todd Rundgren. In turn, Rundgren had immediately reacted by saying that XTC were one of his favourite bands - he'd once seen them live in Chicago - and he'd love to produce them.

The band were flattered and thought it was a wonderful idea. Dave was particularly delighted. He hero worshipped Todd Rundgren, and saw the combination of Andy and Todd in the same room as a potential marriage made in heaven.

Virgin agreed on a package with Rundgren whereby he would supply all travel and accommodation plus per diem expenses, as well as the studio, session musicians and, of course, himself for an all in fee of $150,000. In return Virgin would get an album that would transform XTC's career.

A few weeks before work was due to start, Rundgren requested copies of all demos for the album. Within two days of receiving them he contacted both XTC and Virgin to say that he had worked out the concept for the record. It would take the form of a passing day. Side One would start at dawn and end at midday. Side Two would end at midnight. Furthermore, he had pieced a running order together from the demos. All the songs that revolved around the themes of either nature or love were in. Anything with any sociological or political inference had been left out.

"Todd kept using this expression," Jeremy Lascelles recalls. "He said, 'I know all the songs that fall in the circle, and the songs that fall outside the circle.' He said it with such confidence that you were persuaded that he knew what he was doing."

But already alarm bells were going off in Andy's head. He wasn't completely happy with Todd's choice, feeling that he had omitted some of the best songs. And on a broader level, he wasn't happy about such a big decision being taken without some degree of consultation with the band. Even Colin had doubts: "Todd was saying 'When you come over, we'll start recording track one, side one and carry on in that order! We'd never worked that way before. It was usually a case of recording as much as we could and choosing the best of the bunch. This was all very foreign to us."

XTC arrived at Newark airport, New Jersey, on April 6 and were met by Rundgren's assistant Mary Lou Arnold, who drove them to Rundgren's Utopia studio/home complex in the Catskill Mountains near Woodstock in upstate New York. For the first couple of days they waited apprehensively for Todd to return from San Francisco where he was visiting his family. Although he was based on the West Coast, Utopia was where he preferred to work.

"This place was in the middle of nowhere," says Colin. "It was very pretty, quite mountainous with fir trees everywhere, but it was really cut off. We had the use of a van but Woodstock, about ten miles away, was only a village. Todd's house looked like a fuckin' spaceship! It was this big round thing surrounded by a huge glass conservatory. Whether he designed it himself, I don't know. Below the house was the studio, which was a large wooden cabin with a control room in the roof. About 20 yards further down the hill, in amongst the trees, was this colonial looking wooden guest house. The whole place had an element of rock star decay about it. The TV never worked properly so we amused ourselves by watching mice scurry around the living room."

The day after Todd arrived from San Francisco, recording got underway, concentrating on basic guitar and keyboard parts before moving to San Francisco where Rundgren had booked session musicians to work on drum-tracks and other overdubs.

Right from the off it was obvious that Todd and Andy weren't going to get on. Andy was used to having a large measure of control over everything XTC did and Todd wasn't letting him have any say - barely paying lip service to his ideas and suggestions. Andy Partridge, the irresistible force, had finally met his match in Todd Rundgren, the immovable object. One was a producer determined to produce, the other an artist determined to resist.

Nothing Andy said or did could soften Todd or dent his arrogant demeanour. His sense of humour - often used as a way of getting people on his side - had no effect. Todd would deal Andy's jokes a fatal blow with a deadpan comment like "Stop, you're killing me", and offered none of the deference Andy was used to receiving. To Andy this was all a way of trying to break his morale. "At times he'd launch into me in an abusive fashion," he says. "He'd say things like 'Where *did* you get those jeans from? God, they look like you bought them from Russia! Christ look at them!' It was all a way of making you feel small so that he could stand on top and you'd accept his ideas without question."

On the occasions that Andy stuck by his guns and refused to give in, Todd would walk out of the studio saying, "You can dick around with this all day. I'm going up to the house, and when you've realised that my way is the right way to do it, you call me."

After a few weeks of this ritual humiliation, Andy was ready to quit. "I'm not enjoying this," he told the rest. "I'm thinking of knocking the album on the head. It's like having two Hitlers in the same bunker."

Dave was appalled. "Don't be daft," he said. "Just go along with it and we'll do another record as soon as we get back. We've still got plenty of songs that Todd hasn't chosen."

If not swayed by Dave's reasoning, Andy at least agreed to see the project through. "In the end I think the only thing that stopped him was the knowledge that if he did leave, the band would disintegrate. He knew that we had to come out of this with something."

Indeed, Colin and even Dave also found Rundgren difficult to work with. Todd made no comment about performances and gave them no reassurances. "If you'd done a good take you wouldn't know it," says Dave. "As long as he didn't ask you to do it again you assumed you'd done your bit."

Finally, one day, Andy confronted Todd and told him that unless he made the experience a more pleasant one, he was taking the next plane home. Afterwards an uneasy truce was made between the two of them, but the atmosphere would always remain volatile.

Todd had defined the boundaries of his relationship with the group from day one by keeping his distance from them - both emotionally and physically. None of the customary camaraderie between band and producer was allowed to develop. Although his house was just yards away from where they were staying, Todd kept a purposeful distance.

XTC were also worried by Rundgren's occasional slapdash approach. As well as producer and engineer, Todd was arranger and occasional session musician. One song he picked from Andy's demos was an exuberant pop song called 'That's Really Super, Supergirl'. The band hadn't really wanted to record it and had left the keyboard arrangement to Todd.

"I remember watching him do the overdubs," says Dave. "He had one hand on the tape machine and the other hand on the synthesiser. I could see two keys going down, when he was only meant to be playing one. It was really sloppy. After he'd run through it once, Andy said 'That could sound really good!' Todd said 'What do you mean *could* sound really good. That was it.' Andy said 'Well, could you play it again a bit tighter?' 'Ah, what d'ya mean tighter? That was good enough!'"

For all his other shortcomings, however, as an arranger Todd Rundgren couldn't be faulted. Even Andy grudgingly acknowledged this. Some of the songs were turned on their heads and because Todd's ideas were backed up with solid musical grounding, they nearly always benefited from these transformations.

The best example was 'The Man Who Sailed Around His Soul', a song which according to Andy originally sounded like "Leonard Cohen with Can backing him up". Todd said the song's chords, melody and title reminded him of a spy film, and suggested recording it in that style. "At first I thought, 'Oh Christ, he's flipped his wig'," says Andy. "But as he started to show me what he meant, I thought 'Hey! This is really good! I never thought of doing it this way'."

After one month at Utopia, the band and Rundgren moved to San Francisco. At Soundhole Studio - which was housed within a dilapidated warehouse complex owned by The Tubes - another month of recording followed during which various session musicians, including ex-Tube Prairie Prince, another hard hitting drummer in the Terry Chambers vein, came and went.

XTC were allocated two apartments in an apartment block called Crystal Tower on Taylor Street in mid-town San Francisco overlooking the majestic bay. After tossing a coin it was decided that Andy and Dave would share one apartment and Colin would have the other to himself. But rather than enjoying the extra space and privacy, Colin felt cut off from the other two and generally homesick. This all contributed to the growing tension.

The change of environment did nothing to improve relations between Todd and Andy either, and the bad atmosphere in the studio triggered off an abnormal number of petty arguments within XTC. Dave and Colin were placed in the difficult position of having to compromise between the often polarised demands of Todd and Andy.

One such disagreement arose over a song of Andy's called 'Earn Enough For Us', on which Colin was recording his bass part. Andy complained he was playing notes in the wrong key and seemed to be spoiling the song on purpose. "We got into this silly argument about certain chord changes," says Colin, "and what the component notes of those changes were. Andy accused me of playing a note that wasn't in the chord, but it sounded okay to me."

Tempers flared and - without the calming influence of Dave, who was off on a shopping trip - the argument steam-rollered out of all proportion. It reached a head when Colin threw his bass down and marched out of the studio shouting, "Stick it up your arse. I'm quitting the band!"

Back at Crystal Tower, Colin phoned Carol to say he was coming home - he'd left XTC. Later he phoned Dave to break the news and to explain himself before he heard Andy's version. Colin told Dave, "I'm just calling to tell you I've left the band. I've just had enough of Partridge. I've fuckin' had enough and I'm going."

"He sounded really, really upset," Dave recalls. "He was crying - he was in a terrible state. I thought 'This is more than just an argument over a bass part. This is something far more serious.' I pleaded with him not to do anything hasty. I said 'Just think about it for God's sake'."

Full of remorse, Andy went round to Colin's apartment that evening to apologise, but Colin could not be won over. He was adamant. He told Andy he was sick of being under his thumb. He had left the band and that was it.

Todd Rundgren was equally concerned that Colin was quitting. He had already been paid three parts of his fee by Virgin and had a duty to deliver a completed album. The following morning he called in at Crystal Tower to try and persuade Colin to finish it. "That way at least you'll get the royalties from your songs," he reasoned.

"I had to agree with that," says Colin. "I told Todd I'd do the rest of the bass tracks so long as Andy was kept out of the picture. I didn't want him in the studio leaning over me all the time." Work continued, but Colin remained very sullen for the next few weeks.

In June, Rundgren and XTC returned to Woodstock to add the finishing touches. Once again Andy and Todd were constantly trying to undermine each others' authority, and as mixing finally got underway the studio atmosphere became unbearable. Todd wanted to mastermind the mixing alone without the band present all the time. Naturally, Andy was dead against this, though Colin and Dave were happy to let Todd work alone.

After a few days the tension peaked with a particularly memorable band fight in the kitchen of Todd's guest house. "For about an hour we were bawling our heads off," recalls Andy, "saying exactly what we thought of each other."

"I'd feel a lot more sympathetic towards you," Dave told Andy, "if our track record had been more successful. But every time we do it your way, it never works."

"I reminded both of them that my songs were 75% of the band's character," remembers Andy, "and without my input there would be no XTC! It's the only time in our career that all three of us have been locked in a really terrible row."

That night XTC packed their bags to return to England, agreeing that it was the only way of avoiding further conflict. After telling Todd they wanted copies of the mixes as soon as possible, they left Woodstock the following day. On the flight home Colin sat away from the other two. Since their monumental argument in San Francisco, Andy and Colin had given each other a wide berth. The album may have been completed, but there was still uncertainty about whether Colin was still in the group. "For a while we didn't know if he was going to stay or go," says Dave. "We just played it by ear."

The finished mixes to the new album were posted to XTC in mid-July and, in keeping with the rest of this long unhappy saga, the band didn't like them. "They sounded awful," says Dave. "We told Virgin it was rubbish!"

XTC insisted that Todd should remix the album and he finally agreed. At three o'clock one morning, he rang Dave and demanded, "What exactly is it you want me to do with this record?"

Dave reeled off a list of complaints and Todd replied, "You guys have got me doing what I really love. I just love to remix. It's my favourite occupation!"

"He was really sarcastic about it," sighs Dave. "He just didn't want to do it."

A couple of weeks later a second batch of mixes arrived but the band still weren't happy with several of them. After the third set it was formally reported to Virgin that "Todd (was) unable to spend any more time on this project". Like it or loathe it, XTC and Virgin had their finished album.

Despite everything, 'Skylarking' - a title that belies the friction and bitterness that went into its making - was a gorgeous record, by far the most satisfying since 'English Settlement'. Saturated with rich vocal harmonies (credited to the Beech Avenue Boys!), stirring string arrangements and warm, mellifluous textures, 'Skylarking' celebrated the re-emergence of the pop sensibility that had been largely obscured on the previous two albums. For all his sins, Todd Rundgren had brought more outside musical influences to XTC than they had known before and used them to very good effect.

"The band was at a point in their career where if they didn't get some kind of response to their records, they weren't going to be making any more records," says Rundgren. "I had to constantly emphasise the experience that the listener was going to have when they listened to the record. It wasn't just an album that the band could take home and listen to. It had to be a record that people would listen to and enjoy. There were times when I was at loggerheads with Andy's natural propensity for excess."

Recording as The Dukes Of Stratosphear had affected XTC's output. Some of the songs had an unmistakable tint of psychedelia. This was most strongly heard on Colin's 'Big Day' - a song that had in fact been offered up for '25 O'Clock'.

To begin with Andy hated 'Skylarking'. The studio run-ins, the clash with Todd Rundgren and the fact that many of his initial projections for the songs had been overturned, left a sour taste in his mouth. Jeremy Lascelles recalls: "When the record was finished Andy was saying 'I think this is a piece of shit. I don't like the mixes. Everything's so sloppy . . .' I said 'Andy, you're wrong. There may be some faults, but it's brilliant in its way. It has an identity and integrity that absolutely works'."

At least Andy and Lascelles agreed on one point: they both disliked the one song that everyone around them was saying should be a single, 'Dear God'. Described by Andy as "a one-way letter to God", Lascelles was put off by its controversial lyrics and didn't like the sound of "the whiny American kid singing the first verse" (a ten-year-old girl called Jasmine Veillette, who'd been drafted in by Rundgren).

Andy disliked 'Dear God' for very different reasons. "It failed for me. Man's belief is such a vast topic and I really wanted to write a song specifically about religion and my failure to grasp the whole thing. After I'd written 'Dear God' I could think of a billion other things I wanted to say which were almost impossible to précis into three and a half minutes. It's such a massive subject I could've done it in three and a half albums . . . maybe."

". . . and all the people that you made in your image

See them fighting in the street
Because they can't make opinions meet
About God
I can't believe in you

Did you make disease and the diamond blue?
Did you make mankind after we made you?

And the devil too!"
'Dear God'

The failure of both Andy and Virgin's head of A&R to perceive 'Dear God' as the outstanding track of the 'Skylarking' sessions was extraordinary. With its impassioned, pleading vocal and its swooping string arrangements (not to mention a glorious tune!), it may have been controversial but it was the most accessible XTC had sounded in ages. Even more surprising was the eventual decision to drop the song from the album's running order altogether. Dave and Colin were exasperated.

"Everyone I'd been playing the album to was going nutty over 'Dear God'," says Colin, who had now decided to remain in the band. "I rang Andy and said 'You can't take that off!'."

Andy said: "I'm not happy with it. It's not turned out how I wanted it to."

"He wouldn't listen," recalls Colin. "He wanted to replace it with a song called 'Another Satellite' which wasn't part of Todd's original running order. Jeremy Lascelles was also keen to get 'Another Satellite' on the album. So the decision was taken over our heads."

At least Colin could console himself with the knowledge that one of his songs, 'Grass', was chosen as the first single from 'Skylarking'. With 'Dear God' on its B side, 'Grass' - a charming ode to alfresco teenage passion - was released on August 26. It bombed. Colin: "We thought, 'That's the first nail in the coffin. Here we go again'."

The release of 'Skylarking' itself had to be delayed because of a dispute between the band and Virgin over the album's sleeve. A mock-up of a concept, as usual, by Andy - a tasteful display of the male and female pubis with interwoven meadow flowers - was rejected. "It was meant to have a *Lady Chatterley's Lover* 'risquéness' about it," Andy explains. "All you could see was pubic hair. You

152

didn't even know it was pubic hair unless you stared very carefully at it. You just had the impression of flesh and hair and meadow flowers intertwined. I thought it described the outdoor, summery, slightly erotic atmosphere of some of the songs."

Worried about offending high street shoppers, Virgin conducted market research which suggested that the artwork would have a damaging effect on sales. Although record stores said they would be prepared to stock the album, some large retail chains said they wouldn't display it. Andy subsequently got a call saying passions were running high on the subject at Virgin and suggested he come for a meeting.

"I'd never seen so many people in one room at a Virgin meeting before," says Andy. "There were 30 or 40 people sat round in a huge circle. Some of them were agreeing with me saying 'What's all the fuss about? It's really tasteful.' But this one girl - I don't know what department she was from - was up in arms over it. She was saying 'This is filth! This is disgusting! This is degrading to women!' In the end there were too many people against it, so it had to be dropped. It was the worst case of over-reaction over what? Hair!" And so the 'Dick and Fanny' sleeve passed into band legend . . .

'Skylarking' was released on October 27 in the UK (in a re-designed sleeve featuring a wholly inoffensive Hans Erni print) and reached a paltry No 90 in the charts. The band would've been utterly dejected but for an unexpected twist of fate in America.

XTC's fortunes in the States had been steadily slipping since the semi-success of 'Black Sea' and Geffen, who'd released 'Mummer' and 'The Big Express', were at the point of letting them go. Indeed Virgin America had already been lined up to take over from Geffen right after the release of 'Skylarking'.

Fortuitously, the delayed release of the album allowed time for a few thousand import copies of 'Grass' to find their way into America and into college and university campuses. College radio, the influential underbelly of the American music industry, had picked up on the single and were playing it to death. Not the A side, though, the B side - 'Dear God'.

Jeremy Lascelles got a panic call from Geffen. "What's this track 'Dear God' that's all over college radio?" they demanded. "Where is it? It's not on the album. College radio's going fuckin' nuts over it - we're getting calls about it and we don't know anything about it - it's very embarrassing!"

"I was embarrassed myself," admits Lascelles, "because we'd totally misjudged the potency of the song."

Geffen swung into action fast. The album was re-pressed, restoring 'Dear God' to the running order and dropping another song, 'Mermaid Smiled'. A short time later it was released as a single in its own right. 'Dear God' picked up mainstream airplay all over America, and although it wasn't an actual hit, it acted as a sales catalyst for the album.

As 'Dear God's' polemic lyrical message rang across the States, reaction was predictably polarised. One Florida radio station received threats from a fanatic who said he would "blow up the station if ('Dear God') is played again". Later, At Binghamton in New York State, an 18 year old high school student called Gary Pullis held the school secretary at knife-point in the principal's office one morning and demanded that 'Dear God' be played over the school's communication system. He was later arrested and taken away for "psychiatric evaluation".

Overall, the controversy did XTC no harm at all. On the back of 'Dear God', 'Skylarking' spent over six months in the lower reaches of the US album charts, selling a very respectable 250,000. It wasn't exactly the blockbuster Simon Draper had been waiting for, but it was enough to improve the situation overall. Virgin was happy and, most of all, XTC were back in business.

10

SEASON CYCLE

With the success of 'Dear God' in America, XTC found themselves back in demand. Their talent was personally requested by the music supervisor for the John Hughes Film Corporation, Tarquin Gotch, who wanted XTC to contribute a song for the forthcoming Hollywood baby boom movie *She's Having A Baby*. Starring Elizabeth McGovern and Kevin Bacon, this was to be the follow up to Hughes' previous movie *The Breakfast Club* which had provided a massive US hit single for label mates Simple Minds in 'Don't You Forget About Me'. Gotch wanted to make his soundtrack as interesting and varied as possible, so he approached all the artists he adored. XTC thought it would be good exposure for them and they badly needed the £15,000 he was offering, half of which went straight to Virgin.

Andy dusted off his old composition 'Happy Families' - which had originally been submitted for the 'Mummer' album - and in April 1987, XTC spent a few days at The Manor recording a new version for the film soundtrack. In the event, less than 30 seconds of 'Happy Families' was featured in *She's Having A Baby* when it was eventually released in April 1988, thus confirming Andy's worst feelings towards Hollywood.

Although now in the film industry, Englishman Tarquin Gotch had many years' experience of the music business. As an A&R man at Arista for several years he had signed groups like The Beat (who he later also managed), Wang Chung and Stray Cats. He also produced Rowan Atkinson's hit comedy album 'Live In Belfast'. After moving to WEA he signed Elaine Page and The Associates, among others.

He began working for the John Hughes Corporation in 1986, but kept his hand in the music business, managing groups as diverse as General Public, Dream Academy and The Lilac Time. After meeting XTC he was keen to add them to the list.

Although they liked Tarquin - he had an irreverent ex-public school air about him - the band were hesitant about getting involved with another manager. Their association with Ian Reid had left them highly wary of all such offers. But Gotch was persistent . . .

In May 1987 the band - along with drummer Ian Gregory - travelled to Sawmill Studios at Golant, near Fowey in Cornwall, for more recording as their alter-egos The Dukes. Inspired by the success of '25 O'Clock', Virgin encouraged them to record a second Dukes album. At first Andy had resisted, feeling that what was intended as a one-off joke should not be repeated, but he eventually gave in after much arm-twisting, especially by John Leckie.

This time around Virgin stepped up the budget to £10,000. It was still a comparatively tiny amount, but it meant that they could afford to record ten songs over three weeks. As with '25 O'Clock' most had already been written or demoed and some had been intended for XTC at one time or another. For instance, Colin's song 'Shiny Cage' had originally been offered during 'The Big Express' sessions, while another, 'The Affiliated' was written immediately after 'Skylarking' in anticipation of its successor. Similarly, Andy's song 'You're My Drug' dated back to 'Big Express' and 'Little Lighthouse' was partially recorded during 'Skylarking'. Going even further back, 'Collidea-scope' had been hanging around as a lyrical idea since 'Drums And Wires'. All were poached by The Dukes and subjected to their psychedelic mincing-machine.

Sawmill Studio - set in a remote river creek and accessible only by boat - was an idyllic location for the latest round of musical forgery. It seemed that whenever XTC donned The Dukes' jumbo cords and Paisley shirts, their petty arguments and financial worries were forgotten. They simply concentrated on having fun.

One casual visitor to Sawmill was Tarquin Gotch. Although he was ostensibly catching up with an old friend - he'd known John Leckie since his A&R days at Arista when Leckie produced Simple Minds' first album - it gave him a good excuse to continue his thinly veiled courtship of XTC. Over the ensuing months, Gotch would re-appear all over the place.

In June 1987, just weeks after completing the second Dukes project, XTC were invited to appear on the CASBY show (Canadian Artists Selected By You), a whole evening of performances and award presentations that was to be televised right across Canada by CBC Channel 5. As in the States, the band's fortunes in Canada had picked up considerably since the release of 'Dear God' and the single had topped a listeners' poll on the Toronto based CFNY-FM, the radio station sponsoring the prestigious event.

When Andy first heard about the invitation from Virgin's international department he was less than delighted. He had never been keen on glitzy Hollywood-style awards ceremonies and, more importantly, he was told all bands had to perform - lip-sync - in front of a very large 'live' audience. Against Colin and Dave's wishes, he turned the offer down.

A few days later Virgin International phoned Andy back to say that the CASBY show organisers were very keen to have XTC on and were prepared to take exceptional measures to get them to agree. If the band wished, they could record their slot prior to the main event in an empty theatre. Although still wary, Andy eventually agreed under pressure from Colin, Dave and the record company who all thought it would be invaluable promotion.

XTC arrived in Toronto on June 17 and were billeted in the plush L'Hotel, beneath the city's landmark, the CN Tower, along with other British guests OMD and The Fixx. Everything seemed to be going according to plan until Andy discovered that he was expected to present an award to an up-and-coming Canadian group at a gala dinner and awards ceremony before the 'concert'. Andy flipped. No one at Virgin had told him about this beforehand. Indeed, he was so angry he was ready to turn around and go straight back home. But again the event's organisers told him not to worry, he wouldn't have to make the presentation if he didn't want to.

The following day the band filmed their CASBY show slot in the huge empty convention centre, a day ahead of the event itself. They 'performed' two songs: 'Dear God' - with Colin's son Lee miming the opening verse - and 'Grass' backed up by a small string section and a hired drummer. The rest of the day was given over to routine promotional press interviews.

Next morning the CASBY show sponsors gazed with dismay at the headline in the *Toronto Star*, which read: 'XTC not thrilled by CASBY's'. Among other things the contentious newspaper feature quoted Andy as saying: "I fought not to do (the show). And I might have gotten out of having to present those useless pieces of metal. I dunno, we may not even go to the dinner. I'm not into that sort of thing personally, which is why I fought. But they'll throw us out of our hotel room unless we go."

Understandably outraged by this apparent slap in the face, after all

157

they'd done to try and accommodate XTC's whims, the organisers called on Andy for an explanation. He told them he'd been quoted out of context and that none of his comments had been made with any malicious intent. To placate CASBY, XTC had to call a press conference later that afternoon to explain what Andy had really meant. "Basically we just sat there and apologised for being so rude about the CASBY show," winces Dave. "It was excruciatingly embarrassing!"

Additionally, under pressure from CASBY, Andy later photocopied a handwritten apology, which was placed on every seat of the theatre. It read: 'I feel I should write a few lines in an attempt to set the record straight here. In a recent newspaper article I did a lighthearted interview about the CASBY awards. Much to my disgust, 95% of what I said was either misquoted/chopped up/taken out of context and used by this empty headed reporter in an attempt to make an article for himself out of nothing. So, without more waffle, I want to tell you some truths - We (XTC) won't be performing at the CASBY show along with everyone else because in 1982 we took the decision to stop live performing (simple), but we DO wish to support the CASBY principle and are pre-recording our slot with their cooperation. Truth 2, I don't enjoy the penguin suit circus of most awards ceremonies, so I don't do them (CASBY does not appear to fall into the above category!). This negative smart assed attitude the paper appears to give us in relation to good Canadian music is lies. Truth 3, support CASBY, support good sounds. It's all for you! Thanks for your time.'

While the apology seemed to satisfy the organisers, the incident made XTC no friends. They left Canada the following day with their tails between their legs.

Tarquin Gotch's continuing flirtation with the band was beginning to reap results. Although XTC were still very wary of entering into contractual commitments, they liked him and liked having him around. Besides, Tarquin was a useful and influential ally to have, as Colin soon discovered.

Colin had mentioned that he was interested in doing some session work and he asked Tarquin to put some his way if he heard of anything appropriate. That July, Colin's phone rang. It was Tarquin. "Dave Gilmour's just about to give you a call," he said. "What, the guy from Pink Floyd?" Colin asked incredulously. Tarquin had been friendly with Gilmour since he'd produced Dream Academy a couple of years earlier. Sure enough, moments later the phone rang again.

During the ensuing conversation Dave Gilmour told Colin that he'd just won back the right to use Pink Floyd's name for the first time since his acrimonious split with Roger Waters in 1983. The Floyd were about to embark on a massive world tour and would be needing a bass player. Gilmour liked what he'd heard of Colin's playing and wanted to know if he was interested in auditioning for the tour. It would be worth a considerable sum of money to him if he got the job.

"When he told me the tour was going to last a year, I knew I wouldn't be able to do it," says Colin. "But I told him I wanted time to think about it. It was very tempting but obviously my commitment to the band came first. After I'd put the phone down on him, I picked up my bass and started playing 'Money'. I thought 'Fuck me! I've got to start learning all these bastards!'" In the end, Colin decided against going to the audition and the job went to The Hothouse Flowers' bass player, Peter O'Toole, instead.

August saw two new arrivals. On Monday the 17th, Andy and Marianne's second child, Harry, was born and a week later The Dukes' second album 'Psonic Psunspot' was released. Concentrating on the major Sixties influences they'd left out first time around, 'Psonic Psunspot' didn't upstage its predecessor. Although still an enjoyable, affectionate parody, it sounded more mannered and less spontaneous than '25 O'Clock'. Indeed, because the dividing line between The Dukes and XTC was growing progressively thinner, parts of 'Psonic Psunspot' didn't sound like pastiche at all! It worked best where the plagiarism was strongest: 'You're My Drug', which leaned heavily on the West Coast 12-stringy-ness of The Byrds, and 'Vanishing Girl', with its heavy Hollies influence. Best of all was The Beach Boys' 'Smiley Smile' pastiche, 'Pale and Precious', a song that Dave accused Andy of needlessly throwing away by sacrificing it on The Dukes altar!

On the back of the single 'You're A Good Man Albert Brown', a good-time pub singalong tune in the mould of The Small Faces or The Kinks, 'Psonic Psunspot' managed to equal the sales of '25 O'Clock'. The two albums were later amalgamated and released on the CD-only 'Chips From The Chocolate Fireball (An Anthology)', after which Andy announced that The Dukes had hung up their guitars.

For a while, however, there was talk of various Dukes spin-off projects. For instance, a project had been conceived to make a film based around the '25 O'Clock' EP, to be funded by Godley and Creme's video company, Media Lab. It was to have included a Kit

Williams-style treasure hunt for a solid gold 25-hour clock, which was to be buried somewhere in Britain, clues to its whereabouts to be included in the screenplay. The whole concept had been story-boarded after several meetings between the band and the producer, Steve Blood. But before any filming got under way, Media Lab pulled the plug on the project.

A while later there were plans for a Dukes rock opera, or concept album at least, tentatively entitled 'The Great Royal Jelly Scandal'. It concerned the robbery of vast quantities of honey, wax and Royal Jelly from bee-hives across the countryside and the bees' attempts to retrieve it and punish the perpetrators! This would have been a follow-up to 'Psonic Psunspot' but the concept was never fully realised and subsequently abandoned.

Although sad to see the demise of The Dukes, John Leckie has special cause to remember them with affection. "More people have come to me because I'd worked with The Dukes Of Stratosphear than anything else," he says. "The Stone Roses asked me to produce them because of The Dukes!"

When the fun was over, the band turned their attention to serious matters again. The most sobering was the ongoing case against Ian Reid. Litigation had now dragged on for over three years and was putting an intolerable financial burden on XTC. The band's solicitor Alexis Grower continued to advocate pursuing the claim against him. This meant was that the band's only sources of income were loans from Virgin and their PRS royalties from radio and TV broadcasts.

Because the Virgin loans were offset against the frozen publishing royalties, this posed its own problems. The bulk of the publishing and PRS royalties belonged to Andy, since he wrote most of the songs. Colin was responsible for roughly a quarter of XTC's output and received a proportionate cut of the royalties. But Dave, who wrote no songs, had no specific entitlement to any royalties. Colin and Andy had agreed he should receive a share for his general contribution to the band: thus he was attempting to survive on a 10% share of royalties, plus a rapidly diminishing savings account. When the band were making an album he was okay: they'd receive a record company advance and split this three ways, which would last for a while. But the periods in between LPs, with no tour revenue, recording royalties permanently in the red - not to mention the ever-mounting legal bills - were very lean indeed.

Towards the end of 1987 Dave resorted to taking any small jobs he could get: session work, writing occasional album reviews for *New Hi-Fi Sound* and he even worked for a few months as a part time van driver for the Reading-based Bratts van hire company, whose Swindon branch was being managed by XTC's old friend, singer/songwriter Dave James. No one in XTC was wealthy - Colin also helped out at Bratts occasionally - but Dave's situation was becoming desperate. Luckily a new album was looming.

XTC spent much of the early part of 1988 writing and rehearsing in Andy's attic in preparation for the follow-up to 'Skylarking', their biggest selling album to date. For a group as fascinated by the nature of England as XTC, it was ironic that America had become their biggest sales base. Virgin were obviously keen to sustain and nurture that success by suggesting that they record their next album in the States with a producer sympathetic to American tastes. But Andy wanted to avoid another Todd Rundgren experience at all costs.

After some inconclusive ruminating, Jeremy Lascelles suggested a young American called Paul Fox, who'd just done a Boy George re-mix for Virgin. "They played me this Boy George track, which was George singing over a drum machine and a few sounds pattering along," says Andy. "I thought 'Oh dear, not very good.' Then they played me Paul Fox's re-mix. He'd literally thrown everything away - just kept George's voice - and the track he'd built behind George was great. It was really shiny, powerful and impressive. I thought 'Wow! This bloke's got his head screwed on'."

A short while later Paul Fox flew to England to meet with Andy in Swindon. "I gave him a beer and a sausage roll and we chatted all afternoon. He was obviously a huge fan of the band and was willing to translate what we wanted onto tape. I thought 'Yeah. It's worth taking a chance'."

Armed with a generous recording budget of £150,000, XTC flew to Los Angeles on May 12, accompanied by the Moulding and Partridge families. They stayed in the Oakwood Apartments, a big apartment complex in north Hollywood, favoured by itinerant rock stars and wannabes. Los Angeles being traditionally the showbiz town where dreams are made and broken, during their residency at Oakwood the band met their fair share of the latter.

"We met a lot of people who were going to do big things, but never did," says Colin. "Mostly long haired characters who'd sit out by the pool strumming their guitars and saying things like 'C'mon guys, it's lyrics night tonight'."

Four days after their arrival in LA, rehearsals began with Mr Mister's drummer Pat Mastelotto at Leeds studio in North Hollywood. On June 6 recording of the drum tracks started at Ocean Way Studio One, next door to Studio Two where Elvis Costello recorded his album 'Spike'. On June 30, work on the main bulk of the album got underway at Summa Music Group Studios.

With 23 songs already demoed, Paul Fox chose 15 to concentrate on, including one, 'Merely A Man', which the band had unanimously decided they didn't want to record. 'Merely A Man' started life as a deliberate attempt by Andy to write an American AOR hit at the instigation of Jeremy Lascelles. "After he'd done it, I didn't think it was great, nor did the band," says Lascelles. "But Paul Fox really liked it. So in deference to Paul, Andy rewrote the lyrics and they recorded it".

Even from the demos it was clear that the sheer variety of the songs was going to place this among XTC's better albums. Now entitled 'Oranges And Lemons', it included flashes of Sixties influence on songs like 'Garden Of Earthly Delights', 'The Loving' and 'Here Comes President Kill Again' which indicated that The Dukes were still alive in spirit, if not in body. But others like 'King For A Day', 'Poor Skeleton Steps Out', 'Hold Me My Daddy' and 'Across This Antheap' (a song originally written for 'Skylarking' but rejected by Todd Rundgren) heralded completely fresh directions.

While the three months at Summa remained mercifully free of the petty squabbling that had marred the 'Skylarking' sessions, recording was slow and meticulous which didn't suit everyone. Neither XTC nor Jeremy Lascelles had realised quite how inexperienced Paul Fox was as a producer; indeed, it wasn't until one month into the recording that they learned this was his first major project. The band would look back on the 'Oranges And Lemons' sessions with varying degrees of affection.

Both Colin and Dave felt that Fox pandered too closely to Andy's propensity for studio indulgence; 'Andy-ness' as it has become known. But Andy considers Fox - along with John Leckie - as one of the most caring and nurturing producers he's ever worked with. This underlines the polarity of feeling on the subject of producers that has always existed within XTC. It's a debate that re-emerges every time XTC make a record.

162

Colin and Dave are both of the opinion that Andy's reluctance to be produced is the main reason why XTC haven't sold many more records in their long career. They feel he exercises too much control over their albums during the recording and mixing stages, and is not always the best producer, and midwife, for his own songs. Both of them feel that most producers the band have worked with have too readily given in to Andy's demands.

Andy, not surprisingly, views it differently. "Because most of the songs are mine, most of the time is taken up with me wanting to get the song right. I want my babies to be born correctly. I don't want to rush them out and then say 'It could've been good if I'd thought about it a bit more.' We don't take an inordinate amount of time over our records. I know of bands who take two years to make an album. I know a band that takes a month to get a snare drum sound."

Tarquin Gotch was a frequent visitor throughout the 'Oranges And Lemons' sessions. His work for the John Hughes Corporation meant that he was based locally. One day Tarquin turned up at Summa with River Phoenix, the rising star of movies like *Stand By Me* and *Mosquito Coast*. Through his film industry connections Tarquin had heard that Phoenix was a big XTC fan and was as keen to oblige the young prodigy as much as he wanted to impress the group. He was still anxious to manage the band and was about to pop the question formally.

XTC rewarded Tarquin's patience and support by agreeing to an open ended management deal, which would last one album at a time. In return he would receive the usual 15% royalty commission. Tarquin was well placed to liaise with the American record company Geffen, who had superseded Virgin in importance in XTC's eyes. But his first priority was to do something about the greatest mill stone around their necks - the dispute with Ian Reid.

When Gotch learned the full details of the case, he disagreed with the legal and accountancy advice the band were receiving. He could see hundreds of thousands of pounds being paid out to various QC's, accountants and lawyers, when he believed that XTC had little chance of getting anything from Reid, even if they won the case. Tarquin suggested the band cut their losses and pull out of the dispute before it ruined them.

"XTC spent the whole time worrying about the court case," says Gotch. "Finally it dawned on the chaps that what I was saying was correct. Even if they won, they probably wouldn't get a thing. The mess I found the band in when I first took over was appalling."

On September 7 the MTV awards were held in New York and the video for 'Dear God' was up for three awards: Best Director (Nick Brandt), Best Concept and Best Innovation. Chastened by their experience at the CASBY show, XTC didn't attend even though they were still in America finishing recording. They were thus saved any blushes when in the event the video didn't win any of the prizes. However, it did romp home with the *Billboard* Best Video award.

When recording of 'Oranges And Lemons' was completed a week later, mixing began, still at Summa. With no more recording to preoccupy his mind, Andy began to dwell on the huge XTC debt and with no family support - Marianne, Carol and the children had left Los Angeles two months earlier - gradually slid into a deep depression.

He had just completed what he considered to be another master-piece of a record, but he could see only the futility of the situation. If 'Oranges And Lemons' was a huge success, so what? Whatever funds it generated would only go to pay off the endless tax bills and lawyers' fees. Very uncharacteristically, Andy voluntarily left the mixing totally to Fox and flew back to England on October 7.

"I started to worry too much about everything," Andy explains. "The amount of money that had left our hands was shocking. Literally half a million pounds had gone flapping out the window to various people and it depressed me incredibly. I started to drink heavily in those last few weeks and went off the rails a bit. I had to get back to England and calm myself down."

Fox continued mixing until October 22 when, £30,000 over budget, everyone approved of the finished tracks.

The first single from 'Oranges And Lemons' was released on January 16, 1989. 'Mayor Of Simpleton', a happy slice of simple, melodic, 12-string guitar rock, was widely playlisted in the UK, but only reached No 46 in the charts. Interviewed by *Sounds*, Andy spoke dispassionately about the fact that Britain seemed to have forsaken XTC.

"It's like a butcher wondering why this vegetarian character hasn't been in his shop recently. Obviously we don't sell what Britain wants - we'll stick to the meat eaters. Maybe we're too run of the mill to people over here. Besides we have this awful war crimes record from

1977, which the English pop press won't forgive us for - smart-ass techno punks or whatever . . ."

On February 27 - a day earlier than the States - 'Oranges And Lemons' was released. Although it didn't surpass 'Skylarking' artistically, 'Oranges And Lemons' at least equalled it. It could've benefited from a slightly less fussy production, but the collage of disjointed musical styles and lyrical themes showcased XTC's talent for plundering the musical recipe book and re-emerging with something convincingly, invigoratingly different. The sleeve, taken largely from a Milton Glaser pop poster and, according to Andy, "redrawn as if Heinz Edelmann was responsible", focused unnecessarily on the occasional Sixties reference (and made it an all too inevitable critical sticking point) but the record's highlights showed an extraordinary diversity of design and thought.

Colin's 'King For A Day', with its brisk Steely Dan-ish step, stood alongside 'The Loving', an Eighties rewrite of the 'All You Need Is Love' theme, as the most overtly commercial songs on the album. But as always, deeper investigation unearthed greater pleasures. Other gems included 'Hold Me My Daddy', a son's emotive plea for his father's love, which ended with an incongrous burst of African style guitar, 'Across This Antheap', a whirling dervish of funk-pop sound and the album's comic side-step, 'Pink Thing', a thinly disguised paean to Andy's penis! ('Pink Thing' is also how Andy and Marianne referred to their children as babies!)

The LP's closing track, 'Chalkhills And Children', with its haunting echoes of a Beach Boys 'Pet Sounds' ballad, summarised Andy's ambivalent feelings towards his career. Admitting his ill-at-ease attitude towards the world of showbusiness, he had come to realise only two things really mattered in his life: his family and the familiar landscape of home.

> "I'm floating over strange land
> It's a soulless, sequined, showbiz moon
> I'm floating over strange land
> And stranger still there's no balloon
> But I'm getting higher
> Wafted up by fame's fickle fire
> 'Til the chalkhills and children anchor my feet . . ."
> 'Chalkhills And Children'

"'Chalkhills and Children' is a great deflater song," Andy told *Sounds*. "If you start getting famous or whatever and people start giving you awards, changing a shitty nappy is a brilliant leveller. I think everyone should wipe at least one other person's arse before they die."

In America 'Oranges And Lemons' built substantially on the success of its predecessor. Within six months of release, 'Oranges And Lemons' had sold almost half a million copies, almost double what 'Skylarking' had sold in the same period. Reaching No 44 on the *Billboard Top* 100 and number one on the college album chart, 'Oranges And Lemons' also spawned the first XTC single to make the *Billboard* Top 100. 'Mayor Of Simpleton' reached No 72.

Even in the UK, where 'Oranges And Lemons' met with a low key, but generally favourable, reaction from the press, it managed to reach No 28 - their highest chart placing in a long while.

In February 1989 the long, bitter and very expensive dispute with Ian Reid was settled out of court. Badly bruised and battle scarred, the band had survived to fight another day - but only just.

Indeed the financial situation forced the group to renegotiate their contract with Virgin for the third time. In addition to committing themselves to a further four albums they had to agree to certain unfavourable royalty adjustments. In exchange, Virgin covered their immediate debts.

With considerable Stateside success to draw on, and the Ian Reid case safely out the way, Tarquin Gotch focused on trying to get the band to promote 'Oranges And Lemons' in the US. Andy sensed that he was about to come in for a barrage of pressure to resume touring and pre-empted Tarquin and everyone else by coming up with his own suggestion. Although he wasn't prepared to face a live audience in a conventional concert setting, Andy said he wouldn't mind performing live on radio or TV with acoustic guitars.

Cautiously taken up at first - this had never been done before (although it has since been widely copied by bands like REM) - the idea mushroomed until between them Gotch and Geffen had arranged a tour of around 30 US radio stations. In the end they were having to turn down appearance requests of three times that number. It wouldn't make the band any money *per se*, which Dave was particularly unhappy about, but it would be good promotion for the album.

Equipped only with three acoustic guitars, XTC headed off for

America on May 13. Two days later they made their first radio appearance on Boston's WBCN-FM. "That first one was absolutely petrifying for all concerned," says Andy. "It was the classic old gig syndrome where suddenly a little red light went on and everyone immediately forgot how to play! Our hands froze, we couldn't remember lyrics - it was a total shambles. The fact that we suddenly realised we were broadcasting to millions of people made us fall apart. But after the first radio appearance it was absolutely fine. We were relaxed and I started to enjoy it."

"It was like the old fashioned way of touring," Colin laughs. "It was like something Joe Brown would've done in an early Sixties film!"

Performing up to three times a day, the set list was made up chiefly of 'Oranges And Lemons' material: 'King For A Day', 'Mayor Of Simpleton', 'Blue Beret' (a song written for 'Oranges And Lemons' but never recorded), 'Scarecrow People'; plus three medleys: 'Senses Working Overtime'-'Grass'-'Love On A Farmboy's Wages', 'Great Fire'-'Dear God'-'Big Day' and 'One Of The Millions'-'Pink Thing'-'Garden Of Earthly Delights'. At one station they even played impromptu renderings of a handful of old Dukes' songs.

Stripped down to basic melodies and forced to stand on their own merits, these were fascinating re-interpretations of some of XTC's best loved songs. It was also re-affirmation, after so many years, that XTC were great live performers.

On the last day of the two week tour, on May 31, the band arrived at Toronto's Eastern Studios for a show that was destined for live syndication on radio across Canada. As well as performing the usual acoustic set, they would be interviewed on air. "When we got there we found a large hall with three microphones and three stools," Colin recalls. "It was like The Spinners or something!"

In addition to three microphones, there was also an audience of about 150 people - which immediately put Andy on the defensive. In a panic, he approached Tarquin. "You never told me this was going to happen!" he complained. "This is a gig!"

Both Colin and Dave feared the worst, but Tarquin managed to calm Andy down and the show proceeded without a hitch. "Andy was his normal witty self - he enjoyed it," marvelled Colin. "Of course Tarquin used that as a lever from then on. He'd say 'You've played to an audience of 150. You can play to an audience of 250 . . .' It was a way of trying to increase Partridge's confidence."

The radio tour was capped a month later when the band made

several high profile US TV appearances. On June 28 XTC played a mini acoustic set on MTV before a live audience of approximately 150, without Andy suffering unduly. Indeed, he also became a guest MTV presenter for a week, recording his links in advance on a spare day. Then on June 30 - the same day that Tarquin Gotch was fired by John Hughes, a notorious hire 'em and fire 'em merchant - they performed the new single 'King For A Day' with the house band, live on *The David Letterman Show*.

With a real chance of 'King For A Day' becoming a major American hit, Tarquin was desperate for the band to play a few live dates. He knew that the time for trying to persuade Andy back on the road was never better - Andy had enjoyed the radio tour and he could no longer use stage fright as an excuse for not playing live. He had proved he could do it.

Aware of the sensitivity of the situation, Tarquin adopted a softly softly approach. First he suggested a very leisurely tour which would involve just a handful of gigs with alternate days off. Andy could bring his family along too if that would make things more comfortable. When that didn't work Tarquin hit the band with cold economics: he had already gone through the exercise of arranging a hypothetical US tour with Ian Copeland's FBI agency in New York. Between them they had calculated that if XTC were to undertake a modest three to four week tour, culminating with a gig at Madison Square Garden (which they were confident they could sell out), they'd walk away with an estimated $100,000 each. Dave, understandably, was very interested in this, Colin mildly so. But Andy still gave a resolute "No".

Tarquin was at the point of giving up altogether when he came up with a plan that had to be admired for its underhandedness. Since Andy was unwilling to play live, but Colin and Dave were, he cooked up this story whereby he persuaded Colin and Dave to say they had agreed to team up with Thomas Dolby and tour America as XTC. With Thomas Dolby fronting they would play an assortment of 'Oranges And Lemons' material, Colin's songs and Dolby's songs. Tarquin phoned Andy ostensibly to get his blessing for the tour.

When Andy heard that Thomas Dolby would effectively be taking his place for the duration of this mythical tour, he seemed genuinely upset. "Couldn't I just play on a couple of songs?" he asked. "Of course you can you fool," said Tarquin. "You can play on the whole bloody tour if you like!"

While Andy was seriously considering taking part, he discovered that the Thomas Dolby collaboration was a complete fabrication and changed his mind - none too amused that he had been so easily tricked. But Tarquin's plan had so very nearly worked.

Disappointed, Gotch had nevertheless proved a point. Andy's refusal to tour could no longer be attributed to an emotional inability to do so. He was simply sticking to a stubborn principle: he didn't enjoy touring so he wasn't going to do it. "It annoyed me that we weren't getting anywhere with Andy because we could all see he'd got over his stage fright problem," says Colin. "Now he was just making excuses. There was a time when no one loved an audience more than Andy Partridge."

In August 1989 Virgin released 'The Loving', the third single from 'Oranges and Lemons', but apart from being voted 'Single of the Week' in *NME*, courtesy of guest reviewers The Wonder Stuff, it stiffed. The dust had settled and 'Oranges And Lemons' had clearly done the bulk of its business. XTC slipped into what had all the outward appearance of two and a half years of hibernation.

The following month the first ever international XTC fan convention took place in Manchester, attracting visitors from all over Europe, North America and Japan. September also saw the release of an album by Italian singer Alice, well known in her native country and over much of Europe. 'Il Sol & Nella Pioggia' featured Dave playing guitar on four tracks. He had been approached by Alice's manager/producer/boyfriend Francesco Messina, who had been impressed by Dave's guitar work on 'Oranges And Lemons'.

Dave also contributed guitar to a solo album by Clark Datchler, the former lead singer of Johnny Hates Jazz. In what Dave describes as "a real 'Heaven's Gate' of a production", Datchler spent a fortune on this album. It was recorded over many months in numerous studios, and some of the world's top session musicians had been drafted in, some of whom had played on Michael Jackson's 'Thriller' album. But when the first single from it flopped, Virgin shelved the album's release. When Johnny Hates Jazz re-formed a year later, Dave played on two songs on their new album. This too was subsequently shelved!

Andy, meanwhile, produced four tracks of Peter Blegvad's new album 'King Strut', followed by most of an album called 'All For Love And Love For All' for The Lilac Time, featuring former pop idol Stephen 'Tin Tin' Duffy. During the same period Dave made several TV appearances around Europe with Italian star Alice, followed, in

February 1990, by a session with Marc Almond, during which he contributed guitar on two tracks of Almond's forthcoming album 'Enchanted'.

By the new year Colin and Andy had written more than enough new material to start concentrating on the next album. As a first step, they sent a batch of 20 new songs to Jeremy Lascelles. Within days of receiving them, the Virgin executive contacted Andy saying the songs weren't good enough - though he quite liked one song and half of another! Regrettably he insisted that Andy and Colin would have to write some more. Disappointed but not disheartened, they wrote several new songs. Again Lascelles rejected them. By this stage Andy was getting frustrated and, foreseeing another 'Mummer' saga on the horizon, he arranged a meeting with Lascelles.

The meeting didn't go well. According to Andy, even though he knew his new songs were among the best he'd ever written, Lascelles was attempting to get him to come up with ten hit singles. According to Lascelles, though, much of the material was either substandard or sounded like virtual re-writes of old XTC songs.

"I was trying to encourage Andy to stretch himself a bit," he explains. "Although I have the highest regard for his talent and him as a person, Andy can be very lazy in my opinion. He doesn't really want to push himself beyond his self-defined limits. He thought he had written the album and he didn't want to do any more work."

Having reached a stalemate over the subject of songs, Jeremy Lascelles agreed with Andy that they should nevertheless start to look for a producer. Lascelles hoped that by the time they had found one, Andy would've come up with some more songs. The story of what happened next would take another full length book to relate in detail.

Briefly, over the next 12 months XTC began negotiations with several producers, many of them well-known studio hands like Stephen Hague, Chris Hughes, Steve Lipsom, Bill Bottrell (an engineer who'd worked with Madonna and Michael Jackson), John Leckie and Tony Bourge and Tom Lord-Alge. But all were ditched, or cut themselves out of the running for a variety of reasons: changes of heart by the producers, changes of heart by the band, excessive financial demands, record company disapproval. On one occasion, Jeremy Lascelles inadvertently put noses out of joint by giving two producers the impression that they'd got the job. Unluckily for him, the men in question happened to meet and mention it to each other!

But the ultimate act of heresy, in Andy's eyes, was committed by

170

Steve Lipsom, who wanted to rewrite most of the song lyrics. "He said he wanted to make an album that would appeal to a young girl putting her make up on and getting ready to go out for the night!" says Andy. "He wanted to know what words like 'Rook, rook, gaze in your brook' were going to mean to a 16-year-old girl."

In April 1990 Tarquin Gotch departed gracefully from the scene. He'd had little to do in the way of managing XTC once the hubbub of activity immediately following 'Oranges and Lemons' died down and he had just been hired again - on a higher salary than before - by his old boss John Hughes. One stipulation, however, was that he had to drop his band managing activities (which had been the main reason for John Hughes sacking him one year earlier). On balance it was too good an offer to turn down.

"I'd had a great time working with XTC," says Gotch, "but the difficulty for me was the fact that they wouldn't tour. Without a tour I couldn't make any real money - so it was frustrating in that sense. But in every other way I couldn't have wished for an easier band to work with."

Dave wasn't about to turn down any opportunities either. Also in April, with the band's recording plans put on ice, he accepted an offer to produce a single for indie band Cud, whom Dave describes as being "very serious about having a daft time!" The track 'Hey! Wire' went on to be something of an alternative dance classic.

On May 5 came another noteworthy event. Colin and Barry Andrews joined forces with a young Swindon based singer/songwriter called Dave Marx, and his group The Refugees, for what was meant to be a record company showcase pub gig. Sadly for Marx, none of the A&R men who had promised to turn up, did. So nothing came of it.

In the same period Andy's brother-in-law, Rob Wyborn, called round at his house late one evening, just as Andy and Marianne were about to go to bed. His band, called coincidentally King Strut, were about to play a gig at the Prince of Wales in Swindon and needed to borrow some guitars and strings. Andy was drunk, having already spent the evening in the pub and, at Marianne's suggestion, pulled on a pair of pyjamas and left with Rob to see his band.

King Strut had just lost their bass player and struggled with the sound throughout their first set. During the interval, having had even more to drink, Andy offered to help out. Borrowing a bass from the pub's dooorman, he joined King Strut for the whole of the second set.

"I was so drunk I don't remember much about it," says Andy. "I

171

just remember being on stage, soaked in sweat with my hat on, my pyjama jacket, some green cord trousers, me boots and this borrowed bass! I had to watch the others' hands so I knew which chords to play. Actually it was good fun."

Dave spent the whole of August producing an album for Cud called 'Leggy Mambo', released by Imaginary Records.

By October 1990 the continuing disagreement with Jeremy Lascelles - who was still not satisfied with the material - had reached breaking point for Andy. Angry and frustrated, he phoned Simon Draper to ask why Virgin seemed to be doing everything in their power to prevent the band from making their next album. "You haven't sent us any demos yet," Simon Draper replied. At that point Andy flipped: "I said 'Look, you've got to take Jeremy Lascelles off the job. I can't deal with him any more'."

Lascelles was, in any case, on the move. He was just about to manage Virgin's sister label Ten and relinquish his control over XTC, admitting he'd not been able to give the band his full attention. As far as Andy was concerned, another combative figure was out of the picture. After hearing the demos, Simon Draper told the band he was happy for them to start recording as soon as possible.

In November, having drawn up another shortlist of potential producers, the band was back in touch with Steve Lillywhite. It had been ten years since they'd last worked together, but Andy had liked Steve's work on some recent records, especially The La's album and Talking Heads' LP 'Naked'. Ironically, David Byrne had first contacted Lillywhite because he liked his production on 'Black Sea'. Steve loved the idea of working with them again and suggested a nostalgic reunion of the Lillywhite/Padgham team - just for XTC. They would even cut their respective fees by half to make the project financially viable.

Over the next five months, however, a number of setbacks kept delaying the project. Twice Lillywhite, who was also busy producing an album for his wife, Kirsty MacColl, postponed the start of recording. Lillywhite and Padgham also both failed to turn up to rehearsals as promised. Just days before recording was due to start for a third time, Lillywhite went on holiday without telling the band. Finally, Hugh Padgham's manager made several unacceptably rigid last minute changes to his contract. By late March 1991 the band had lost patience and told Virgin to sack the pair.

At least one thing was going right. XTC's search for a drummer for the new album had brought them into contact with one of the best in the business. Dave's brother Ian Gregory was a big Fairport Convention fan and he particularly admired their drummer Dave Mattacks, one of Britain's best known session drummers who'd worked with Paul McCartney, Elton John, The Who, Chris Rea and many other stellar names. During one of their regular British tours, Ian had caught up with Fairport Convention at the Oxford Apollo. In the 1991 tour programme, Dave Mattacks had listed a few bands and artists he'd most like to work with, and hadn't already. Sandwiched between Ry Cooder and Randy Newman were XTC. Ian took this back to Swindon to show the band.

Days later the Fairport's tour reached the Wyvern Theatre, Swindon. Dave Mattacks arrived to find a message taped to his drum stool asking him to call Andy Partridge. "I thought it was the crew winding me up," Dave laughs, "because they knew XTC was a Swindon based band. I phoned the number and when Marianne answered I thought I'd got one of those sex lines!"

Soon realising it wasn't a wind-up, Dave and Andy spent most of an afternoon chatting on the phone. Dave was amazed that Andy could recall many of the albums he'd appeared on - including one of his favourites, Brian Eno's 'Before And After Science'. Andy was flattered that Dave had heard of XTC, even more flattered to learn that he was a fan - particularly of 'Oranges And Lemons'. By the end of their conversation Mattacks had agreed to play on XTC's new album.

The band spent the next few months working their way through another list of potential producers which very gradually narrowed down to two who were keen to work with them: John Paul Jones, the former bassist and keyboard player with Led Zeppelin, who subsequently ruled himself out by asking for an exorbitant fee, and Gus Dudgeon, perhaps best known for his work with Elton John, with whom Dave Mattacks had worked many times before.

Not a moment too soon, recording of the new album began on July 15 at Chipping Norton Recording Studios in Oxfordshire. In Gus Dudgeon, XTC had found a producer who was not obviously compatible but who was unquestionably the most experienced they'd ever worked with. His career spanned 25 years and dozens of established mainstream artists like Elton (12 of whose albums he'd produced), Joan Armatrading, David Bowie, Bruce Hornsby, Elkie Brooks, The Beach Boys, Jennifer Rush and Chris Rea. Against this list XTC made unlikely clients.

173

From day one it was clear that both band and producer were in for another rough ride. In what Andy would later cite as one of the three most difficult albums to for him to work on (after 'Go 2' along with 'Skylarking'), it developed into a classic XTC saga. Although Gus and Andy got on well personally, they frequently didn't see eye to eye in the studio. On one or two occasions their differences of opinion boiled over into intensely personal rows.

Andy wanted his songs to be recorded, as faithfully as possible, in the way he perceived them and found Gus unable to grasp how passionate he was about carrying his ideas through. On one occasion, after recording a song called 'Rook' - which Andy rated as the most personal and introspective he'd ever written - Andy complained that it hadn't turned out how he wanted. He thought they should have another go at getting it right. But, far from being one of his favourite songs, 'Rook' wasn't even on his list of songs considered for recording, and Gus responded unsympathetically by suggesting that if he wasn't happy with 'Rook' after it had been mixed, he should "bin it".

Andy was outraged. It was the last thing to say to him about what he considered to be the very peak of his songwriting. "It's like saying 'If you're not happy today . . . just off yourself'," says Andy indignantly. "It was the biggest mental kick in the balls that anyone could give me."

But Gus Dudgeon exercised a different set of priorities. He believed it was about time XTC's record sales matched their reputation. He felt XTC's songs impressed people, but often failed to touch them. As far as Gus was concerned he'd been hired by XTC on the strength of his track record - a track record which had made him one of the most successful producers in the world. The only person who was preventing him from doing his work properly, he felt, was Andy.

"I really love the guy," says Dudgeon. "He's amusing, he's charming. But you can flip between thinking Andy's superb and having a great time working with him, to wanting to fucking kill him, in a matter of minutes. Half the time he really doesn't realise the effect he's having on people. It goes right past him.

"Dave Mattacks said he'd never worked so hard in his life. Here's a man who's recorded with most of the top names in rock. At one point, when Andy picked his drumsticks up and started trying to show him how to play a drum pattern, Dave was ready to hit him. It's almost impossible to upset Dave Mattacks - that takes some doing!"

"It was bloody hard work!" Dave Mattacks would confirm. "But I put up with being pushed because the material was great and I liked the guys. If they'd been arseholes and the material wasn't any good, I would have definitely walked out. But in the end I enjoyed the challenge and the results were great. I'm more proud of what I've contributed to those tracks than anything else to date."

Colin and Dave, meanwhile, stood cautiously on the sidelines. Although they sympathised with Gus Dudgeon, they were afraid of upsetting the apple-cart. The wrestling between Andy and Gus was wearing at times, but the results were impressive and that, ultimately, was what mattered most. During the Chipping Norton sessions both regained a supreme sense of confidence and enjoyment that neither had felt since the recording of 'English Settlement'. The further they got into the recording, the more convinced they both became that the new record was going to be biggest and best of their careers.

As recording at Chipping Norton drew to a close in mid-October, a dark cloud hung ominously in the air. After a short three week break the album was due to be mixed at Rockfield Studios with Gus Dudgeon and (Chipping Norton Recording Studios' in-house engineer) Barry Hammond at the controls. But Dudgeon was so convinced that if Andy was allowed to oversee the work at Rockfield he would wreck the fragile chemistry of what he personally saw as the "big, big breakthrough" for XTC, he banned him from the mixing sessions. Not surprisingly, Andy took this as nothing less than a gross insult and fought the decision all the way.

Eventually, after the intervention of Simon Draper, a compromise of sorts was reached. Andy would be allowed to look in during the mixing but wouldn't be allowed to supervise the whole session. In addition, any comments he had to make would be noted but wouldn't necessarily be acted upon. It was an unworkable compromise, but one which Andy appeared to go along with in order to keep the peace.

Andy turned up at Rockfield on day one of the mixing and, predictably enough, tempers flared within hours. He was heavily critical of the first mix that Dudgeon had completed and wanted it done again. Conversely, Andy was living up to Dudgeon's worst expectations - this was precisely the reason he'd wanted Andy banned from the sessions.

After a heated debate which lasted about eight hours and was left unresolved, Andy left Rockfield and went home. A week later Dudgeon was sacked and replaced by Nick Davis, a young engineer/producer who'd worked on the recently released Genesis LP 'We Can't

Dance'. Although Gus Dudgeon had been bracing himself for such an eventuality, it didn't diffuse his anger.

"I've known some pretty insular artists in my time," he says, "people like Joan Armatrading, who has never in her life made any compromises with her art. But nowadays she at least produces herself, whereas these guys have made a point of hiring good producers. Now why hire good producers if you're either going to completely interfere with what they do to the point that you're not going to get the best out of them, or you don't actually want a good production?"

By Christmas, mixing of the album was at last completed to everyone's satisfaction. Now titled 'Nonsuch' - meaning, appropriately enough, 'unrivalled' - the trials and tribulations of the previous two and a half years had, at least, resulted in what all those close to them considered an outstanding record. Possibly their most accomplished yet . . .

XTC - EPILOGUE

Afer 15 years of making records, XTC remain an enigma: they don't tour, they have few hits, they refuse to conform to the rudiments of the music industry, yet perversely that industry still recognises them as a rare and precious commodity. They invoke a respect - in some a passion - that would dwarf many artists selling ten times the volume of records.

Yet for three musicians so obviously at odds with the mainstream rock world, there's a surprising lack of cohesion within the ranks. While all three remain totally committed to swimming against the tide of mediocrity, there's a split set of priorities at work. All three of them agree that if they have any commercial success these days it's despite their efforts to do what they believe in, but Colin and Dave are both strongly in favour of allowing producers to take a firmer control. "That's what we pay them for and it's a complete waste of time not letting them do their thing," says Colin.

Colin and Dave also long to tour again and are considering doing so whether as XTC, or not. For Colin it's not just a question of wanting to be seen and heard. More crucially, he feels his songwriting has suffered from years of not playing live. "Although I've got more time on my hands now, if anything my songwriting libido has gone down," he explains. "I find it harder to write because I haven't got the musical influences going in. I need to play with other musicians. When we were touring you'd get an idea for a song during a soundcheck and you knew that when you got back home you'd be working on that.

"I suppose it's only laziness that's really stopped me from finding other musicians to play with. I've made my mind up that from now on I'm going to become more musically active with other bands. If this band doesn't rehearse, doesn't get together, then obviously I have to seek an input from elsewhere."

As managing director of Virgin Records, Simon Draper has unequivocal expectations of the band, even at this advanced stage of their career. "What I would like them to do - and this goes right back to the very beginning of my relationship with the band - is let other people have a bit more room," he says. "I don't think they've ever let anyone fully produce their records," he says. "Andy allows producers in because at this point the other two guys won't make records unless there's a producer present - otherwise they'd just get trodden all over by Andy. However brilliant he is, I don't think he's the best producer of his own records."

But Andy balks at all suggestions of compromise. He regards attempts to make his art more acceptable for mass consumption as nothing short of contemptible. Hit records aren't his priority, in fact they're not even a goal. If they happen it's by accident, not by design. Andy Partridge will admit he's interested only in pleasing himself and if by sticking to his principles that makes XTC's music unpalatable to a wide audience then so be it.

"People who like XTC like us for precisely the reason we aren't like everyone else," he argues. "If you like cheesecake, you don't like it because it reminds you of some other form of cake so you'll put up with the cheese element. You like it because it's cheesecake. If you like Picasso you don't complain that a lot of his work isn't quite in perspective and it's a little too blue occasionally. You like it because it's Picasso. If you have the taste for what XTC is then fine, but I don't want to radically change the formula just because somebody I don't know from Adam doesn't like the way our songs go la-la-la."

If there's a pervasive theme throughout XTC's existence it's that what Andy wants, XTC usually gets. He is simultaneously the reason they exist and the reason why, since 1982, they have effectively been a semi-dormant studio entity. While Andy is determined to reverse the current trend of ever-lengthening gaps between albums - he says XTC would release an album every six months if Virgin would allow it - he is never likely to reverse his decision about playing live. Whether that decision, taken when it was, destroyed the band in terms of denying them success on a huge scale, no one can ever say for sure. The only certainty is that it will remain the most contentious issue facing XTC for the rest of their career.

"We make good records but I don't think we're born entertainers," Andy concludes. "At one point in our career, we were a well oiled performing machine, but it wasn't very enjoyable. My priorities have changed dramatically over the years. I don't want to get on stage and suffer, not even for vast amounts of money.

"I have a recurring nightmare. It's that we're on stage somewhere and every person who's ever been in the band is on stage with us: Dave Cartner, Nervous Steve, Barry Andrews, Steve Hutchins, Terry Chambers . . . they're all there like this mass orchestra. The house lights are on and they're all looking at me saying 'What number are we gonna play?' I'm thinking 'God, he wasn't in the band when he was, so he won't know that. He hasn't drummed for five or six years, so he won't be able to do that. He doesn't know that album, because he'd left the band by then . . .' And the audience is going 'Come on!'"

WHERE ARE THEY NOW?

BARRY ANDREWS: Since leaving XTC in 1979 Barry has been involved with a number of bands, including The League Of Gentlemen (with Robert Fripp), Restaurant For Dogs, Shriekback and Illuminati, with varying degrees of success. He's currently in the process of reforming Shriekback who disbanded in 1988.

DAVE BENNETT: Former manager of Star Park. Last heard of working in the Seychelles.

DAVE CARTNER: Former member of Clark Kent, Star Park and The Helium Kids. Still lives in Swindon where he recently married for the second time.

TERRY CHAMBERS: Emigrated to Australia on December 28, 1982 (although still retaining his British passport) and in August 1983 married Donna Blanchard who gave birth to their second child, daughter Corrie, in 1985. Continued working with bands for a while, most notably Sydney-based New Zealand rockers Dragon, and featured on their platinum selling album 'The Body And The Beat', released in 1984. Group disbanded in 1986 after their American guitarist died from a drug overdose. Has since lost interest in the music business and hasn't played drums for several years. Instead, he's been doing "bits and pieces here and there . . . nothing much" which has included various gardening and manual labour jobs in and around Newcastle, New South Wales. In October 1991, Terry returned to Swindon for a few weeks - the first return to England since December

1982 - and visited his three former XTC colleagues at Chipping Norton recording studios.

AL CLARK: Emigrated to Australia in 1986 where he runs his own Sydney based film production company. He is also planning to follow up his 1982 book *Raymond Chandler In Hollywood* (Proteus) with another book which . . . "could well feature certain very recognisable West Country characters".

DENNIS DETHERIDGE: Still works in PR, most recently as Press Liaison Officer for the Avon Office Centre in Bristol. Currently lives in Abergavenny, Wales.

TONY GORDON: Former manager of Helium Kidz. Continued to manage rock and pop acts throughout the seventies and eighties, achieving major success with Culture Club and Curiosity Killed The Cat. Currently runs Wedge Music Ltd in London, managing Boy George.

TARQUIN GOTCH: Still produces films in Los Angeles, but was recently fired by John Hughes for the second time. Doesn't rule out the possibility of working with XTC again in the future.

STEVE HUTCHINS: Former lead singer of The Helium Kidz and XTC. Current whereabouts unknown.

ALLAN JONES: Current editor of *Melody Maker*.

JEREMY LASCELLES: Since September 1991 he has been managing director of Offside Records, a Virgin-owned label which has among its acts Belinda Carlisle, Wendy and Lisa and . . . Mary Margaret O'Hara!

JON PERKINS: Former member of XTC. Perkins' band The Stadium Dogs signed a deal with Magnet and released an album 'What's Next' in 1978. Has since been a member of The Original Mirrors and has released several albums under his own name. Most recently he's also been a member of Dave Stewart's Spiritual Cowboys.

PETER PHIPPS: As well as continued with session drumming, he has recently re-formed The Glitter Band.

IAN REID: Last heard of running a sports shop in Cheltenham. Present whereabouts uncertain.

MARTIN VINCENT: Former lead singer of Stray Blues. Last heard of working in Swindon TAX Office. Present whereabouts uncertain.

STEVE WARREN: Andy Partridge's teenage friend has worked as a parts purchaser for Mitsubishi motors in Cirencester since October 1982. Still living in Swindon, his wife Nora gave birth to a son, James, in April 1991.

COMPLETE XTC UK DISCOGRAPHY

XTC SINGLES

SCIENCE FRICTION/SHE'S SO SQUARE (10/77)	Virgin VS 188 3-D EP:
Science Friction/She's So Square/Dance Band (12", 10/77)	Virgin VS 188 12
TRAFFIC LIGHT ROCK (live) (c/w Tangerine Dream, The Motors & U-Roy,	
freebie with 'Record Mirror'. no p/s, 12/77)	Virgin VR 08 10274
STATUE OF LIBERTY/HANG ON TO THE NIGHT (1/78)	Virgin VS 201
THIS IS POP?/HEATWAVE (4/78)	Virgin VS 209
ARE YOU RECEIVING ME?/INSTANT TUNES (10/78)	Virgin VS 231
LIFE BEGINS AT THE HOP/HOMO SAFARI (30,000 on clear vinyl 5/79, No.54)	Virgin VS 259
LIFE BEGINS AT THE HOP/HOMO SAFARI (5/79)	Virgin VS 259
MAKING PLANS FOR NIGEL/BUSHMAN PRESIDENT/PULSING, PULSING	
(gameboard p/s/ with playing pieces, 9/79, No.17)	Virgin VS 282
MAKING PLANS FOR NIGEL/BUSHMAN PRESIDENT/PULSING, PULSING (9/79)	Virgin VS 282
TEN FEET TALL (b/w The Skids, 'The Olympian', red vinyl flexi free with Smash Hits)	Smash Hits HIT 002
WAIT TILL YOUR BOAT GOES DOWN/TEN FEET TALL (US Version) (3/80)	Virgin VS 322
GENERALS AND MAJORS/DON'T LOSE YOUR TEMPER/SMOKELESS ZONE/	
THE SOMNAMBULIST (double-pack, 8/80, No.32)	Virgin VS 365
GENERALS AND MAJORS/DON'T LOSE YOUR TEMPER (8/80)	Virgin VS 365
TOWERS OF LONDON/SET MYSELF ON FIRE (live)/BATTERY BRIDES (live)/	
SCISSOR MAN (double-pack, 10/80, No.31)	Virgin VS 372
TOWERS OF LONDON/SET MYSELF ON FIRE (live) (10/80)	Virgin VS 372
TAKE THIS TOWN (b/w The Ruts 'Babylon Burning', 11/80)	RSO 71
SGT ROCK (Is Going To Help Me)/LIVING THROUGH ANOTHER CUBA (live)/	
GENERALS AND MAJORS (live) (first 20,000 in poster sleeve, 1/81, No.16)	Virgin VS 384
SGT ROCK (Is Going To Help Me)/LIVING THROUGH ANOTHER CUBA (live)/	
GENERALS AND MAJORS (live) (1/81)	Virgin VS 384
RESPECTABLE STREET/STRANGE TALES, STRANGE TAILS/OFFICER BLUE (3/81)	Virgin VS 408
SENSES WORKING OVERTIME/BLAME THE WEATHER/TISSUE TIGERS	
(poster sleeve, 1/82, No.10)	Virgin VS 462
SENSES WORKING OVERTIME/BLAME THE WEATHER/TISSUE TIGERS (1/82)	Virgin VS 462
SENSES WORKING OVERTIME/EGYPTIAN SOLUTION/BLAME THE WEATHER/	
TISSUE TIGERS (12", 1/82)	Virgin VS 462 12

LOOKING FOR FOOTPRINTS (free flexi with 'Flexipop' mag, on red,
    blue, green or yellow vinyl, 2/82)   Flexipop 16

BALL AND CHAIN/PUNCH AND JUDY/HEAVEN IS PAVED WITH BROKEN GLASS
    (2/82, No.58)   Virgin VS 482

BALL AND CHAIN/HEAVEN IS PAVED WITH BROKEN GLASS/PUNCH AND JUDY/
    COCKPIT DANCE MIXTURE (12", 2/82)   Virgin VS 482

NO THUGS IN OUR HOUSE/CHAIN OF COMMAND/LIMELIGHT/OVER RUSTY WATER
    (9" die-cut g/fold sleeve, 5/82)   Virgin VS 490

NO THUGS IN OUR HOUSE/CHAIN OF COMMAND/LIMELIGHT/
    OVER RUSTY WATER (5/82)   Virgin VS 490

GREAT FIRE/GOLD (with outer p/s, 4/83)   Virgin VS 553

GREAT FIRE/GOLD (4/83)   Virgin VS 553

GREAT FIRE/GOLD/FROST CIRCUS/PROCESSION TOWARDS LEARNING LAND
    (12", 4/83)   Virgin VS 55312

WONDERLAND/JUMP (picture disc, 7/83)   Virgin VSY 606

WONDERLAND/JUMP (7/83)   Virgin VS 606

LOVE ON A FARMBOY'S WAGES/IN LOVING MEMORY OF A NAME/
    DESERT ISLAND/TOYS (double-pack, 9/83, No.50)   Virgin VS 613

LOVE ON A FARMBOY'S WAGES/IN LOVING MEMORY OF A NAME (9/83)   Virgin VS 613

LOVE ON A FARMBOY'S WAGES/BURNING WITH OPTIMISMS FLAME (live)
ENGLISH ROUNDABOUT (live)/CUT IT OUT (live) (12", 9/83)   Virgin VS 61312

ALL YOU PRETTY GIRLS/WASHAWAY (with outer die-cut p/s, 9/84, No.55)   Virgin VS 709

ALL YOU PRETTY GIRLS/WASHAWAY (9/84)   Virgin VS 709

ALL YOU PRETTY GIRLS/WASHAWAY/RED BRICK DREAM (12", 9/84)   Virgin VS 70912

THIS WORLD OVER/BLUE OVERALL (with postcards, 10/84)   Virgin VS 721

THIS WORLD OVER/BLUE OVERALL (12", 10/84)   Virgin VS 72112

WAKE UP/TAKE THIS TOWN/MANTIS ON PAROLE (11/84)   Virgin VS 746

WAKE UP/TAKE THIS TOWN/MANTIS ON PAROLE/MAKING PLANS FOR
    NIGEL/SGT. ROCK (Is Going To Help Me)/SENSES WORKING OVERTIME
    (12", 1/85)   Virgin VS 74612

GRASS/DEAR GOD (8/86)   Virgin VS 882

GRASS/EXTROVERT/DEAR GOD (8/86) (12")   Virgin VS 88212

THE MEETING PLACE/THE MAN WHO SAILED AROUND HIS SOUL (clear vinyl
    with printed transparent sleeve, 2/87)   Virgin VSY 912

THE MEETING PLACE/THE MAN WHO SAILED AROUND HIS SOUL/TERRORISM
    (home demo)/LET'S MAKE A DEN (home demo)/FIND THE FOX (home demo)/
    THE TROUBLES (home demo) (12", 2/87)   Virgin VS 91212

DEAR GOD/BIG DAY (6/87)   Virgin VS 960

DEAR GOD/BIG DAY/ANOTHER SATELLITE (live) (12", 6/87)   Virgin VS 96012

DEAR GOD/HOMO SAFARI SERIES 1-6 (5" CD, 6/87)   Virgin CDEP 3

SENSES WORKING OVERTIME/BLAME THE WEATHER/TISSUE TIGERS (3" CD, 7/88)	Virgin VS CDT9
MAKING PLANS FOR NIGEL/SENSES WORKING OVERTIME (11/88)	Old Gold OG 9819
MAYOR OF SIMPLETON/ONE OF THE MILLIONS (1/89, No.46)	Virgin VS 1158
MAYOR OF SIMPLETON/DEAR GOD/SENSES WORKING OVERTIME/ MAKING PLANS FOR NIGEL (12", 1/89)	Virgin VS R1158
MAYOR OF SIMPLETON/ONE OF THE MILLIONS/ELLA GURU (12", 1/89)	Virgin VS T1158
MAYOR OF SIMPLETON/ELLA GURU/LIVING IN A HAUNTED HEART (home demo)/ THE GOOD THINGS (home demo) (3" CD, 1/89)	Virgin VSCD 1158
KING FOR A DAY/HAPPY FAMILIES (4/89)	Virgin VS 1177
KING FOR A DAY (12" version)/(7" version)/HAPPY FAMILIES (12", 4/89)	Virgin VS T1177
KING FOR A DAY (12" version)/(7" version)/MY PAINT HEROES (home demo)/ SKELETONS (home demo) (3" CD in crown-shaped box, 4/89)	Virgin VSCD 1177
KING FOR A DAY/HAPPY FAMILIES/GENERALS AND MAJORS/TOWERS OF LONDON (cassette, 4/89)	Virgin VSC 1177
THE LOVING/CYNICAL DAYS (8/89)	Virgin VS 1201
THE LOVING/CYNICAL DAYS/THE WORLD IS FULL OF ANGRY YOUNG MEN (12", 8/89)	Virgin VST 1201
THE LOVING/CYNICAL DAYS/THE WORLD IS FULL OF ANGRY YOUNG MEN (3" CD, 8/89)	Virgin VSCD 1201
THE LOVING/THE WORLD IS FULL OF ANGRY YOUNG MEN (cassette, 8/89)	Virgin VSC 1201

XTC LP's

WHITE MUSIC (with black inner bag, 1/78, No. 38)	Virgin V 2095
GO 2 (first 15,000 w/'Go +' 12" EP: Dance With Me Germany/Beat The Bible/A Dictionary Of Modern Marriage/Clap, Clap, Clap/We Kill The Beast plus insert, 10/78, No.21)	Virgin V 2108
DRUMS AND WIRES (first 15,000 with free 7":Chain Of Command/Limelight plus gatefold insert, 8/79, No.34)	Virgin V 2129
BLACK SEA (initial copies had green paper outer sleeve and lyric insert, 9/80, No.16)	Virgin V 2173
ENGLISH SETTLEMENT (double LP, initial sleeves had textured sleeves, 2/82, No.5)	Virgin V 2223
WAXWORKS (first 50,000 came with free LP, 'Beeswax', 11/82, No.54)	Virgin V 2251
MUMMER (with inner sleeve, 8/83), No.51)	Virgin V 2264
BEESWAX (mid-price re-issue, 1983)	Virgin OVED 9
WHITE MUSIC (mid-price re-issue, 3/84)	Virgin OVED 60
GO 2 (mid-price reissue, 3/84)	Virgin OVED 61
THE BIG EXPRESS (initial copies in circular sleeve and inner bag, 10/84, No.38)	Virgin V 2325
BLACK SEA (mid-price re-issue, 1986)	Virgin OVED 83
DRUMS AND WIRES (mid-price re-issue, 1986)	Virgin OVED 113

MUMMER (mid-price re-issue, 1986)	Virgin OVED 142
SKYLARKING (initial copies had embossed sleeve and inner bag 10/86, No.90)	Virgin V 2399
THE BIG EXPRESS (mid-price re-issue, 1988)	Virgin OVED 182
ORANGES AND LEMONS (double LP with inner sleeves, 2/89, No.28)	Virgin V 2581
NONSUCH (1992)	Virgin X?

XTC CD's

SKYLARKING (10/86)	Virgin CDV 2399
WHITE MUSIC (plus Science Friction/She's So Square/Dance Band/Hang On To The Night/ Heatwave/Traffic Light Rock/Instant Tunes, 3/87)	Virgin CDV 2095
MUMMER (plus Frost Circus/Jump/Toys/Gold/Procession Towards Learning Land/ Desert Island, 3/87)	Virgin CDV 2264
BLACK SEA (plus Smokeless Zone/Don't Lose Your Temper/The Somnambulist, 3/87)	Virgin CDV 2172
GO 2 (plus Are You Receiving Me?, 7/87)	Virgin CDV 2108
DRUMS AND WIRES (plus Limelight/Chain Of Command, 1987)	Virgin CDV 2129
THE COMPACT XTC - THE SINGLES 1978-1985 (1987)	Virgin CDV 2251
ENGLISH SETTLEMENT (without Leisure/Down In the Cockpit, 1987)	Virgin CDV 2223
THE BIG EXPRESS (plus Red Brick Dream/Washaway/Blue Overall, 1987)	Virgin CDV 2325
ORANGES AND LEMONS (2/87)	Virgin CDV 2581
ORANGES AND LEMONS (limited edition box with three CD's, 10/89)	Virgin CDVT 2581
EXPLODE TOGETHER (The Dub Experiments 78-80) (8/90)	Virgin CDOVT 308
RAG & BONE BUFFET (8/90)	Virgin CDOVT 311

SELECTED COMPILATIONS

GUILLOTINE (10" w/inner sleeve and poster, including 'Traffic Light Rock' (studio version), 2/78	Virgin VCL 5001
HOPE AND ANCHOR FRONTLINE FESTIVAL (double LP, blue vinyl, with insert, including live versions of 'I'm Bugged' and 'Science Friction', 9/78)	WEA K 66077
DOA - DEAD ON ARRIVAL (luminous vinyl, with poster insert, includes 'Radios In Motion', 10/78)	Virgin VD 2508
CASH COWS (including 'Respectable Street', 11/80)	Virgin MILK 1
MACHINES (including 'The Somnambulist', 1980)	Virgin V 2177
HALF POUNDER (including 'Radios In Motion', available to Record Mirror readers)	RM BURG 1
URRGH! A MUSICAL WAR (double LP, including 'Respectable Street' (live), (9/81)	A&M AMLX 64692
MUSIC AND RHYTHM (double LP, including 'It's Nearly Africa', released in conjunction with 1982 WOMAD Festival)	WEA K 68045

LIFE IN THE EUROPEAN THEATRE (including 'Living Through Another Cuba', 1/82) WEA K 58412
FAST 'N' BULBOUS (including cover of Capt. Beefheart's
   'Ella Guru', 1988) Imaginary Records ILLUSION 002
SHE'S HAVING A BABY (including 'Happy Families', 7/88) IRS 6211

DUKES OF STRATOSPHEAR SINGLES

THE MOLE FROM THE MINISTRY/MY LOVE EXPLODES (4/85) Virgin VS 763
YOU'RE A GOOD MAN ALBERT BROWN/VANISHING GIRL (first 5,000 on multi-coloured
   vinyl, 7/87) Virgin VSY 982
YOU'RE A GOOD MAN ALBERT BROWN/VANISHING GIRL (7/87) Virgin VS 982
YOU'RE A GOOD MAN ALBERT BROWN/VANISHING GIRL/THE MOLE FROM THE
   MINISTRY/MY LOVE EXPLODES (12", 7/87) Virgin VS 98212

DUKES OF STRATOSPHEAR LP's

25 O'CLOCK (4/85) Virgin WOW 1
PSONIC PSUNSPOT (gatefold sleeve, first 5,000 on multi-coloured vinyl, 8/87) Virgin VP 2440
PSONIC PSUNSPOT (gatefold sleeve, 8/87) Virgin V 2440
CHIPS FROM THE CHOCOLATE FIREBALL (CD, includes '25 O'Clock' and 'Psonic
   Psunspot/ LP's, plus inner booklet, 1987) Virgin COMCD 11

ANDY PARTRIDGE LP

TAKE AWAY (THE LURE OF SALVAGE) (with textured sleeve, 2/80) Virgin V 2145
TAKE AWAY (THE LURE OF SALVAGE) (mid-price re-issue, 1986) Virgin OVED 130

THE COLONEL SINGLE

TOO MANY COOKS IN THE KITCHEN/I NEED PROTECTION (10/80) Virgin VS 380

THREE WISE MEN SINGLE

THANKS FOR CHRISTMAS/COUNTDOWN TO CHRISTMAS PARTYTIME (11/83) Virgin VS 642

JOHNNY JAPES AND HIS JESTICLES SINGLE

BAGS OF FUN WITH BUSTER/SCROTAL SCRATCH MIX (Available through 'Viz' comic, 12/87)   VIZ 1

VIDEO

LOOK LOOK (compilation of promos, 1978-82)   Virgin VIRV 013D